Warbirds
Alive

The World's Top 25 Flyable Historic Military Aircraft

Paul Coggan

MIDLAND
An imprint of
Ian Allan Publishing

This book is dedicated to
Debra and Polly

Warbirds Alive
© 2004 Paul Coggan
ISBN 1 85780 143 1

Published by Midland Publishing
4 Watling Drive, Hinckley, LE10 3EY, England
Tel: 01455 254 490   Fax: 01455 254 495
E-mail: midlandbooks@compuserve.com

Midland Publishing is an imprint of
Ian Allan Publishing Ltd

Worldwide distribution (except North America):
Midland Counties Publications
4 Watling Drive, Hinckley, LE10 3EY, England
Telephone: 01455 254 450   Fax: 01455 233 737
E-mail: midlandbooks@compuserve.com
www.midlandcountiessuperstore.com

North American trade distribution:
Specialty Press Publishers & Wholesalers Inc.
39966 Grand Avenue, North Branch, MN 55056, USA
Tel: 651 277 1400   Fax: 651 277 1203
Toll free telephone: 800 895 4585
www.specialtypress.com

Design concept and layout
© 2004 Midland Publishing and
Sue Bushell

Printed in England by
Ian Allan Printing Ltd
Riverdene Business Park, Molesey Road,
Hersham, Surrey, KT12 4RG

Front cover: A fine piece of formation flying by three aircraft all owned at the time by Charles Osborn. Leading is P-47D 44-90368/N4747P Big Ass Bird II, followed by FG-1D BuNo 92399/ N448AG (now N451AG with the Cavanaugh Flight Museum) and P-51D 44-73206/N3751D Hurry Home Honey. Tom Smith

Title page: Joe Tobul rebuilt F4U-4 Corsair BuNo 97143/N713JT and flew it for the first time following rebuild on 8th December 1991. Sadly, ten years later the aircraft crashed on 10th November 2002 killing the pilot. Ed Toth

Below: After the end of World War Two, large numbers of Allied aircraft, including these 8th Air Force P-51Ds (note some of the FG markings are still clearly visible even though some of the codes have been crudely painted out), were assembled at Oberpffafen, Germany. Several went to the Swiss Air Force and other foreign air arms, including Sweden. Though several of the ex-Swedish Air Force P-51Ds survive today, the Swiss simply chopped up their Mustangs for scrap following their retirement from service.
Warbird Index

Contents

Introduction

As I write this book, the number of hours flown by warbird and vintage aircraft around the world has reached a record high. The standards of airframe and engine restoration have also attained new levels, with the emphasis now being on 'stock military restorations'.

As early as 1942 the United States Congress had begun to discuss the disposition of surplus military equipment, including aircraft. Congress passed the Surplus Property Act on 15th February 1944, and this defined the policy and objectives and saw the establishment of the Surplus War Property Administration. In October of that year, the Surplus Property Board was launched with W Stuart Symington as Chief Administrator. The Reconstruction Finance Corporation, founded by Congress in 1932, took over the sale of aircraft from the Defense Plant Corporation and continued this until the estab-

lishment of the War Assets Administration in January 1946.

A large number of organisations were involved in the disposal of thousands of surplus Army Air Force, Navy and Marine Corps fighters and bombers that had returned to the United States after the cessation of hostilities. Many were pressed into service as instructional airframes at technical institutions and trade schools in the United States, only to be 'more thoughtfully' disposed of later to museums and in some cases, private collectors. Sadly, because there simply wasn't the same level of interest then that exists today, tens of thousands of other aircraft were simply scrapped without a second thought. It is now a matter of record that of more than 300,000 combat aircraft manufactured in the United States during the World War Two period, only a very small percentage survived into the 1950s.

The sad sight of several Mustang mainplanes languishing at the Asplin's Supplies scrap yard in New Zealand during the late 1950s. The Royal New Zealand Air Force sold all of its Mustangs to scrap merchants. Jim Winchester

In 1946 the Office of Foreign Liquidation was established to handle the sale of surplus aircraft in Europe. This in turn led to the Foreign Liquidation Commission that sold aircraft to Australia, New Zealand, various countries in Central and South America as well as several other nations around the world. By this means the United States managed to recoup a little of its huge investment in World War Two aircraft manufacture. In addition, dozens of military aid programmes were established which led to hundreds more surplus aircraft being passed on to air arms around the world.

When it came time for these second-hand aircraft to be phased out of service by their respective owners and operators, some were returned to the United States as part of the Mutual Defense Assistance Program (MDAP) agreement. However, large numbers did not return home and were either scrapped in situ, consigned to commercial scrap yards and left to rot, or were properly stored in reserve for potential onward sale if the respective military aid programme permitted it.

Few dispute that the activity of actively recovering, restoring and flying warbirds goes back to a few celebrated individuals. In the summer of 1951, a crop-duster pilot by the name of Lloyd Nolen purchased a Curtiss P-40M (43-5778) from Bill March in Phoenix, Arizona, to fulfil his ambition of continuing to fly military aircraft following his military service. Though the aircraft was a challenge to fly, Nolen decided to part with it to finance the acquisition of the aircraft he really wanted – a North American P-51D Mustang.

Although jets were starting to replace the higher performance piston-engined fighters in military service, there were still a significant number of the latter on strength with the US Air Force. However, just as Nolen was about to realise his dream of owning a Mustang, the Korean War erupted and the Pentagon recalled all F-51s to military service. It is well known that several of the recalled aircraft went on to serve in Korea.

Though Nolen had to wait a further five years, he did eventually acquire a P-51D with finance he and a group of colleagues raised. In October 1957, P-51D-30-NA 44-74843 was registered N10601 to Lloyd Nolen of Mustang & Co in Mercedes, Texas. The aircraft, fresh out of military service, required little attention to get it flying and the group members were soon flying it. It is still airworthy today.

A couple of years after acquiring the P-51D, Nolen was alerted to the availability of a Grumman F8F Bearcat for sale at a US Navy storage facility at NAS Litchfield Park, Arizona. Though the type did not see

Now registered to the Federal Express Corporation of Memphis, Tennessee, P-40E Kittyhawk AK979 is seen here registered N5672N in 1948. Warbird Index

Formerly RCAF1064, this P-40E was registered N151U to the EAA Museum, then at Hales Corners, Wisconsin, in June 1967. Warbird Index

Hugh Wells of Baltimore, Maryland, owned Lockheed P-38L Lightning N25Y when this photograph was taken at Harbor Field, Maryland, in April 1959. Dick Phillips collection

Lockheed P-38L Lightning 44-27183/ N517PA was modified for civilian aerial survey duties and is seen here at Santa Barbara, California, in July 1971 when owned by Wally D Peterson. Erich Gandet

This oddly coloured P-38 (or an F-5) was photographed at Las Vegas in May 1968. It was clearly engaged in photo survey duties at some stage of its career. Warbird Index

NAS Litchfield Park, Arizona, circa 1959. This Grumman F7F Tigercat is one of thousands of surplus naval warbirds offered for sale/scrap at the facility at the time. Brian Baker

This derelict F7F-3 Tigercat is now believed to be in store with warbird collector Kermit Weeks at Octillo Wells. Warbird Index

combat during World War Two, it is one of Grumman's most beautiful aircraft and remains as sought after today as it was then. In fact Nolen's expedition to Litchfield Park resulted in the purchase of not one, but two F8F-2s (BuNos 121614 and 122619) for the princely sum of $800.00 each.

The sight of so many thousands of warbirds stored in the open at NAS Litchfield Park dismayed Nolen. Investigative telephone calls to his associates revealed the story was the same everywhere. He reached the conclusion that there was little effort being made to preserve any examples of the aircraft that were 'under the axe', let alone any interest being shown in keeping them in flying condition. A few were being sidelined for museums, but these would not fly. Nolen's opinion, however, was that flying these 'warbirds' was the best way to preserve them. How prophetic.

The Smithsonian Institution had began to collect types for its aviation museum in Washington, DC, and the US Navy, in the early 1960s, made a policy decision to acquire types for its Museum of Naval Aviation which was to be built at NAS Pensacola, Florida. Some far-sighted individuals had also begun collecting isolated examples around the United States, but there was no

Sis-Q Flying Service of Santa Rosa, California, has been a major source of Grumman F7F Tigercat airframes. This one is seen in 'active service' as a fire-bomber in 1970.
Warbird Index

One that didn't make it: F8F-2 Bearcat BuNo 121699 was registered N7826C to John Dorr of Orinda, California, in 1958. It was destroyed in a crash at Amarillo, Texas, in August 1966.
William T Larkins

Seen here in the early 1960s, Grumman F8F-2 Bearcat BuNo 121752/N7827C was raced as Tom's Cat. *William T Larkins*

coordinated effort to keep these aircraft airworthy. For its part, the US Air Force was in the process of formulating an important initiative, and had launched plans to methodically collect examples of all the aircraft types that had been operated by the Air Force and its forebears, including important World War Two combat types. Yet, although these aircraft would be subject to a high standard of preservation, they would not fly; instead they would be exhibited at the massive US Air Force Museum at Wright-Patterson AFB in Dayton, Ohio.

There is a story that the first Mustang acquired by Lloyd Nolen and his colleagues was adorned with the name 'Confederate Air Force', painted by a practical joker during the hours of darkness. The name stuck and undoubtedly the Confederate Air Force (CAF, renamed the Commemorative Air Force in 2002) was the basis for what has since grown into an international movement of private owners and collections of airworthy historic combat aircraft, kept airworthy by a serious industry dedicated to their safe operation.

By 1960 the CAF was an increasingly powerful voice in the quest to preserve World War Two aircraft in flying condition. On 6th September 1961 the CAF became a nonprofit Texas corporation, formed to 'preserve and restore World War Two combat aircraft'. By the end of that year the group already had nine aircraft. The organisation went from strength to strength, and by 1965 had established a creditable 'living museum' with support services and its first museum building. In 1968 the CAF took up residence in its new headquarters at the appropriately named Rebel Field in Harlingen, Texas.

Besides the continuing operation of several rare and valuable aircraft and its ambitious restoration programmes, being undertaken by various CAF 'Wings' across the United

The Confederate Air Force were desperate to get a Mustang – this was one of their first aircraft. Warbird Index

Vought F4U-7 Corsair BuNo 133722 in service with the French Aéronavale. The aircraft ended up in Half Moon Bay, California, with Gary Harris who had it rebuilt to airworthy condition over a ten-year period. Warbird enthusiasts in the United Kingdom were treated to several years' residence in the custody of Lindsey Walton, but it stayed on the US civil register as N1337A. It was eventually sold to Jack Erickson in Oregon in 1993. P Lucas

N1337A in April 1993, being dismantled prior to containerisation and shipment to the United States. Trevor Moore

Being raced at Reno in 1968 with a then-fashionable civil (and gaudy) colour scheme and named Lancer II, F4U-4 BuNo 97259 is now on display in the EAA Museum at Oshkosh, Wisconsin. Warbird Index

Vought FG-1D Corsair BuNo 88368 was recovered from Lake Washington on 14th June 1984. Aircraft in similar condition have been rebuilt to fly; this one is now exhibited aboard the USS Yorktown. Erich Gandet

Argentina was a major source of Corsair airframes. This aircraft, one of the last to come out of the country, is believed to be in airworthy condition in France. Warbird Index

Assigned to the Royal Australian Navy in March 1952, Sea Fury FB.11 WG630 was transferred to the Experimental Building Station at Ryde, New South Wales, where it is seen in action as a wind machine. It is now being rebuilt to fly for the Royal Australian Navy Historic Flight at NAS Nowra, New South Wales. via Peter Anderson

P-51D Mustang 44-64005 served with the 361st FG. Flown by Lieutenant George Vanden Heuval, it saw combat and downed several Luftwaffe aircraft. It was then transferred to the Royal Canadian Air Force, in whose markings it is seen here as RCAF9561 before it was struck off charge in 1960. It is now active as N5ICK. Dave Menard.

States, the next landmark event occurred in 1991 when the organisation moved to Midland, Texas. Today, the CAF has over 11,000 members worldwide, several hundred of whom perform essential duties as maintenance crew and pilots. Privately funded and self-supporting, the CAF currently own more than 140 aircraft (registered to the American Airpower Heritage Flying Museum), 33 of which are currently being restored to airworthy condition. The organisation is an all-volunteer group and membership is open to anyone over the age of 18. Undoubtedly, the foresight of the founding fathers of the CAF was a significant milestone in the history of the warbird movement.

In the early days of the warbird movement, the extent of operation of ex-military aircraft varied from country to country; and the degree of interest shown by private individuals in acquiring these aircraft was far below that of today. For example, in Australia, which now has a buoyant warbird movement, the Department of Civil Aviation regulated the civil operation of ex-military aircraft. Immediately after World War Two, such operation was limited to those aircraft types deemed suitable for use in a commercial aviation role, plus a small number of types that could be used in a private role. In the case of those types selected for commercial use, the aircraft had to be suitably modified to civilian standards. This included types such as the Douglas C-47 (plus previously impressed civilian DC-2s and DC-3s), and Lockheed 'twins' such as the Hudson.

Hawker Sea Fury FB.11 WG567 was assigned to the Royal Canadian Navy in August 1951 and was phased out of service in February 1957. It was then registered CF-VAN to Robert P Vanderveken, of Pierrefonds, Quebec, in September 1961. It was heavily modified for Unlimited air racing and named Miss Merced. *Currently incumbent with J & S Aviation of Oconomowoc, Wisconsin, it is seen here as N878M* Super Chief *in 1988.* Warbird Index

Australia had no equivalent to the United States' flexible 'Experimental' category, which was used to cover a gamut of early warbirds there; no fighter types and the like were permitted. There were a few exceptions, notably the UK registration of an ex-Royal Australian Air Force CAC Mustang for Ron Flockhart as an air racer and the Australian civil registration of another Mustang, which seemed to escape the attention of the authorities.

The unwillingness of the Australian aviation authorities to cooperate with certifying warbirds combined with the general lack of interest in such types exhibited worldwide

at that time, resulted in extensive scrapping of ex-military aircraft in Australia. It wasn't until the 1970s that the first real warbirds received official sanction to fly as civil aircraft in Australia, and even then restrictions on their operation were quite severe.

Canada was another major source for warbird aircraft, particularly B-25 Mitchells, P-51D Mustangs, T-6 Texans, P-40 Kittyhawks, Bolingbrokes, Harvards, Hurricanes, Cansos and Catalinas, Venturas, Lysanders and Lancasters.

As related earlier, the United States Government sold a large number of aircraft to overseas air arms, and there were even

some isolated cases of smuggling (to Israel amongst others). Legitimate sales of what we now call warbirds effectively extended the period of time available to civilians for the acquisition of aircraft for civil use.

For example, the P-47 Thunderbolt, now a comparatively rare warbird, went into service with air arms of numerous countries including Bolivia, Brazil, Colombia, Guatemala, Mexico, Nicaragua, Peru, Venezuela and Yugoslavia. The aircraft provided excellent platforms for their recipients and gave long service. When they were retired they were stored, and almost all of the countries mentioned duly yielded airframes for museums and for private collectors to restore and put back in the air, many in the recent past. One such aircraft has recently been restored by Pacific Fighters in Idaho.

It is an interesting exercise to analyse the surviving P-47 Thunderbolt population and its various sources. The United States Air Force Museum, as mentioned earlier, was a comparatively efficient collector in the early days and now has six P-47 airframes at various locations, all but one (an ex-Peruvian Air Force P-47D) coming from Air National

Blain Fowler of Camrose, Alberta, has operated F4U-7 Corsair BuNo 133710/C-GWFU Alberta Blue *since October 1983. The aircraft is up for sale at the time of writing.* Blain Fowler

Neal Melton's P-47D was one of several such airframes recovered from Brazil in recent years; this shot shows another example mounted on a pylon at Santa Cruz Air Base, Brazil. Warbird Index

Guard stocks. Peru yielded some eight P-47s, four of which are now in the hands of private collectors and four in museums; one of the airframes has a 'split personality'.

Brazil has perhaps yielded the majority of flyable or potentially flyable P-47s. Of the 13 examples, eight (one of which is flyable) are thought to still be on charge with the Brazilian Air Force in various museums, and a further two are currently being rebuilt to fly. Of the ex-Yugoslav Air Force airframes – five in total – three are in museums, one is being rebuilt to fly, and one is in the Yugoslavian Aviation Museum in Belgrade. In Venezuela four P-47s have survived, three as museum exhibits and one as airworthy.

It is also worthy of note that two examples of the rarer P-47G Thunderbolt variant were acquired from Technical Institutes. The Air Museum Planes of Fame 'razorback' was rescued from the famous Cal-Aero Technical Institute in Glendale, California. The other P-47G (apparently modified to TP-47G standards quite early in its career, making it truly unique), currently owned by Flying A Services, came from the Aero Industries Technical Institute and was transferred to Oakland Airport, California as long ago as 1946. It was later used as a ground-running engine test rig with the Flying Tiger Line at the same airport and only really became a true warbird when ownership was transferred to Ray Stutsman in December 1979. Other rare warbirds have survived due to the fact that they were employed in similar roles. Other countries that still have P-47 airframes include Chile, China, Colombia and Cuba.

The surviving North American P-51 Mustang population – over 300 in number – can also claim a variety of sources, and these are outlined extensively in the author's companion work, *Mustang Survivors* (Midland Publishing, 2003).

While the Confederate Air Force can rightly claim to be pioneers of warbird operations, there are several notable individuals who deserve recognition for collecting, restoring and establishing the airworthy operation of warbird aircraft.

Paul Mantz was one of the first pioneers of the warbird movement. The now legendary character set an international aviation record

by performing 46 consecutive outside loops on 6th July 1930 whilst flying a Fleet 2 above San Mateo, California. This outstanding record stood for almost 50 years. The following year he founded United Air Services at Burbank, California, where he performed in motion pictures as a stunt pilot. Mantz became well known for his flying prowess and his ability to

deliver exactly what film directors required.

Mantz also served as technical advisor to the famous aviatrix Amelia Earhart, painstakingly planning her ground-breaking flights in the 1930s. During World War Two he served as a USAAF Colonel in the Special Services Motion Picture Division. Making morale-boosting films for public release, he

utilised many servicemen as actors, including the likes of Ronald Reagan, Alan Ladd, Clark Gable and George Montgomery. Now-famous training films were also made for instructional purposes.

At the close of World War Two, many people thought Mantz unstable when he purchased 475 surplus military bombers for a mere $56,500. However, when he drained the fuel from the aircraft to sell and finance his venture, he proved his worth as an astute businessman.

Paul Mantz's exploits in air racing have also gone down in history. Having been placed third in the 1938 and 1939 Bendix Races flying a Lockheed Orion, he then became the first aviator to win the Bendix Trophy three times consecutively, starting in 1946. His mount for these remarkable achievements was his red North American P-51B Mustang.

The 1960s saw Mantz team up with another aviation movie pilot, Frank Tallman. Together they formed the now famous Tallmantz Aviation, based at Santa Ana Airport in California, setting up the Movieland of the Air Museum with several aircraft, all of which were put to work to earn their keep. Sadly, Paul Mantz lost his life in a flying accident during filming of the closing scenes of *Flight of the Phoenix* on 8th July 1965, in Buttercup Valley, Arizona.

North American P-51D-25NA Mustang 44-72777 seen here in Rhode Island ANG markings. Eventually the aircraft passed to Cavalier Aircraft Corporation of Sarasota, Florida, and was later employed by the Indonesian Air Force. It was recovered by the late Stephen Johnson of Van Pac Carriers, Oakland, California, in the late 1970s. The aircraft is currently owned by Steve Seghetti (registered N151D) and is a genuine combat veteran, having been flown by 'Doc' Watson during World War Two. William T Larkins

P-51D Mustang 44-73275 in North Dakota Air National Guard markings. After being sold as 'surplus' via McClellan AFB, California, in September 1957, it became N119H in 1966 and still carries these markings with its current owner, James Elkins of Salem, Oregon. Dick Phillips collection

Curtiss P-40N 44-7983 in September 1968 when owned by the Tallmantz Collection. It is now airworthy in the United States and owned by Ice Strike Corporation. Warbird Index

Frank Tallman of the now famous Tallmantz Aviation operated this rare, dual-control, factory-built Curtiss TP-40N in the early 1960s. It became part of the Movieland of the Air Museum until it was purchased by aircraft collector Kermit Weeks who has the aircraft on rebuild in Florida. P Bowers

Ed Maloney of the Air Museum took delivery of this FG-1D Corsair in 1958. It is seen here leaving the custodianship of the Military Aircraft Restoration Corporation at Chino en route to the Midwest Aviation Museum of Danville, Illinois, in January 1994. Mike VadeBonCoeur

Photographs on the opposite page:

Top left: *Photographed in Air National Guard markings, P-51D Mustang 44-63542 became N5450V. It is now N51HR with the Ted Contri family in Yuba City, California. Dick Phillips*

Top right: *P-51D Mustang 44-63542 photographed at Yuba County Airport, California, in April 1977. Boardman C Reed*

Centre: *P-51D Mustang 44-72777 was flown by Major Ralph J 'Doc' Watson of the 52nd FG during World War Two. It was later reworked by Cavalier (as 72-1537) and transferred to the Indonesian Air Force, with whom it stayed until recovered by Stephen Johnson of VanPac Carriers in 1978. It is now owned by Steve Seghetti and registered N151D. Steve Seghetti*

Among the first true American pioneers of the warbird movement, as we know it today, was Ed Maloney. One of Ed's great inspirations was General 'Hap' Arnold, the World War Two USAAF Chief of Staff, who advocated the preservation of at least one example of every type of USAAF aircraft for future generations. Despite this, though some types were ordered to be stored for display at the Smithsonian and the nascent Air Force Museum, many others were simply scrapped with little or no regard for Arnold's dictum.

Close to Ed Maloney's home in Southern California was the Cal Aero Academy (now

Chino Airport), where he saw over 5,000 aircraft scrapped. From news reaching him, Maloney was aware that thousands more such aircraft were being similarly scrapped across the United States. Personally enthused by 'Hap' Arnold's strong advocacy of preservation, Maloney began his own crusade to save as many warbirds as was practicable. He methodically visited scrap yards and auctions of surplus aircraft, and trade schools where warbirds were being utilised as instructional airframes. Some aircraft were dramatically pulled from the scrappers' clutches at the very last opportunity. It

is only now that we can truly appreciate this pioneering work.

At the beginning, Ed Maloney's aircraft collection was stored in his 'back yard'. However, by January 1957 storage space was quickly running out, which led to a decision to open a museum to the public. Located in Claremont, California, and simply christened The Air Museum, Ed Maloney's venture grew at a dramatic pace, changing venues several times in the process. Today it is The Air Museum – Planes of Fame and is located at Chino, known to many as the centre of warbird restoration in California.

At the outset it was Ed Maloney's intention to restore as many as possible of the aircraft in his collection to flying condition. Today, Ed Maloney serves on the Museum's Board of Directors, has authored numerous books and continues his efforts in support of the preservation of aviation history.

For many students of the warbird movement, the making of the 1969 film *Battle of Britain* was certainly a major catalyst in launching airworthy warbird collections. The chief 'mover and shaker' in providing aircraft for the film was T.G. 'Hamish' Mahaddie of Spitfire Productions. A few years earlier, Mirisch Films had made the film *633 Squadron*, for which Mahaddie acquired two Mosquito bombers.

Mahaddie's task for production of *Battle of Britain* was much more difficult. His main concern was mustering the Luftwaffe aircraft; no Messerschmitt Bf 109s or any of the German-engined bombers were available.

Hispano HA-1112-M1L Buchon C4K-169 dressed as a Royal Air Force Hurricane for the filming of Battle of Britain *by Spitfire Productions Ltd in 1968. Like so many of its warbird sisters, this aircraft (as N9939) was damaged in a ground-loop accident at Harlingen, Texas, in October 1976. It was acquired by Harold Kindsvater who lovingly restored it to fly once more as N109W. Warbird Index*

The same aircraft as N9939 loaded aboard a trailer for the move to its new owner, Harold Kindsvater. Robb Satterfield

The roll-out of Hispano HA-1112-M1L C4K-169 as N109W in July 2000. Wayne Gomes

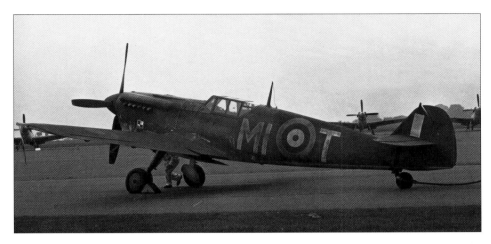

Photographs on the opposite page:

Japanese aircraft have only recently come to the fore in the field of airworthy restorations, but they are gaining popularity amongst collectors. No doubt those worried about accidents (as opposed to museum fires) would be quite worried if this unique Mitsubishi J2M3 Raiden, FE320, was to be restored to fly. It is on the inventory of the Air Museum at Chino, California, and is see here on a rare airing at the Planes of Fame airshow. Joe Cupido

Hurricane Mk IIc PZ865 'dressed' by the film studios and looking the part for its appearance in the film Battle of Britain. *Warbird Index*

However, Mahaddie quickly turned his attention to Spain where the Ejericto del Aire (Spanish Air Force) was operating Hispano HA-1112-M1L Buchons – essentially Merlin-engined Bf 109s. Some 24 Buchons were acquired by Mahaddie on behalf of Spitfire Productions, along with three Spitfires and two CASA-2.111s (Merlin-engined Heinkel He 111s).

On completion of filming, most of the Buchons were disposed of, some to another warbird collector, Wilson 'Connie' Edwards of Breckenridge, Texas. Edwards sold many of the aircraft over the years but still has several stored away, including a rare HA-1112-K1L two-seater. When interviewed by the author in 1968, Hamish Mahaddie, a man of great modesty, refused to take any credit for being a catalyst for the warbird movement.

One of the most prolific private vintage aircraft collectors in the history of the world-wide warbirds movement was Doug Arnold, perhaps best known for forming the company Warbirds of Great Britain Ltd. There is not a major private collection in the world that does not have an aircraft owned by Doug Arnold at one stage or another during his career. His activities included dealing with several foreign governments, resulting in dozens of warbirds being rescued from obscurity. His experience in successfully closing deals with foreign governments was the envy of many others who had failed previously.

Doug Arnold was a man with a reputation for being tough; a shrewd character with an eye for a good investment based on years of experience. He was a personality for whom the attraction of publicity was unimportant, yet the size of his aircraft collection inevitably raised a lot of interest. His interest in warbirds stemmed from his activities immediately after World War Two. Undoubtedly his main interest was in the Supermarine Spitfire and its many variants. Over the years he owned almost every mark of the type extant; the records show he had owned as many as 14 Spitfires and a Seafire. His ultimate ambition was to own one of every mark – and he came quite close to achieving it.

Doug Arnold is perhaps best known for his activities on the Indian sub-continent, where he was directly responsible for the recovery of no less than seven Hawker Tempests and several Spitfires. Additionally, he was responsible for the retrieval of many of the ex-Spanish Air Force CASA Ju-52 variants that now reside in collections in France, Germany, South Africa, the United States and other parts of the world. Four Hawker Sea Furies, which otherwise may have been scrapped following use as target tugs in West Ger-

Warbird collector Charles Church sadly lost his life in this Spitfire, built up pretty much from scratch by Spitfire restorer Dick Melton as a 'modified Mk Vc', when it crashed following a catastrophic engine failure on 1st July 1989. *Author*

The unique Seafire III PP972 in the Warbirds of Great Britain hangar at Biggin Hill, Kent, in 1989. It is currently nearing the end of a rebuild to fly in Norfolk. *Author*

Spitfire PR.XI PL983 during filming of the controversial UK TV series Piece of Cake, during which Ray Hanna of the Old Flying Machine Company famously flew Spitfire IX MH434 through the spans of a bridge. Sadly the latter aircraft crashed following an engine failure at Rouene, France, on 9th June 2001, killing pilot Martin Sargeant. The airframe is now being rebuilt. *Mike Shreeve*

This unidentified Sea Fury T.20S shows its German target tug origins in the form of its red and orange colour scheme. Warbird Index

M.D.N. 'Bill' Fisher acquired Hawker Sea Fury FB.11 WJ288 from Hawker Siddeley Aviation for the Historic Aircraft Preservation Society at Biggin Hill in 1966. It was registered G-SALY to Patrick Luscombe of the British Air Reserve in July 1983. Photographed in transit at Duxford at around that time, the aircraft ended up with Warbirds of Great Britain before being exported to the United States for Ed Stanley of Portland, Oregon, in 1990. It is now owned by David Peeler of Memphis, Tennessee. Michael Shreeve

many, were also acquired and introduced to the warbird community. He also made the first arrangement with the United Kingdom's Ministry of Defence to release several gate guard Spitfires in exchange for aircraft provided to the RAF Museum at Hendon.

All in all, but not including Douglas DC-3s and C-47s, some 79 warbirds have been owned at one time or another by Doug Arnold's companies, the main one being Warbirds of Great Britain Ltd based at Blackbushe, Bitteswell, Biggin Hill and later Bournemouth. The aircraft in question include three Lancasters, one Lincoln, two P-63 Kingcobras, two B-17 Flying Fortresses, two CAC Mustangs, one PBY Catalina, seven CASA Ju-52s, one CASA 2.111, one B-24J Liberator, one P-40N, one Mosquito (now in the USAF Museum), one Fw 190, three Gnats, one Meteor, one F6F Hellcat, one F8F Bearcat, two TBM Avengers, one FM-2 Wildcat, five Hawker Fury/Sea Furies, one Hurricane, seven Tempests, one HA-1112-M1L Buchon, one P-38 Lightning, three Bf 109s, two Noorduyn-built AT-16 Harvards, five P-51 Mustangs, two B-25 Mitchells, three P-47 Thunderbolts, fourteen Spitfires, one Seafire, three F4U Corsairs and one Lysander.

Highlights included returning a Lockheed P-38 to the United Kingdom for the first time since World War Two, on 16th May 1989. Despite his activities in the warbird field, Doug Arnold kept a low profile right up until his death in November 1992.

Another prolific warbird collector based in the United States is David C Tallichet. Perhaps most famous for his recovery of several B-26 Marauder bombers from 'Million Dollar Valley' in British Columbia in 1971 and his exploits with P-40s and Beauforts, Tallichet has been associated with approximately 100 warbirds over the years. His Military Aircraft Restoration Corporation has been the most active of the companies he has used; at the time of writing, some 36 aircraft were still registered to MARC along with several unregistered hulks held in store as potential future projects.

Tom Friedkin, a long-established warbird collector based in the United States, is perhaps best known for his role as a movie pilot. His interest in warbirds goes back to his father, Kenneth, who trained pilots during World War Two and undertook combat missions with the RAF. Post war, Kenneth started a flight-training establishment in San Diego, California, perfectly located due to the area's excellent flying weather. In 1949

Seen here in June 1988, F8F-2 Bearcat BuNo 121752 in a civilian paint scheme when owned by World Jet Inc of Fort Lauderdale, Florida. It later passed to Warbirds of Great Britain and is now owned by the Heritage Flight Museum of Eastsound, Washington. Thierry Thomassin

Hawker Sea Fury T.20S G-BCOW was ferried from Germany to Blackbushe in October 1974 where Warbirds of Great Britain imported it. The aircraft is now in the United States with the Zager Aircraft Corporation of Cupertino, California, registered N281L. Gary R Brown

Hawker Tempest II MW848 masquerading as HA623 of the Indian Air Force, marks which it wore with that air arm when it served in the late 1940s. The aircraft is now on charge with the Indian Air Force Museum in Palam, New Delhi. Several Tempests were recovered from India and though one (of three aircraft held) with Tempest Two Ltd is close to completion, with its registered owner at Gamston Airport in Nottinghamshire, the others are far from airworthy. Simon Watson

he launched the now famous Pacific Southwest Airlines (PSA), which commenced operations with a leased Douglas DC-3.

Kenneth Friedkin was a flamboyant 'people person', his trademark being colourful shirts and an insistence that all of PSA's flight crew mixed with the passengers. He was also a true pioneer of low cost fares: with PSA you could fly from San Francisco to San Diego for less than $20. The airline – known affectionately as the 'Poor Sailors Airline' due to the patronage of hundreds of Pacific Fleet personnel – expanded rapidly.

Sadly, Kenneth Friedkin passed away in 1962 aged just 47, and just 12 months later Tom Friedkin lost his mother too. As the major shareholder, Tom soon found himself on the PSA board while continuing to fly full time as a pilot.

By the late-1980s, PSA had been acquired by US Air and with his share of the proceeds, Tom launched several successful ventures and began collecting warbirds, in which he has a passionate interest. Initially a number of jet warbirds were acquired, including types like the F-5 Freedom Fighter, a beautiful F-86 Sabre and MiG-15. Currently the Friedkin Collection, previously operated under the Cinema Air banner, is known as Chino Warbirds and includes single examples of a rare A-36 Invader, FM-2 Wildcat, F6F Hellcat and F8F Bearcat, two P-51 Mustangs and several Grumman J2F Ducks.

Originally surplussed in 1957 via NAS Litchfield Park and registered N7195C to George Kreitberg of Salem, Oregon, this Tigercat was owned by Gary Flanders and Mike Bogue when it was photographed at Oakland, California, on 14th May 1982. The photographer also supplied the details for the authentic paint scheme. William T Larkins

Fast forward ten years: BuNo 121752 Wampus Cat at Reno in September 1998 wearing a US Navy colour scheme. Tom Smith

Rene Bouverat's F8F-2 Bearcat in June 2000, dressed in newly applied French Aéronavale markings and registered F-AZRJ. Thierry Thomassin

Photographs on the opposite page:

P-38L Lightning 44-53186/N505MH being painted as Miss Behavin' at Chino in 1989. Larry Smigla

Mike Wright prepares to ferry P-38L Lightning 44-53186/N505MH to the United Kingdom in May 1989. It stayed only briefly before it was transferred to the Evergreen Vintage Aircraft Collection, where it remains today. David Arnold

The current holder of the biggest warbird fleet in the United States, Fantasy of Flight founder Kermit Weeks, has some 70 warbirds either airworthy, under restoration or in store at the Polk City, Florida, visitor attraction's storage hangars. The opening of the 'aviation-themed attraction' represents the pinnacle of Weeks' lifelong passion for aircraft and aviation history.

Weeks earned recognition both for his accomplishments in the air as a pilot, and on the ground for his technical expertise in designing and building aircraft. For the past 30 years, he has constantly promoted aviation and in particular warbird aircraft restoration.

At the tender age of 17, while still studying at high school, Weeks began building his first home-built aircraft, which he completed and flew four years later. In 1973 he competed in aerobatic flying for the first time. He also began pursuing an aeronautical engineering degree at Miami-Dade Junior College, the University of Florida and later Purdue University. Just three years later, he had designed and built the 'Weeks Special', an aerobatic aircraft qualified for the United States Aerobatics Team. In 1978, he was runner-up out of 61 competitors, earning three Silver Medals and one Bronze in the World Aerobatics Championships staged in Czechoslovakia. This was the start of a distinguished career in competition aerobatics.

By the late 1970s Weeks' aviation interests had began to embrace the collection, restoration and preservation of antique and warbird aircraft. He acquired aircraft and projects at a rapid rate, contracting out some of the restoration work and performing other restorations in-house. In 1985, he opened the Weeks Air Museum in Miami, a non-profit facility housing much of his private collection and other antique aircraft owned by the Museum.

As his own collection grew, Weeks began planning an ambitious move to a custom-built facility that would enable him to exhibit his aircraft collection to the general public. By the late 1980s he had acquired a 300-acre site close to Polk City, Florida, just 20 miles south-west of Walt Disney World. His dream was to create an aviation-themed attraction that he christened Fantasy of Flight.

Ironically, as Weeks' plans for Fantasy of Flight neared completion Hurricane 'Andrew' decimated much of the Miami area, heavily damaging sections of the Weeks Air Museum facility and taking its toll on some of the rarer warbirds. However, Kermit continued undaunted and the Fantasy of Flight attraction opened shortly afterwards. It houses almost all of his collection of aircraft and one of the biggest aero engine collections in the world.

One of the warbird collections that has evolved dramatically is The Fighter Collection, based at Duxford, Cambridgeshire. Stephen Grey began collecting warbirds in 1980, three core aircraft being acquired in a relatively short space of time. The first of the trio, P-51D Mustang 44-73149, was purchased in California and ferried to the UK to

Nelson Ezell restored Kermit Weeks' F4U-4 BuNo 97286, seen here in 1994, which had just three previous owners. Warbird Index

Kermit Weeks' Vought F4U-4 Corsair, BuNo 97286/N5215V, was rebuilt to flying condition by Nelson Ezell and his crew at Breckenridge, Texas. It is now based at Polk City, Florida. The Warbird Index

Recovered from a Scouts adventure area, F6F-3 Hellcat BuNo 43014 was first registered to John R 'Jack' Sandberg as N7537U. Sandberg went on to found JRS Enterprises, which supported the warbird restoration industry with rebuilt warbird engines until May 2003. Jack was killed in 1993 in the crash of his custom-built racing aeroplane Tsunami. *The Hellcat, seen here in 1986, is now with Kermit Weeks at Polk City, Florida.* Author

Photographs on the opposite page:

Top left: *Elmer Ward's Grumman F8F-2 Bearcat in its stunning fire orange and black colour scheme, being restored in the early 1990s. The aircraft suffered considerable damage when it was force-landed at Oshkosh, Wisconsin, on 2nd August 1993.* Gary R Brown

Top right: *Grumman F8F-2 Bearcat BuNo 121748, now in France with Rene Bouverat as F-AZRJ, seen here in a civilian paint scheme as N200N with Sonoma Valley Aircraft.* Rene Bouverat

Bottom: *Kermit Weeks added an ex-Indian Air Force B-24J Liberator to his collection in September 1994 – seen here on a ferry flight into Florida in May 1998.* Tom Smith

Seen here in 1978, Grumman F8F-1B Bearcat BuNo 122095 sat outside Government offices in Bangkok, Thailand, for many years before being recovered by the world-famous Salis Collection in 1986. After passing through Jersey-based Patina (as G-BUCF) and then the Yankee Air Corps, ownership passed to its present custodian, Tom Wood of Indianapolis who has it registered as N2209. Philippe Denis

Lockheed P-38J Lightning 42-67543 California Cutie seen in service with The Fighter Collection during an overseas trip to France in 1996. Pilot 'Hoof' Proudfoot tragically lost his life when the aircraft crashed and was totally destroyed at Duxford on 14th July 1996. Thierry Thomassin

Iraqi Single Seat Fury 37534 painted in authentic Iraqi Air Force markings by the Old Flying Machine Company. One has to ask if such markings would now be considered 'politically correct' in a world gone mad, but it did look most impressive back in 1994! The airframe has since been repainted in more sombre Royal Navy markings and exported to South Africa where it flies with the Jayesse Trust as ZU-SEA. Thierry Thomassin

make its UK debut at the Biggin Hill airshow, flown by Ray Hanna, on 2nd May 1981. Spitfire IX ML417 was also acquired in the United States as a project and shipped back to the United Kingdom for restoration. A flyable F8F Bearcat, one of Grey's favourite airshow performers, completed the trio.

Though it was not Stephen's original intention, the three core aircraft represented the start of a formidable collecting and trading habit that has resulted in an impressive and meaningful warbird collection – the best of its type in Europe and some would say the world, for variety and uniqueness. There has also been a trading policy that has assisted other collections to start up all over the world, for example the Alpine Fighter Collection in New Zealand and the Flying Legend organisation in France. Additionally, the engineering arm of The Fighter Collection has undertaken work for other collections, including the RAF Museum, producing some quality static exhibits into the bargain.

Not only has the The Fighter Collection grown in stature, it has become the focus of public attention and a dedicated team also produce an airshow – aptly named Flying Legends – which takes place at Duxford each summer over a weekend. This event has become the gathering-point for Europe's warbird owners and is watched enthusiastically by warbird aficionados from around the globe. The Fighter Collection has seen more than 50 warbirds pass through its hands since its inception, and has kept a core fleet airworthy for the viewing delight of thousands all over Europe.

Also resident at Duxford, Ray Hanna's Old Flying Machine Company (OFMC) was formed in 1981 with Ray's son Mark as Managing Director. At the core of the company's philosophy is the intention of preserving and

The late Mark Hanna of the Old Flying Machine Company in Curtiss P-40E AK933, taxying in after a flying display at Duxford on 9th June 1985. Michael Shreeve

Spitfire LF.XVIe SL542 at RAF St Athan when in storage for the Ministry of Defence. Warbird Index

The Ministry of Defence, in its wisdom, decided to auction one of the Battle of Britain Memorial Flight's Spitfire XIXs, PS853. Ownership passed to Euan English for a brief period before the aircraft was sold to Rolls-Royce plc, which operates the aircraft today as G-RRGN. Author

maintaining rare vintage aircraft in flying condition. The company's policy is based on a commitment 'to display the aircraft in a manner that emulates as closely and safely as possible the roles for which they were originally designed'. This has set OFMC apart from similar collections across the world.

Today the OFMC has grown in size and quality to become one of the foremost warbird collections in the world; the latest aircraft, a Lavochkin La-9, flew for the first time in the United Kingdom as this book was being written. The acquisition and release of this aircraft was negotiated primarily by Ray Hanna over many years from the Chinese government, and has resulted in a rare fighter aircraft being put back in the air after several years' restoration by Pioneer Aero Restorations in Ardmore, New Zealand.

All of the OFMC pilots have exceptional backgrounds in military and aerobatics flying. No other organisation has travelled the globe as extensively as OFMC; it is estimated that the aircraft are seen 'live' by over five million people a year in Europe alone. The

aircraft have flown as far afield in Europe as Italy, Norway and Poland, and have even been disassembled and freighted to New Zealand for reassembly and display. In addition to air display work, OFMC specialise in precision flying for film work and advertising.

The company's profile was raised further when Swiss chronograph manufacturer Breitling decided to sponsor four OFMC aircraft, initially over a two-year period. Dubbed the Breitling Fighters, the quartet would tour Europe, visiting major airshows and providing the spectacle of four high-performance warbirds in formation. The quartet – an FG-1D Corsair, Spitfire IX, P-51D Mustang and P-40E Kittyhawk – were painted in new schemes.

Tragically, the co-founder of OFMC, Mark Hanna, was seriously injured in an aircraft crash in Spain on 25th September 1999 and died the following day. The accident took place at Sabadell near Barcelona where the aircraft was due to participate in a large flying display. The loss of Mark stunned the warbird movement. An ex-RAF fast jet pilot, he had flown over 4,000 flying hours of which 2,300 were on historic aircraft.

Almost coincidental with the growth of The Fighter Collection in the United Kingdom, another major collection developed in the United States. Bob Pond acquired his tastes in warbirds in a similar fashion and there was a good deal of open cooperation between the then aptly named Planes of Fame East at Chino and Flying Cloud Airport in Minnesota, and The Fighter Collection. In more recent years the main collection has been housed at the Palm Springs Air Museum, California, and contains several rare aircraft including the Grumman G-58B N700A, which was essentially the world's first privately owned Bearcat. Named *Gulfhawk* and flown by Grumman President Roger Wolfe Kahn, it was eventually passed to the Champlin Fighter Museum at Mesa,

Boeing B-17G Flying Fortress 44-85643/F-BEEA when in service with the Institut Géographique National at Creil, France, where it had served since June 1948 on survey duties. It went on to appear in the Enigma Productions film Memphis Belle, *during which it crashed at RAF Binbrook, caught fire and was destroyed on 25th July 1989.* Warbird Index

Roger Wolfe Kahn at the controls of the beautiful Grumman G-58B which was registered to the Grumman Aircraft Engineering Company as N700A in January 1950 and named Gulfhawk. *Kahn served as the company's president. After being sold to the Redship Cornell Aeronautical Laboratory in Buffalo, New York, ownership passed through several warbird notables including William Ross. J.W. 'Bill' Fornoff, Doug Champlin and Bob Pond. The aircraft is currently painted in a civilian scheme and registered to Pond Warbirds LLC of Palm Springs, California.* courtesy Grumman Corporation

The history of Grumman F6F-5 Hellcat BuNo 78645 is somewhat vague, having been acquired by Charles F Nichols in 1978 for the Yanks Air Museum. It is seen here at Chino in 1994. Thierry Thomassin

Grumman F8F-1B Bearcat BuNo 122095 fully restored and airworthy outside Fighter Rebuilders in May 1998. Thierry Thomassin

Curtiss P-40N 44-7192/N10626 in April 1990 at the Champlin Fighter Museum. Alan Gruening

Arizona, who sold it to Pond in 1986. The airworthy aircraft in this collection now number some 19, registered to Pond Warbirds LLC in Palm Springs, California, where the majority are housed in a custom-built facility.

Charles Nichols, the principal behind the Yanks Air Museum, started collecting warbirds some years ago and now has a world-class assembly of mainly World War Two warbirds, some on the US register and others simply on static display.

The Yanks Air Museum, currently located at Chino Airport, contains a unique collection of 'strictly American made' historic aircraft that date from the early 1900s to the present day, including jet aircraft. All the collection's aircraft are restored to their original factory specifications. Where possible, aircraft in the collection are restored to airworthy status and there are currently 17 aircraft registered to Charles Nichols.

The museum is a non-profit 501(c)3 organisation with declared assets well in excess of $10 million in donated aircraft and artefacts. Currently the museum occupies a five-acre facility located at the western end of Chino Airport. The museum area has two 30,000-ft^2 buildings coupled with several storage units. The main buildings house almost all of the 80 aircraft in the collection with one building being utilised for aircraft restoration and maintenance.

Santa Barbara, California, 27th July 1971: the incomplete and tired-looking Fw 190D-13 WNr 836017 basks in the sunlight. Transferred to the Georgia Institute of Technology in 1946, it remained there until 1968 when it was acquired by the Nazi Museum in Santa Barbara, California. Doug Champlin then acquired the aircraft and had it shipped to Germany where it was rebuilt to taxiable condition. A recent complete restoration by Dave Goss of Gosshawk Unlimited will see the aircraft technically airworthy, but despite recent media reports it will not fly – owner Doug Champlin says it would be 'simply too risky'. Erich Gandet

The Fw 190D-13 with its engine being run by Dave Goss at the Champlin Fighter Museum at Mesa, Arizona, in January 1990. Alan Gruening

The latest restoration will see the Fw 190D-13 completed as close to factory-like condition as it has ever been. Alan Gruening

Pursuing its goal to develop and grow into a 'major aviation museum resort complex' complete with its own airfield, some 440 acres of land have been purchased in Greenfield, California, by Monterey County to house the new museum. Additionally, the Yanks Air Museum library houses aviation-related publications, including microfiche, in a temperature and humidity-controlled environment.

Doug Champlin can almost certainly be categorised as one of the founding fathers of today's warbird movement. Though his Champlin Fighter Museum also houses a number of World War One aeroplanes, his first recorded foray into the acquisition of World War Two aircraft appears to have been in 1969, when he had P-51D Mustang 45-11586 (since destroyed in a flying accident) registered to himself as N518M. The Champlin Fighter Collection (aircraft are registered to Windward Aviation) has a number of interesting aircraft still registered to it, though they will shortly be transferred to the Museum of Flight in Seattle, Washington.

The most valuable aircraft in the collection has to be the long-nosed Focke-Wulf Fw 190D-13. Shipped to the United States from France in July 1945, the aircraft was transferred to the Georgia Institute of Technology before being released to the Nazi Museum in Santa Barbara, California, as a complete aircraft, in 1968. It was transferred to the ownership of Windward Aviation in 1972, immediately being shipped to Germany where Art Williams restored it. The aircraft is said to be in airworthy condition but is not flown.

The Champlin Collection's Yak-9 is a rare and original aircraft. Doug Champlin discovered it during a visit to Russia in 1992 and soon after, Art Williams was contracted to find and acquire it. Williams flew to Novosibirsk, Siberia, purchased the Yak-9 and arranged for it to be transferred to Moscow via the Siberian railroad. Once the aircraft had been secured, Sergei Kotov arranged its

restoration. In 1996, the restored Yak-9 was shipped to Mesa, Arizona. It is equipped with an original engine, and all instrumentation and all other parts are of original Russian manufacture.

At the end of 2000, the Seattle-based Museum of Flight acquired the majority of the Champlin Fighter Collection; some 25 aircraft, mostly World War One and Two types, many of which are unique. Currently housed in the Champlin Fighter Aircraft Museum in Mesa, they will be transferred to Seattle into the Museum of Flight's expansion wing, which is scheduled for completion at the time of writing.

Doug Champlin has also been responsible for funding and coordinating two very important warbird restoration programmes involving previously 'unavailable' warbirds. Working closely with Herb Tischler and his team at the Texas Airplane Company based in Fort Worth, Doug financed the construction of several Grumman F3F 'Flying Barrels'

which now form important parts of several collections.

More recently, Tischler's team has been concentrating on the similarly rare Nakajima Ki-43 Hayabusa. Based on major components recovered by Doug Champlin some years ago, the projects are nearing completion. A recent chat with George Tischler (Herb's brother) revealed that the fuselages are fairly complete, except for more minor items like access doors, and the installation of control surfaces. The landing gears are being built up from fabricated parts as required for installation into the wings, which are now recognisable after being manufactured from drawings and the major structures acquired by Doug Champlin. Wing No.1 is on hold until some rework to match wing No.2 is completed.

Wing No.2 will be the first flight unit. It has been pulled from the assembly jig and is

currently being 'soft mated' to a fuselage. At the time of writing, assembly of Wing No.3 had just started in the assembly jig. Work on the first flight unit cockpit will not be started until the wing and fuselage are assembled in their final state for flight. Engine cowling work is on hold until the mock-up engine is mounted, which is scheduled after work on the wing and fuselage of the first aircraft is completed. The team are now searching for an original 1,130-hp (843-kW) Nakajima Ha.115 14-cylinder two-row air-cooled radial engine.

Founded in 1979 by Bob Collings, The Collings Foundation's stated aim is to 'to organise and support 'living history' events that enable Americans to learn more about their heritage through direct participation'. Originally the Collings Foundation ran transport-related events such as antique car rallies, and hill climbs. During the 1980s, these

Two-seat Fw 190F-8/U1 at RAF St Athan. Assigned to the Luftwaffe as 'Black 38' it was captured at Grove, Denmark, in 1945. In September 1945 the aircraft, assigned to the RAF as AM 29, was flown to Farnborough from Schleswig, Germany, for evaluation, eventually being transferred to the RAF's Air Historical Branch. Prior to its removal to the Royal Air Force Museum at Hendon in 1990, the aircraft's engine was regularly exercised, much to the delight of its custodians. The Warbird Index

Boeing B-17G 44-85718/G-FORT at Duxford in July 1987 shortly before being ferried to the USA for the Lone Star Flight Museum, then located in Houston, Texas. Michael Shreeve

The newly restored Grumman F7F Tigercat, N800RW/BuNo 80503 was restored by Darrell Skurich at Vintage Aircraft Limited, Fort Collins, CO in the late 1980s. Warbird Index

Grumman F6F-5N Hellcat BuNo 94204/N4998V is now airworthy and housed with the Lone Star Flight Museum; its first civilian owner was the Normandie Iron & Metal Company. Warbird Index

Modified by Cavalier in the 1960s, P-51D-25NA Mustang 44-73206/N3751D Hurry Home Honey, photographed out of Oshkosh in 1991, in an accurate presentation of Pete Peterson's 364th FS, 347th FG colours. Robert S DeGroat

activities developed to include aviation-related events such as airshows. In 1989, Collings decided that the Foundation should launch a Veterans 'Wings of Freedom' tour to show off a fully restored Consolidated B-24J Liberator that flew as a living tribute to B-24 veterans from the European Theatre of Operations.

The B-24 was repainted in 1999 to pay homage to veterans of the Pacific Theatre of Operations. The 'Wings of Freedom' tour also includes the Collings Foundation's B-17G Flying Fortress, representing the operational mate of the B-24 on countless bombing missions during World War Two. It is estimated that between three and four million people see these warbirds each year during the tour.

Additionally, the Collings Foundation operates other aircraft including a 1909 Bleriot XI, Dr.1 Triplane, PT-17 Stearman, AT-6 Texan, TBM Avenger, Fi 156 Storch, UC-78 Bobcat, F4U-5NL Corsair, A-26C Invader, B-25J Mitchell, T-33 Shooting Star, UH-IE 'Huey', TA-4JF Skyhawk and an S2F Tracker. Some of these aircraft are airworthy, others are in restoration at the time of writing.

Robert Waltrip founded the Lone Star Flight Museum. One of his first acquisitions was F6F-5N Hellcat N4998V, purchased from Mike Coutches in November 1986. A new museum facility was constructed on Galveston Island, Texas, to house the museum that now contains a number of restored, airworthy warbirds. Stars in the collection (divided between the Texas Aviation Hall of Fame and Air SRV on the US register) include a B-17 and several Grumman 'Cats' (FM-2, F3F, F6F, F7F and an F8F). In addition, some British warbirds have joined the museum, a restored Spitfire having flown recently while work has commenced on restoring a Hurricane.

Robert 'Robs' Lamplough was one of the first people in the United Kingdom to get involved in the recovery and operation of warbirds. In 1976 he flew to Israel and recovered four Mustangs, three Spitfires, a Hurricane and large chunks of a Mosquito. The majority of these have since been restored to flying condition. In 1977 he rescued a Yak-11 from Israel that had been flown there

Vought F4U-5N Corsair BuNo 121823 was mounted on a pole after being phased out of service by the Argentine Navy. Retrieved by the late Don Knapp in 1990, the aircraft was rebuilt by Ezell Aviation for the Lone Star Flight Museum at Galveston. Warbird Index

by a defecting Egyptian Air Force pilot. It too is now airworthy, though it has seen several changes of ownership over the years.

July 1981 saw Robs visit some of the scrap yards in Italy to rescue a mix of T-6G Texans and Harvards. The trip also resulted in acquisition of the hulk of ex-Italian Air Force P-51D Mustang MM4292 which had been languishing on a dump for more than a decade, after a tip-off from the author. Just two years later, Robs discovered a historic Messerschmitt Bf 109E airframe in poor condition in Spain and it was recovered to the United Kingdom.

Robs Lamplough was also one of the first people to recognise the availability and attractiveness of the Czech Aero Vodochody L-39 Albatros as a jet warbird, acquiring several from Chad. He currently operates one of the Mustangs recovered from Israel and a rare Spitfire VIII (MV154) that was acquired in 1979. The Hurricane and the rare Spanish Civil War Bf 109E are both in storage.

Guy Black's restoration company, Aero Vintage Ltd, is best known for its building and restoration of Hawker biplanes. Following many years of research into the original manufacturing techniques undertaken by Hawker Aircraft, Guy was able to finance a production run of the unique hexagonal spar material necessary for the accurate restoration of several of the Hawker biplanes he has in his possession, and also utilised in the Hurricane fighter. The first Hawker biplane to be restored was a Nimrod I (S1581) that flew for the first time in 2001 and was later traded with The Fighter Collection for a Hurricane. A Nimrod II, Afghan Hind (from Canada), Audax and Swedish Hart are all in the queue for restoration to flying condition.

Seen here in external storage, P-51D Mustang IDF38 was restored to flying condition by an Israeli Air Force Colonel, Israel Yitzhaki. It was flown for the first time at Herzlia in February 1984. Recent research undertaken by The Fighter Collection in conjunction with the Swedish Air Force Museum has revealed that the aircraft is in fact 44-83864, which was assigned to the 78th FG at RAF Duxford during World War Two. Noam Hartoch

Spitfire IX TE566 in Israel shortly before being containerised for shipment to Duxford for Robs Lamplough in 1976. Robert J Lamplough

P-51D Mustang IDF146 in temporary storage along with several Spitfires just before being shipped to the United Kingdom in the late 1970s. Robert J Lamplough

Photographed in Israel, this gaily painted kibbutz plaything is believed to have been recovered by Angelo and Pete Regina of Van Nuys, California, to form the basis of restored P-51D Mustang 44-73210, now owned by Ike Innes of Manitoba, Canada, and registered CF-IKE. Robert J Lamplough

The flyable aircraft are operated by the Historic Aircraft Collection, which also have a rare Yak-1 fighter being restored by Hawker Restorations in Suffolk at the time of writing. The Historic Aircraft Collection also have an airworthy Spitfire V which was part of the aforementioned trade by Tim Routsis with the Ministry of Defence. Thanks to the offices of Guy Black, the future of Hawker's magnificent between-the-wars biplanes is assured.

After following up an initiative undertaken by Douglas Arnold some years earlier, Tim Routsis (who had made his fortune in 'Silicon Fen', Cambridgeshire, with a software business) began his search for a Spitfire in 1986. The target on this occasion was to 'rescue' half a dozen Spitfires held at RAF Stations in the United Kingdom, most of which were literally guarding the gates. These aircraft were held by the Historic Branch of the Ministry of Defence. After several meetings, Tim was able to conclude an agreement whereby ownership of five Spitfires would transfer to him in exchange for several GRP Spitfire and Hurricane airframes (which would replace the real aircraft on the gates) and two real aircraft for the RAF Museum at Hendon.

The first of the five to be recovered was Spitfire XVI RW382 from the gate at RAF Uxbridge on 26th August 1988. This airframe duly became the first candidate for restoration. The work was finished by a new company set up by Tim with Clive Denney and Ian Warren which later moved into a custom-built hangar at Audley End airfield near Saffron Walden, Essex.

The second airframe to undergo restoration was Spitfire XVI TD248, which had been removed from atop a pylon at RAF Sealand. It had been sold to Ed Coventry and flew for the first time following rebuild on 10th

Right: *This Italian Air Force P-51D Mustang sat out in the open at an Italian Air Force Fire Fighting School until 1981 when Robs Lamplough acquired it. It appeared on the United Kingdom register for a short time as G-BMBA before being sold to a buyer in the United States. Its current whereabouts are unknown.* John Legg

Centre: *Spitfire XVI RW382 was mounted on a small pylon when it guarded the gate at RAF Uxbridge in 1981.* Warbird Index

Below: *Historic Flying founder Tim Routsis puts the Vintage V-12's-rebuilt Packard Merlin in RW382 through its paces in the engine run area at Audley End in spring 1991.* Author

Photographs on the opposite page:

Top: *Luxury house-builder Charles Church bucked the trend when he had Spitfire Tr.9 PT462 painted in this gaudy camouflage that 'reflected his company's house colours'. Photographed at North Weald shortly after painting, the aircraft was rebuilt by Dick Melton using a Spitfire hulk recovered from the Gaza Strip in Israel by Robs Lamplough. It was later exported to the United States before coming back home to the United Kingdom once more for Anthony Hodgson, the current owner, in 1998.* Michael Shreeve

Centre and bottom: *The author assisted Clive and Linda Denney of Vintage Fabrics to re-fabric Hurricane IIc PZ865 at RAF St Athan for the Battle of Britain Memorial Flight. The job took three long days and was completed using traditional materials and sheer hard graft!* Author

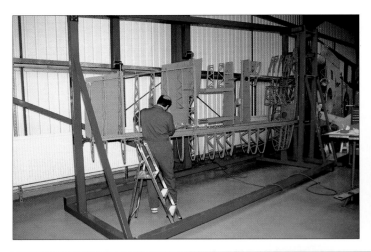

Above left: *The massive wing jig at Audley End was seldom empty during the busiest years of Historic Flying's tenancy at that airfield.* Author

Above right: *Imported as a project from New Zealander Don J Subritzky of Auckland, Spitfire Vc JG891 is seen installed in the fuselage jig at Audley End.* Author

Left: *Spitfire IXc MK912 was acquired from Belgium by the Historic Aircraft Collection for Guy Black. Ownership was later transferred to Historic Flying, who completed a total rebuild. The aircraft had just been sold to a Canadian as this book was written, emphasising the worldwide connections enjoyed by the warbirds industry.* Author

Bottom: *Through the good offices of Clive Denney, a recognised expert in the black art of painting and finishing vintage and warbird aircraft, Historic Flying were one of the first restoration facilities to utilise this state-of-the-art 'spray-bake' unit at Audley End. It did exactly what the name implies – baked the finish onto the airframe; giving a finish far superior to the original.* Author

November 1992. By then all five of the gate guard Spitfires had been retrieved, their places taken by the GRP replacements manufactured by Feggans Brown in London.

The last of the five airframes, TB252, a rare high-backed Spitfire XVI, was sold to Tony Banta as this book was being prepared and was being shipped to New Zealand for rebuild by Pioneer Avspecs at Ardmore. This bought to an end another interesting chapter in warbird recovery. Historic Flying Ltd was sold to Belgian businessman Karel Bos and now operates from a new facility at Duxford.

In the early 1990s Jim Cavanaugh began his collecting activities in grand fashion with the acquisition of several fighter aircraft. Like most collectors, Jim launched with a P-51D Mustang which he purchased in 1990, quickly followed by a number of other valuable and attractive aeroplanes, including a rare Spitfire VIII (MT719) initially recovered from India by Ormond Haydon-Baillie in 1978.

In October 1993 the Cavanaugh Flight Museum opened its doors to the public. Covering nearly 50,000ft² of display area, the

museum is located in the grounds of Addison Airport just outside Dallas, Texas. The museum houses one of the most significant warbird collections in the USA. Almost all of the aircraft in the museum are maintained in airworthy condition, the majority taking to the air on a regular basis. Among these are two recipients of the EAA's Grand Champion Warbird Trophy awarded at Oshkosh, Wisconsin, namely the B-25 Mitchell and F9F-2 Panther. The Cavanaugh Flight Museum currently has 19 aircraft listed in its collection.

The warbirds scene in Australia has been simmering since the early 1960s with two main proponents: Col Pay of Scone, New South Wales; and the late Guido Zuccoli of Toowoomba, Northern Territories, whose death in a T-6 crash at RAAF Tyndall on 6th March 1997 was a major loss for that country. Fortunately, Guido's widow Lynette has carried on the tradition.

Col Pay first became involved with warbirds when he purchased CA-18 Mk 21 Mustang A68-104 in October 1970. He is also well known for his rare Spitfire VIII VH-HET (sold in 2000 to David Lowy) and for his forays into Asia where he purchased some 15 T-28s (Laos, 1988) and six A-37 Dragonflies (Vietnam, 1989). He still owns the Mustang, several Spitfires and some CA-25 Winjeels.

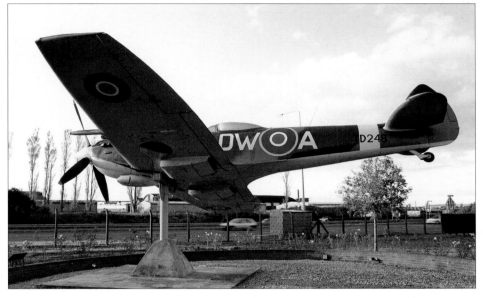

Charlie Brown taxies out at Audley End in newly restored Spitfire V EP120 for its first flight after restoration. Eric Quenardel

Spitfire XVI TD248 abeam the pylon at RAF Sealand shortly before being removed and dismantled for restoration to fly. Phil Parish

Spitfire XVI TD248 undergoing engine runs shortly before its first flight in November 1992. Tim Routsis exercises the Rolls-Royce Merlin engine rebuilt by Mike Nixon/Vintage V-12's. Author

The rare high-back Spitfire XVI TB252 was removed from the gate at RAF Bentley Priory, Middlesex, by a team from Historic Flying in November 1988. Author

The first ex-Dominican Air Force Mustang to arrive in the United States in 1983 went to Elmo Hahn of Muskegon, Michigan. Registered N51EH, 44-72339 is now owned by James A Cavanaugh Jr, and is flown regularly by the Cavanaugh Flight Museum. Warbird Index

Sea Fury FB.11 WG630 awaits its turn in the restoration queue at NAS Nowra. Warbird Index

Guido Zuccoli's entry onto the warbird scene occurred when he purchased three ex-Iraqi Air Force Furies from the Jurist/Tallichet cache in January 1982. He later acquired a rare Fiat G-59 that was restored by Sanders Aviation, then based at Chino, and this flown for the first time following restoration in September 1987. His next acquisition was a CAC Boomerang, also rebuilt by Sanders. Like Col Pay, Guido then became involved recovering some T-28s in Asia and also acquired an A-37 followed by a Commonwealth CA-27 Sabre. The collection continues and a Corsair is now being restored.

More recently, David Lowy's Temora Aviation Museum has come onto the scene with a good mix of jet and piston aircraft, though the former Col Pay Spitfire is registered to David personally. The current collection includes a Vampire, Meteor, Canberra and A-37 Dragonfly. The prospects for the future are exciting.

In New Zealand, Sir Tim Wallis devoted his early years to pioneering New Zealand's heli-borne venison recovery operation. Subsequently he explored the live capture of feral deer in order to establish New

Zealand's deer-farming industry. Concurrent with this, he urbanised the overseas markets to sustain these operations. These developments allowed Tim to indulge his real passion, aviation, which led to the formation of several projects.

Tim Wallis revitalised the warbird movement in the Southern Hemisphere with the establishment of the Alpine Fighter Collection and later the New Zealand Fighter Pilot's Museum. Not only has Tim built a huge collection of high-quality aircraft from scratch, he has participated in a number of projects which have contributed significantly toward the airworthy warbird population across the world. The Alpine Fighter Collection (a division of Alpine Deer Group Ltd), based at Wanaka Airport, Lake Wanaka on the South Island of New Zealand, was built to consist primarily of World War Two aircraft.

In 1984 Tim purchased his first warbird, a P-51D Mustang. Within five years the Mustang had been sold and the nascent collection comprised a Spitfire XVI, with many

High back, Packard Merlin-engined Spitfire XVI TB863 was restored at Duxford by The Fighter Collection for Sir Tim Wallis of the Alpine Fighter Collection. Engine runs were being conducted when this picture was taken, circa 1987. Michael Shreeve

A Hurricane wing section bearing Soviet markings at Airframe Assemblies on the Isle of Wight. Many ex-Soviet machines have been recovered and AA have produced numerous refurbished wing sections for the type. Author

other aircraft projects being researched. By the early 1990s Tim had started additional major projects. He masterminded and funded a major restoration programme in Russia involving several Polikarpov I-16 and I-153 fighters. With Tony Ditheridge in the United Kingdom, he launched Hawker Restorations Ltd, initially handling the restoration of three Hurricane wrecks, one of which would be involved in a partnership project with Air New Zealand, with the completed, airworthy Hurricane destined for the Alpine Fighter Collection.

Amidst this activity, Tim put the wheels in motion to create and fund the New Zealand

Fighter Pilot's Museum, and funded the construction of a large workshop complex. Last but not least, every two years the now world-famous Warbirds Over Wanaka airshows are run. These airshows see a migration of warbird enthusiasts to South Island, often having travelled thousands of miles to see the spectacle that only Wanaka's stunning backdrops can offer.

Sir Tim Wallis narrowly escaped death in a nasty aircraft accident in January 1996, and suffered a major head injury. However, this did not stifle his determination to contribute towards the international warbirds movement and he has subsequently made a sub-

A MiG-3 hulk in the process of being recovered from Murmansk. The centre section of the fuselage and the wing section yielded large numbers of small components. *Boris Osetinsky*

A MiG-3 being carefully disassembled and documented prior to restoration to airworthy condition. *Boris Osetinsky*

stantial recovery. The presence of the New Zealand Fighter Pilot's Museum and the award-winning Warbirds Over Wanaka airshows has firmly established Wanaka as the warbird capital of the Southern Hemisphere.

Brian Reynolds founded the Olympic Flight Museum at Olympia, Washington, in 1998. Some 12 aircraft are now registered with the museum, including several jets. A Corsair is in restoration with John Lane at Airpower Unlimited (one of 18 Corsairs being rebuilt at the time of writing), and there are several jet aircraft waiting in the wings that may be restored to fly in the future.

Undoubtedly the most interesting warbird development in the new millennium has been the formation of a world-class collection by two closely connected organisations based in Seattle, Washington. Between July 1998 and the end of 2002, a core collection of warbird aircraft – piston and jet – was put together for two organisations sharing the same address. The Flying Heritage Collection (April 2001 saw the name change to Flying Heritage Inc) has 14 aircraft registered to it,

the majority of which are being restored to flying condition. Notables include an Fw 190A-5 recovered from Russia almost intact and untouched since its forced landing in 1944, now being restored to flying condition in the United Kingdom; a Curtiss P-40C recovered from the same source in 1991, restored by Fighter Rebuilders in California and first flown following rebuild on 1st September 1998; and a Nakajima Ki-43 Hayabusa, restored to taxying condition by the Alpine Fighter Collection in Wanaka, New Zealand, and inadvertently 'test-hopped' before sale to Flying Heritage in March 2000. The most recent aircraft to be put into restoration for flight is an F-84G Thunderjet, currently being reworked in California.

The sister organisation to Flying Heritage Inc is Vulcan Warbirds, which has ten aircraft registered to it including an Me 262, a rare F-86A Sabre and two F8U Crusaders, all of which will be restored to fly. As if that was not enough, the two organisations also have a Hurricane, Bf 109 and Mosquito waiting in the wings and continue to collect warbirds covertly to add to the ranks of the already

impressive fleet. Not only is the collection world class; it was assembled in record time, the first aircraft being registered in July 1998. All of the companies undertaking restoration work for these organisations are subject to a unique non-disclosure agreement.

Since the late 1970s there has been a surge of interest in aircraft recovery in the former Soviet Union, which has been the source for some wonderful and unique warbird recoveries and has provided much raw material for the global warbird industry to restore and in some cases reconstruct.

Eugene Konoplev, who recovered some aircraft for the museum at Monino, was the first individual in Russia to negotiate such an arrangement, which he completed as early as 1975. He now resides in Ukraine and is currently working with the Antonov Museum. He also recovered some aircraft for the North Fleet Air Force Museum near Murmansk. Mr Khapaev was the head of the group that recovered many historic aircraft for the North Fleet Air Force Museum. Many of this museum's aircraft were later acquired by Jim Pearce and shipped to the West.

Mr Kupratsevich found the MVT 109E. Mr Dmitrinok worked for many years in Karelia and recovered a large number of aircraft including the unique Fw 189 for Jim Pearce. One of the most prolific wreck-hunters in Russia is Mr Dudin. His grand total of recovered wrecks is past the 100-mark and includes the P-40C Tomahawk now with Flying Heritage Inc following rebuild, Brooklands' Hurricane project, as well as some Spitfires including one for The Fighter Collection.

Mr Prytkov found and recovered the now famous Brewster Buffalo that became the subject of an ownership dispute, believed to be unresolved at the time of writing. Boris Osetinsky at Gelengik recovered a Bf 109G-4 from the Black Sea in 1988; it was sent to Italy for rebuild. He also recovered several I-15s, I-16s and I-153s and his company rebuilt them. The latest project is the restoration of four MiG-3 piston-engined fighters based on four recoveries. The first aircraft is well advanced and will fly in Russia.

Oleg Leiko and his company have recovered and rebuilt several aircraft for the Moscow Victory Museum, including a Bell P-63C-5 Kingcobra (44-4011), and are now working on a Bf 109E-7. Undoubtedly this recovery work has been of great value to restoration companies and collectors alike, and it is set to continue for many years to come as new areas are explored utilising modern technology. Who knows what the future holds…

Acknowledgements

As with any work, *Warbirds Alive* would not have been half the book it is without the help and assistance of many different people around the world:

Craig Charleston and Ian Warren of Charleston Aviation Services put themselves out to keep me informed of the progress they were making on David Price's Bf 109E, and test pilot Charlie Brown has been kind enough to allow me to include his piece on flying the restored aircraft.

Graham Warner and John Romain of the Aircraft Restoration Company at Duxford both assisted with information on their Blenheim restorations. Sadly, ten years and three months after its maiden (post-rebuild) flight, and as these Acknowledgements were being penned, the aircraft suffered an accident and was damaged on the evening of 18th August 2003. We wish them the best of luck with the rebuild.

Art Teeters and his crew at Cal Pacific Airmotive in Salinas, California, masterfully restored Kermit Weeks' rare P-51C and I am indebted to Art for assisting me with information. As always, Tom Smith captured the quality of the restoration in pictures; no mean feat.

Aviation Image creator Patrick Bunce generously supplied me with images of the Collings Foundation B-24J Liberator before, during and after restoration at Tom Reilly Vintage Aircraft, as did Jack Flynn whose frequent visits provided me with pictorial progress reports.

Bob Munro helped out significantly with photographs of the Shuttleworth Collection's Bristol Fighter, Gloster Gladiator and Hawker Hind; and the Collection's Chief Engineer, Chris Morris, filled me in on some of the trials and tribulations they endure to keep the Gladiator in the air for us all to enjoy.

Simon Brown, then the 'Head Wrench' at Square One Aviation, supplied important information on the restoration of Colonel Frank Borman's Bell P-63 Kingcobra; and Thierry Thomassin supplied rebuild pictures. Again, Patrick Bunce stepped in to fill the gaps in picture coverage with some spectacular air-to-airs of a difficult-to-photograph aeroplane.

Guy Black of Aero Vintage Ltd was of immense help in relating the story of the research behind and restoration of the spectacular Hawker Nimrod biplane. He also allowed me unlimited access to the aircraft during the restoration process, for which I am most grateful.

On the P-40 front, Pioneer Aero Restorations, operated by Garth Hogan and Charles Darby, has become synonymous with quality work. I appreciate their valuable input on the restoration of the Old Flying Machine Company's P-40, an authentic and original example that was one of the first to establish the company's enviable reputation.

Bob and Donna Odegaard's rare Goodyear F2G-1 Super Corsair is a splendid example of the type, and the aircraft is a tribute to their personal skill and determination to see it fly again after a long period in storage.

Polikarpou I-15bis '19' getting airborne for a test flight. This aircraft is now with Jerry Yagen in Virginia, USA. Boris Osetinsky

They kindly provided photographs and information on the project. Scott Germain of Warbird Aero Press supplied some fantastic air-to-air portraits of the finished aeroplane which took the inaugural Rolls-Royce Heritage Trophy; a worthy first winner.

The South Island of New Zealand holds as treasure one of the world's finest collections of warbirds in the most stunning of settings. Sir Tim Wallis and the Alpine Fighter Collection live at Wanaka and the restoration of their Hurricane, by the UK-based Hawker Restorations Ltd and the Engineering arm of Air New Zealand, ranks amongst their fine achievements. Curator of the sister New Zealand Fighter Pilot's Museum, Ian Brodie, Alpine's Chief Engineer Ray Mulqueen and Chief Pilot Keith Skilling all helped me get the story straight.

The Chino-based Planes of Fame Museum in California has many rare warbird restorations to its name. Steve Hinton is a well-known warbird personality and film pilot/aerial co-ordinator. Though Steve doesn't have the luxury of lots of spare time (he also runs his Fighter Rebuilders restoration shop), he always answers my emails and was most helpful with information on the museum's rare Mitsubishi A6M Model 52 Zero project.

The principal at Hawker Restorations Ltd, Tony Ditheridge, has always extended a very warm personal welcome to me whenever I have visited his workshops at Moat Farm in Suffolk. The Hurricane is notoriously 'over-engineered' and until the company came along, Hurricane restorations were always 'compromises' (even though they were properly certified) due to the lack of original spar material which simply no longer existed. In partnership with the aforementioned Guy Black, Tony was able to research and recreate such valuable raw material. The rest, as they say, is history.

Bryan Wood at the Royal Navy Historic Flight and Lee Rickles at BAE Systems Brough were both most helpful in assisting me to tell the story of the restoration of the RNHF's Sea Fury. With the loss of the flagship Fairey Firefly, the self-funding Trust have difficult times ahead. All we can do is give them the best support we can and wish them good luck for the future; they deserve it.

Tony Ritzman and Carl Scholl at Aero Trader in California are well known for their magnificent B-25 Mitchell restorations. However, as Tony is often heard to say, 'we don't just do B-25s' and the Weeks Air Museum's B-26 Marauder was, on Tony's own admission, not a restoration as such; the aircraft simply had to be made airworthy to get it to its new base at Polk City, Florida. However, it wasn't quite that simple and getting the aircraft back in the air and reliably airworthy was quite a challenge; one to which they rose admirably. Thanks to them both, and to Jack McCloy of Fantasy of Flight, for relating the true story of the rare B-26.

Bob Collings of the Collings Foundation runs an annual US 'bomber tour' with his B-17G Flying Fortress and B-24J Liberator. Wherever they go they attract attention and have become great ambassadors for the warbird movement. Bob figured that, with the vastness of the USA, why not take the 'air-planes to the people'. Using that principle, millions of people, among them many World War Two veterans, have seen the aircraft. Such operations are not without their problems but Bob Collings, Jon Rising and American Aero Services' Gary Norville, aided and abetted by Patrick Bunce, paint an accurate picture of life on the road with the bombers.

In the mid-1980s the 'warbird movement' truly became a warbird industry with record numbers of engineers and volunteers becoming involved in keeping an ever-increasing number of aircraft airworthy. Electronics specialist Tim Routsis, more used to earning a living in 'Silicon Fen', did a job swap for a few years when he founded Historic Flying at Audley End. In partnership with Clive Denney and Ian Warren, Tim set up a new company that would set new standards for Spitfire restorations. To make life more interesting, he came to an arrangement with the Ministry of Defence that saw several Spit-fires 'brought in from the cold' from their gate guard duties. Historic Flying continues to restore Spitfires, but under new ownership and with a base at the Imperial War Museum Duxford. The example featured in this book, BM597, was one of the last aircraft to be restored under Routsis' supervision.

When it comes to the venerable Republic P-47 Thunderbolt, one restoration company stands out from the crowd: Westpac Restorations. Alan Wojciak and Bill Klaers have been involved in the warbird industry for many years and in the last few have become recognised worldwide as Thunderbolt specialists. Alan took the time to explain a little about the pitfalls involved in restoring the huge fighter. Owner Neal Melton elaborated on the joys of ownership to complete the chapter on a most interesting aeroplane.

Many others have given me help and encouragement with *Warbirds Alive* along the way. My apologies in advance if I have omitted anyone. In putting this work together, I have tried to present both a compact history of the evolution of the warbird industry from the early pioneering days and a snapshot of what is happening today. Some readers will by now have noticed that there is no mention of warbird jets. This is deliberate as the two areas are very different and the jets movement is still in its relative infancy. That story can be told another day.

Glossary

A&AEE	Aeroplane & Armament Experimental Establishment	HMS	Her/His Majesty's Ship	R/t	Radio/telephone
AACU	Anti-Aircraft Co-operation Unit	hp	Horsepower	RAF	Royal Air Force
AF	Air Force	IAP	Russian Air Force Fighter regiment	RCAF	Royal Canadian Air Force
AFB	Air Force Base	IAS	Indicated Air Speed	RNAS	Royal Naval Air Station
ALG	Advance Landing Ground	IFF	Identification Friend or Foe	RNAY	Royal Naval Air Yard
AMSL	Above Mean Sea Level	km	Kilometres	RNZAF	Royal New Zealand Air Force
ATC	Air Traffic Control	km/h	Kilometres per hour	RPM	revolutions/rotations per minute
AVG	American Volunteer Group	kph	Kilometres per hour	RV	Rendezvous
BG	Bombardment Group	kW	kilowatts	SoTT	School of Technical Training
BS	Bombardment Squadron	LOA	Letter of Authorization	TBO	Time Between Overhaul
CAA	Civil Aviation Authority	MAEU	Marine Aircraft Evaluation Unit	TMA	Terminal Control Area
CAF	Canadian Armed Forces	MAP	Municipal Airport	UHF	Ultra-High Frequency
CO$_2$	Carbon Dioxide	MoD	Ministry of Defence	USAAC	United States Army Air Corps
CSU	Constant Speed Unit	MU	Maintenance Unit	USAAF	United States Army Air Forces
DFC	Distinguished Flying Cross	NACA	National Advisory Committee on Aeronautics	USAF	United States Air Force
DME	Distance-Measuring Equipment			VC	Victoria Cross
EAA	Experimental Aircraft Association	NAS	Naval Air Station	VFR	Visual Flight Rules
FAA	Federal Aviation Administration	NASA	National Aeronautics and Space Administration	VHF	Very High Frequency
FG	Fighter Group			VMF	Marine Fighter Squadron
FONAC	Flag Officer Naval Air Command	NWC	Naval Weapons Center	VNE	Never-exceed speed
FS	Fighter Squadron	OAT	Outside Air Temperature	VOR	VHF Omni-directional Range (radio beacons)
GPS	Global Positioning System	OUT	Operational Training Unit		
GRP	Glass-Reinforced Plastic	QNH	Altimeter subscale setting to altitude of destination airfield	WNr	Werk Nummer
GvIAP	Russian Air Force fighter regiment	R&R	Rest & Recuperation		

1

Messerschmitt Bf 109E-7
WNr 3579 'White 14'/N81562

This rare Bf 109E-7 was recovered from Russia in 1992, in derelict but essentially complete condition. At the time there was no airworthy Bf 109Es extant, although the Ministry of Defence was close to flying a similarly rare Bf 109G-2/Trop, WNr 10639, which became quite famous as G-USTV/'Black 6'. The two models are very different.

The aircraft had been acquired by warbird specialist Craig Charleston of Charleston Aviation Services on behalf of American warbird collector David Price. Both Craig and the owner were aware of the aircraft's rarity and knew it would be extremely expensive and technically difficult to get it back in the air again. From the outset, Craig realised that both the airframe and engine would need extensive research before the first wrenches were even turned.

After only limited research into the airframe's provenance, it was realised that not only was the aircraft a rare marque, but its individual history was quite incredible. The aircraft had been flown by Hans-Joachim Marseille, one of the Lutfwaffe's leading aces with 158 'kills' (seven during the Battle of Britain) and the leading ace against the RAF.

Considerable research was undertaken and the identity plates located on the aircraft confirmed that the aircraft is a Bf 109E-7, WNr 3579, which served as 'White 14' with I(Jagd)/LG 2. The official Luftwaffe report dated 2nd September 1940 states that 'Cadet Officer H.J. Marseille force-landed 3579 at Calais-Marck on this date after having claimed an RAF Spitfire over the Thames Estuary the same day'.

It was necessary to invest several thousand hours of research into the original manufacturing processes for the '109. After consultation with the owner, Craig decided that the engine should go to Mike Nixon of Vintage V-12's in Tehachapi, California, quite early on in the project to allow the maximum possible time to have the engine restored, tested and made otherwise airworthy for installation in the airframe.

After many hours spent on the telephone, Craig was able to locate a huge number of drawings for the type, the official Luftwaffe repair book and German materials specifications, all of which had to be translated into working copies for the restoration effort. It had been decided at the outset that all of the original German manufacturing processes should be followed and the rare aircraft restored to the same condition it would have been in when it rolled off the manufacturer's production line. Original technical documentation and manuals were essential to ensure the success of the project.

Though there were several Hispano HA-1112-M1L Buchons already airworthy in Europe and the United States, plus a single Bf 109G-2/Trop airworthy in the United Kingdom, this would be the first project to undertake a major engineering process that mirrored completely the manufacturing methods utilised in the Messerschmitt factory.

Messerschmitt Bf 109E-7 WNr 3579 at Craig Charleston's shop shortly after it was unpacked after shipping from Russia in January 1993. Although the aircraft was obviously badly damaged, it yielded an enormous number of minor parts as well as some major structure.
via Craig Charleston

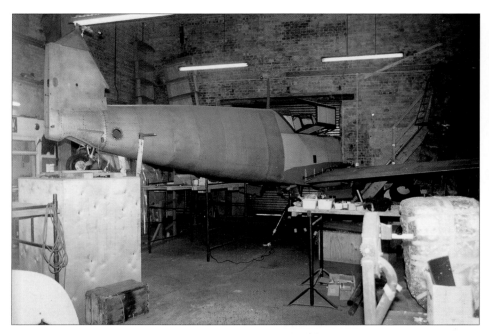

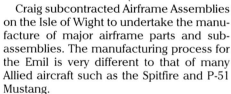

Top left: *The rear fuselage takes shape at Craig Charleston's workshops.* Author

Left: *The port wing, in the jig at Airframe Assemblies on the Isle of Wight, shows the intricate rivet pattern, recaptured again for the first time in over 50 years.* Author

Above: *Ironically, just as a German company currently manufactures propellers for modern-day Spitfires, a skilfully manipulated English Wheel was used to manufacture the complex curved cowling for the Bf 109E-7.* Author

Craig subcontracted Airframe Assemblies on the Isle of Wight to undertake the manufacture of major airframe parts and sub-assemblies. The manufacturing process for the Emil is very different to that of many Allied aircraft such as the Spitfire and P-51 Mustang.

Airframe Assemblies is a professional company working under the auspices of the CAA with an A2 approval (permitting them to manufacture new structures up to and including wings and fuselages plus many more smaller items). They have a drawing office capable of redrawing plans from which parts can be manufactured with a quality assurance certificate. This was an essential factor behind the success of the project.

Project 'White 14' was contributed to by a number of other companies, closely coordinated and driven forward by Craig. A large number of parts were usable from the origi-

nal airframe but because the aircraft was being rebuilt to fly, some of the major and load-bearing structure was newly manufactured. Rear fuselage blocks – necessary to recreate the original rear fuselage sections alone – cost some £30,000 to replicate, though they are now available for other projects. The blocks were required to stretch-form the fuselage sections.

Airframe Assemblies undertook the majority of the production engineering, making the very heavy gauge metal wing ribs with massive flanges and deeply recessed dimples. Ian Warren and Bob and Simone Cunningham worked on the huge amount of metal work, shaping cowlings, fairings and other sheet metal items. Gerry Marshall at Anglia Radiators was contracted to work on the unique oil cooler and radiators for the project.

Philip Hilt was able to help build up the archive of drawings and Chris Van Hee lent

a significant hand in locating many spare parts and miscellaneous items that would add to the originality of the entire airframe. Craig sings the praises of Airframe Assemblies boss Steve Vizard: 'Steve did a lot of running about, following up leads and chasing bits and pieces as well as maintaining close contact with me – we couldn't have completed the project without his input.'

In terms of difficulty, there is no doubt that this was one of the most intricate and enigmatic warbird restoration projects ever to be undertaken. 'Every aspect of the Emil project threw up a new problem and we had significant back up with expertise from a number of technical sources,' recalls Craig. 'One of the main stumbling blocks was a good donor engine and although we had access to several units, it took us several months to get enough cores together to make two good engines – one for the aircraft plus one spare unit, so Mike Nixon stood any sort of chance of getting the powerplant ready on schedule.'

Investment in tooling was also substantial and although the owner and Craig discussed the merits of opting for a Bf 109E 'look-alike' structure that didn't incorporate the genuine engineering foibles of the real thing, that idea was rejected early on in the project. Instead the more difficult but correct path was chosen: adopting the original manufacturing methods, including making the fuselage blocks and producing accurate jigs for the fuselage, wings, flaps, ailerons, fin and other empennage parts.

Ian Warren of Warren Fabrications made items such as the flame guards around the cowlings, detail cowling parts, the internal throttle linkage and assorted other fuselage items such as the secondary bulkhead, as well as assisting Craig directly in the all-important final assembly and structural assembly.

Craig elected to have the engine mounts machined from solid instead of forged magnesium, and Patrick Engineering (a CNC engineering company) was contracted for the job. Many of the forged magnesium castings were replaced by aluminium, a deliberate policy to prevent dissimilar metal corrosion and associated problems in the future. Melton Aviation assembled the undercarriage legs.

So what special problems had to be overcome? Tooling for the wings spars was expensive but, as with the fuselage blocks, now exists for future projects; two more '109 projects have been undertaken since 'White 14' was restored. Dies had to be made to draw the extrusions – named Ripley stringer section – which is both hard and immensely strong. Over 2,000ft (610m) of stringer sec-

tion had to be produced to complete the project task and metallurgist Ron Dak researched modern equivalents that were approved by the CAA. The original (but deactivated!) cannons were put back in the wings and several other valuable and attractive 'trinkets' from a variety of sources (the result of many hours of chasing leads around the world) were able to be installed.

Throughout the entire project, the intention was to produce an airframe totally representative of the original and as authentic as possible, the only caveat being to ensure that flight safety is paramount. With this in mind, modern electrics and avionics were fitted to the airframe and a wooden propeller was developed in conjunction with Michael Barnett at Cambridge-based Skycraft Services. Given the aircraft's penchant for ground-looping, Craig says the adoption of such a unit will ensure minimum damage to the engine in the unlikely event of a propeller strike.

With all the main structural work complete and the majority of the systems installed, it was time to plan the move of 'White 14' to Chino, California, where it would be reassembled, rigged and the painting finished prior to test flying. Clive Denney of Vintage Fabrics had already

painted the majority of the aircraft and had completed the fabric work. He travelled to California with Ian Warren and Craig who had a hangar ready and waiting to accept the aircraft for final assembly.

Preparations were also made to get the aircraft 'packed' and ready for air-freighting to California and the fuselage and wings were then carefully packed and secured on a metal roller pallet in company with several wooden crates. The pallet and crates were then transported to Gatwick Airport where they were all loaded aboard an El Al flight bound for Los Angeles on 14th January 1999.

Following limited flight operations in the United States the aircraft was sold to Canadian Ed Russell in late 2003. Flight Lieutenant Charlie Brown, RAF, who has significant warbird flying experience and who has flown the Bf 109G-2/Trop 'Black Six' on many occasions, was asked to test-fly the Emil and his story is outlined overleaf.

Below left: Front port view of the fuselage. Author

Below right: Wiring and plumbing were in the early stages when this shot was taken. Author

The 'office' of the Emil, faithfully restored by Craig using original instruments and duplicate, authentic placarding which led to some nifty conversion work by the test pilot.
Thierry Thomassin

have been taught or have developed are due to my RAF training as a pilot and flying instructor. The Service has spent a great deal of time and money on me; I am indebted to it. Now to the test programme, which I shall go through on a day-by-day basis

Sunday 26th September 1999
Ian Warren collected me from LA and took me out to Chino, where I met Craig and Gordon. I was taken to see 3579 at various times in the United Kingdom as the restoration progressed, but I was close to speechless when I saw here complete for the first time. The rest of the evening was spent discussing the 'game plan' for the test programme and getting to know Gordon (a reckonable character and partner in the team).

Monday 27th September 1999
Relaxed start, introduced to Flo's Airport Café for an excellent breakfast. Down to business, collating the information that Craig had collected in order to compile my personal set of First Flight Notes. These were to comprise of a set of RAF Enemy Aircraft Evaluation Unit notes titled *Instructions for Flying the Messerschmitt 109*, supplemented by any additional details that I could find. I also visited ATC at Chino, getting to know them and enjoying their splendidly efficient air-conditioning in the cab! Then it was off to AIA at Chino to purchase the excellent *VFR Guide* and a chart for the LA area.

During the early evening, Frank Strickler and Steve Hinton arrived. Frank was to handle the release of the aircraft for flight testing and was to test me on the ground and in the air for the issue of an FAA Authority to flight test Bf 109 series aircraft. Tuesday evening I had dinner with Frank. The conversation went something along the lines of 'What's your flying background, Frank?' For a couple of very pleasant and intensely interesting hours, Frank briefly outlined his flying career. Duly impressed and humbled, I turned in early to revise US Airspace, R/T and procedures for my check flight with Frank the next day.

Tuesday 28th September 1999
Elegant dining with Frank for breakfast at the Burger King near the hotel. At Chino it was time for more revision of the Emil notes that I had collated and time to make some knee-board cribs for my flight suit, such as engine and airframe limitations, pre-start settings, pre-take-off settings and anticipated airspeed for take-off, climb, glide and powered approach. Frank and Craig, meanwhile, were busy reviewing 3579's restoration paperwork.

Introduction
I'll start by saying what a privilege it has been to flight test the only Bf 109E to fly since World War Two. I am extremely grateful to David Price, the owner of this fine aircraft, Craig Charleston and Ian Warren who restored her, and Mike Nixon of Vintage V-12's who restored the DB601A engine.

Why me?
I am, essentially, an ex-fast jet (BAe Tornado GR.1s) RAF Flying Instructor who has some experience of flight testing and displaying historic aircraft, primarily the Spitfire but other types as well and, most significantly, just over half the total post-restoration flying that 'Black 6' ever flew.

Technical Introduction
Bf 109E-4 WNr 3579 – henceforth in this article known as '3579' – is an exceptionally original and authentic restoration. She flies with original instruments calibrated in kph, km, pressures in kg/cm², boost in ATA (1 ATA + 1 standard atmosphere, 0 boost, 29.92 inches etc). All figures quoted in this article are in original units for ease of comparison with original Bf 109E information.

The Test Programme
The fact that I am a current serving RAF Officer is only of background interest. The testing of 3579 was a private venture, using some of my annual leave allowance and my FAA licence. However, any flying skills that I

Mid-afternoon and it was time for Frank to test me in the SNJ-5 from Planes of Fame for the issue of my LOA. The check flight was flown from the rear cockpit and comprised of steep turns, stalls clean and in the Approach configuration, aerobatics, recovery to Chino for a touch-and-go and a flapless full-stop landing. Frank was satisfied with my performance. I was comprehensively briefed on how I was to conduct the test programme, on what my responsibilities were and what entries I was to make in the aircraft's Logbook. Only when Frank had finished his briefing did he give me my LOA.

By early evening the plan came together; the aircraft had been released for flight testing, I had my LOA and now all was set for the first flight.

Wednesday 29th September 1999
After breakfast with Frank at Flo's, Craig taxied 3579 from the hangar to the ASP at the base of the ATC tower. This was the point at which Craig had briefed me he would hand over control of the team to me for the flight testing. A clear and unequivocal brief – a nice touch by Craig, appreciated by me.

Starting and Taxying
The starting was exceptionally straightforward using the electric starter system fitted by Mike Nixon, who was now present with his wife Kim to witness the first flight and to be on hand for technical assistance. The taxying was exactly as I remembered 'Black 6' to be – very tail-heavy with large breakout forces required to counter the large castor

angle of the tailwheel. Turning the aircraft required the control column fully forward and appropriate amounts of rudder, brake and power to get the tail round. Another feature I noticed was how exceptionally patient the aircraft was on the ground regarding coolant radiator temperature. The aircraft was warm following Craig's taxying; I started it and taxied it for a further ten minutes or so and still the coolant temperature was well within limits prior to shutdown (the OAT was 30°C). All was well with starting and taxying – the threatened Santa Anna winds had not manifested themselves – and so all was set for the first flight.

Flight No.1
The start was uneventful but it was a long taxy from the ASP to Runway 08R (about one mile). It was apparent that the brakes were getting warm (and so was I!). I lined up on the runway, took in 'the picture', then noticed that the A/C Bus circuit breaker had popped. This meant no radio, no propeller control, no engine temperature and pressure gauges, etc. So without being able to speak with ATC, I cleared the runway and shut down at the 08R holding area. Rather disappointed, I was driven back to the ASP to tell the team what had happened. I was despatched to Flo's for lunch. Over lunch I realised what a blessing the A/C Bus circuit breaker popping had been: one mile taxying in an OAT of +35°C and the brakes and I were not in the best of shape, to be absolutely honest. Better to have the aircraft cool at the holding point for the first flight with all my wits about me.

Though the majority of the restoration work, assembly and painting was carried out in the UK by Craig Charleston and Ian Warren (with major structures prepared by Airframe Assemblies on the Isle of Wight), it was always intended that the test flying would be carried out in the United States; here the aircraft is reassembled at Chino. Thierry Thommasin

After lunch it was back to the ASP, where Craig said that the aircraft was ready. After transport out to the 08R holding area, courtesy ATC, I was ready to go.

Once again the start was easy, the checks unhurried and I found myself lined up on the runway full of confidence and anticipation. My game plan was as per 'Black 6': take off 1.0 to 1.2 ATA monitoring the rpm, keep the tail down until 100kph (62mph), raise it slightly (being prepared to catch any tendency to swing) and then fly her off at 150kph (93mph). What I found was that the tail felt like it should be raised just as the airspeed started to register, that is at 50-60kph (31-37mph). Once the tail was off the runway the familiar extreme change in directional stability became apparent – from almost absolute stability to almost absolute instability. The aircraft flew herself off at 110kph (68mph), much sooner than I had anticipated.

Once off the ground, I checked the rpm: 2,400, still well inside the limit of 2,500. I applied the brakes and selected the undercarriage up. The undercarriage functioned correctly and as I approached 200kph (124mph) in a shallow climb I noted the rpm approaching 2,500. Using the propeller pitch control switch on the throttle, I trimmed it back to 2,400 (5-minute limit), raised the flaps and established a 270kph (168mph) climb, which seemed a little too fast for this aircraft. Later I settled upon 250kph (155mph) as the best climb speed.

Once at 270kph, I trimmed the rpm down to 2,300 (30-minute limit). I levelled off below the TMA above the airfield that was at 2,700QNH – Chino's elevation is 650ft (198m) AMSL – giving me just below 0.8km (2,640ft) on the altimeter. I set 2,000rpm and 0.8ATM and checked around the cockpit. To my consternation, the outlet oil temperature was well above the maximum of 90°C, at 115°C; the inlet oil temperature too was well above its maximum of 75°C, at 95°C. I called the tower and said I had an oil temperature problem and that I might need priority for landing. I reduced boost and rpm to try to reduce oil temperatures, which did reduce a little, but they were still well above the stated maximums.

Keeping a watchful eye on the engine gauges and ensuring I was always in a position to force land, engine out if necessary, I carried out the essentials of a first flight test profile; namely stalls, clean and in the landing configuration, the selection of a suitable threshold speed based upon the information gleaned from the stalls, and assessment of aircraft attitude and controllability. Much to my surprise, I established a speed of 200kph (124mph) to enter the downwind leg, 150kph (93mph) at the end of the downwind, a curving final approach aiming to reduce speed to 130kph (81mph) halfway around, 120kph (74.5mph) with 30° to go to the centreline and a threshold speed of 110kph (68mph) with a dribble of power to stabilise the rate of speed decay. Compare this with 'Black 6', where I aimed to be at 200kph at the end of the downwind leg and not less than 165kph (102.5mph) at the threshold. Content that I had obtained the necessary information to attempt to land, I flew the aircraft to the numbers I had planned and was rewarded with an uneventful and, I am pleased to say, presentable landing. The first sortie from take off to landing was 20 minutes.

The one thing I have not yet mentioned was the trim of the aircraft; this was truly exceptional for a first flight – it was 'hands and feet off'. Sometimes it is a real struggle, distractingly so, just to keep an aircraft's wings level or flying straight. None of that with 3579 – a real credit to the quality of the restoration work Craig and Ian had done. For the debrief, the team gathered in the welcome shade of the gazebo next to the ASP. I was full of praise for the team; they were full of concern regarding the oil temperature problem. I also mentioned that in the fullness of time the throttle friction should be improved and that I was not sure that the turn indicator was working. The team reminded me that at one point in the flight I had achieved the situation where I got one undercarriage leg down and one up –

I said that, yes, I had realised, and that I thought it was a teething problem as the subsequent selections had been OK.

The aircraft was taxied back to the hangar and the cowlings removed to inspect for leaks and any other faults. That evening, the debriefing carried on at the Chino Airport lounge.

Thursday 30th September 1999
Flight No.2
Reassured by Mike Nixon's advice that the modern oil in the engine was good for 120°C outlet temperature and 95°C inlet temperature, and that the oil in 3579 seemed not to have suffered from the temperatures reached on the first flight, I was confident to fly the aircraft for a second time to see what effect changing the oil cooler control door setting would have. What I found was that changing the oil cooler flap setting had little effect on oil temperatures, which were well above the maximums allowed.

Originally intended to be a short flight of 20 minutes or so, flight No.2 was extended to one hour by a light twin bursting a main wheel tyre on the threshold of 26L (bearing in mind 26R/08L was out of action for the time I was at Chino with Work In Progress). Whilst in the overhead at Chino, I took the opportunity to carry out some more tests:

a. Stalls
b. Undercarriage timing
c. Fuel gauging and operation of low fuel light
d. Electrical system
e. Cruise trim

Flight No.3
It was decided that as the oil cooler flap had little effect on oil temperatures, we should remove it and see what effect that had. Flight No.3 was uneventful in all but the fact that the oil temperatures were still well above the maximums

Friday 1st October 1999
Flight No.4
To be flown in the relative cool of the morning with the oil cooler flap back on (20°C as opposed to 30-35°C for previous flights). Flight No.4 lasted 40 minutes, during which time the oil temperatures were considerably lower but still well above the maximums. The opportunity was taken on this flight to investigate the effects of changing the settings of the coolant radiator flaps. The range of speeds achieved vs. flaps settings were as follows:

Coolant flaps setting	Speed	Temp
Fully open	280kph (174mph)	80°C
Half open	325kph (202mph)	80°C
Quarter open	350kph (217.5mph)	95°C

The coolant temperature limit varies with altitude; it is not a pressurised system. At low levels it is 100°C.

The coolant radiator flaps operated beautifully and clearly reflected the care and attention to detail that went in to restoring the system. I landed from flight No.4 at 0835 local time. Shortly afterwards, David Price arrived in his Cessna Centurion. While I debriefed with Craig and Mike, David got some cockpit time.

Flight No.5
For this flight the ducting around the face of the oil cooler was aluminium-taped to seal it against any loss of cooling airflow around the edges of the oil cooler. The taping was found to have little or no effect. On flight No.5 the opportunity was taken to investigate the gliding characteristics of 3579 and to establish recommended gliding speeds for the clean and landing configurations. A recommended clean glide speed of 200kph (124mph) and a landing configuration speed of 130kph (81mph) were established.

After flight No.5, due to the fact time was of the essence, it was decided to take the aircraft back to the hangar and clear the throttle friction snag and work on the oil temperature problem at the same time. Once back at the hangar, the team set about removing the oil cooler to check the oil pressure relief valve which is intended to protect the oil cooler if the oil pressure is too high, by bypassing the oil cooler core completely. At the same time, Ian set about fabricating an oil cooler inlet guide vane, which is seen in some Bf109E model pictures. Sadly, due to the work now in progress, it was becoming clear that David would not get to start or taxy the aircraft that day. David was cheerful and stoical as ever and set about reading the information I had gathered together on flying the aircraft.

It was dark by the time the oil cooler oil pressure relief valve had been adjusted, the throttle friction material replaced and the problem with the turn indicator identified. It would have been tempting to go for fitting the inlet guide vane as well as adjusting the pressure relief valve, but Gordon kept us on the right track by reminding us that we should try only one thing at a time. David and I went back to the hotel and had dinner together, discussing 3579 and other topics as aviators do.

Saturday 2nd October 1999
Flight No.6
After the oil cooler oil pressure relief valve adjustment, I flew the aircraft and eureka, the oil temperatures were well within limits. The throttle friction was now excellent and the turn indicator worked. Of interest is that the venturi for the turn indicator is mounted in the outlet part of the port coolant radiator duct; as such, it does not function on the ground but works perfectly in the air.

Having got the oil temperature in hand, I decided to open the engine up a bit to check its responses prior to committing myself and the aircraft to a performance climb check. The result was that at 0.8km (2,640ft) altitude and +35°C OAT and with the 2,300rpm, above 1.0ATA, there were small boost variations. I resolved to climb on the next sortie without the distractions of taking down figures every 30 seconds to check the engine's response to fairly high power settings and changes in altitude.

After flight No.6, David had to depart to attend to business.

Flight No.7
The first flight away from the Chino overhead! The boost variations noted on flight No.6 proved to be transient and only present at about 0.8km (2,640ft) altitude in the temperatures that prevailed. I climbed to 3.0km (9,900ft) at 1.15ATA (2,300rpm) and conducted the following tests:

a. Incipient spin tests (from the academic spin entry and from manoeuvre)
b. Maximum achieved speed at 3.0km, 1.15ATA/2,300rpm = 440kph (273mph) IAS
c. Aerobatics: looping and rolling manoeuvres
d. Rate-of-roll tests
e. Dive to VNE

Briefly, I was amazed at how docile the aircraft was and how difficult it was to depart, particularly from manoeuvre. In a level turn there was lots of warning from a wide buffet margin and the aircraft would not depart unless it was out of balance. Once departed, the aircraft was recovered easily by 'centralising the controls'. I established a recommended minimum looping speed of 450kph (280mph) and found that the 'gearing' of the propeller control was just right for looping; with a little practice it was easy to keep the

rpm at 2,300 throughout looping manoeuvres. I would not, however, describe looping as easy. Rolling, on the other hand, was simply astounding. The ailerons were light and extremely effective. The rate of roll is at least 50% faster than a Mk V Spitfire with full-span wing-tips. During the VNE dive, I achieved an IAS of 660kph (373mph). The original limit was 750kph (466mph). I was only limited by the height available, not by any feature of the aircraft, which was extremely smooth and stable at 660kph.

Flight No.8
On this flight I undertook a performance climb at 1.15ATA and 2,300rpm (30-minute limit). A climb speed of 250kph (155mph) gave an average rate of climb of 2,145ft/min (11m/sec). Bearing in mind the maximum boost limit of 1.35ATA, the 'all out' climb must be impressive. But I did not wish to thrash the aircraft, merely to set a baseline against which further tests could be conducted in the future.

After the climb, I descended to RV with John Maloney and Jerry Wilkins in the Planes of Fame SNJ-5 for ten minutes air-to-air photography before recovering to Chino.

Flight Nos.9 and 10
At this stage the flight test was complete in terms of the information I wanted and I had flown five hours and ten minutes aircraft logbook time, that is take-off to landing. The test programme demanded a minimum time of five hours' flying and ten take-offs and full-stop landings. So far I had done only eight take-offs and full stops, therefore I had two to do, hence flight Nos.9 and 10.

Given that the aircraft was so patient in terms of its coolant temperatures, I planned to fly the two flights with a stop-go in between. I got airborne, did a low approach and go-around and landed, stopped in less than 1,500ft (457m) of runway, cleared on to a link taxiway for pre-take-off checks, then took off again for a circuit and landing.

That evening, after we had put the aircraft in the hangar and cleaned it, the team enjoyed a bottle of Champagne that had been given to us by one of the team's many friends at Chino. Another nice touch from Craig – I have the cork.

Sunday 3rd October 1999
Administration day and the day I am due to depart, at lunch-time, for the evening flight from LA back to London Heathrow. Sunday morning and I am going ten to the dozen to complete all the paperwork such that there are no loose ends remaining. Robert, another valued member of the team, helped me out by copying all the documentation. With only 15 minutes to spare before I must depart Chino, the job is complete. Robert and I set off from Chino to LA by car.

As I depart Chino, I reflect on what a perfect aircraft 3579 has turned out to be – way in excess of my expectations – and the outstanding hospitality and kindness shown to me by the team, the members of Planes of Fame Museum and by ATC at Chino.

The Emil looks menacing on the ground, stunning in the air. Test pilot Charlie Brown looks very snug in the cockpit. Warbird Index

2

Bristol Blenheim
G-BPIV

The story of Graham Warner's Bristol Blenheim (actually a Bolingbroke IVT built by Fairchild of Canada) has, over the years, been related many times. It is a story of dogged determination; a struggle against all the odds that saw not one but two aircraft restored.

Following service with the RCAF, the Bolingbroke IVT in question (RCAF10038) eventually ended up with Wes Agnew of Hartney, Manitoba, in 1969. In 1974, with ownership having passed to the truly legendary Ormond Haydon-Baillie, the aircraft arrived at Duxford, Cambridgeshire, to be put into storage. Though registered G-BLHM, this identity was not taken up and the aircraft was transferred to the British Aerial Museum as G-MKIV in March 1982.

Lovingly restored at Duxford, the aircraft first took to the air on 22nd May 1987, only to crash in spectacular fashion almost exactly a month later at Denham, Buckinghamshire, a victim of pilot error.

While the shock, genuine horror and gnashing of teeth that the aircraft had been so cruelly snatched from the victorious restoration team after such a short flying career were still tangible, the entire team

met to discuss the possibility of starting over and repeating the whole restoration experience. Almost all of G-MKIV had been damaged beyond repair in the crash at Denham. The aircraft had cartwheeled wing-tip to wing-tip; the port engine ended up resting behind the starboard wing and the all-important centre section was twisted by the impact. Only an aileron and a few other parts were considered to be usable in the restoration of the second aircraft.

Despite having a very tall mountain to climb, the decision was made to proceed and a second aircraft, Bolingbroke IVT RCAF10201, the second aircraft in the last batch of Fairchild-built Bolingbrokes, arrived at Duxford in January 1988; it was registered G-BPIV in February 1989. The team had made a point of saying that their aim was to restore the aircraft to flying condition within five years. Anyone who has anything to do with restoring vintage aircraft, especially warbirds, will tell you that the team's promise constituted a bold opening statement. (In fact, parts from two Bolingbroke airframes were used in the restoration of G-BPIV; the wings were to come from RCAF9073 and the fuselage from RCAF10201.)

The first Blenheim restoration at Duxford masquerading as V6028/GB-D of 105 Squadron. Mike Shreeve

Whilst the engineering team pushed the project forward by putting in the hours, Graham Warner was busy in other ways, constantly seeking publicity for the project and furthering the aims of the Blenheim Society. It had always been one of the British Aerial Museum's key aims to bring the Blenheim well and truly into the public spotlight, and in Graham they had a past master in the art of garnering first-rate media coverage with his persuasive manner and total enthusiasm for all things Blenheim.

Additionally, it is worth pointing out that the aircraft was restored at a time when the United Kingdom was in a deep economic recession. Graham was determined that the restoration project would reverse the image of the Blenheim as a type now consigned to the history books. With consummate skill and endless perseverance, he would turn the 'Forgotten Bomber' into a highly visible warbird.

On the restoration front, to make the climb towards airworthiness ever steeper,

several of the companies that had assisted with the first restoration were either no longer in business or had cut back on spending due to the recession. British Aerospace's Lostock plant had restored the propellers for the first aircraft, but due to its closure the units for the second restoration had to go to Canada to be overhauled; this was a commercial undertaking, which meant not only extra expense but added shipping charges too. The propellers were the only major items to be sent out for restoration or overhaul – everything else on the aircraft, plus the engines, was worked on in-house.

Despite the fact that this was 'second time around' for the team, problems still manifested themselves, and it must have been soul-destroying to have to go over old ground. The biggest hold-up was the wait for the raw material required for the wing spar. Like many other warbirds, each and every rivet in the structure had to be renewed. Each outer wing spar alone contained a staggering 8,000 rivets. There are eight sections in all, which means 64,000 rivets.

The structural integrity of the fuselage had been compromised by two large holes cut in the rear to aid dismantling in Canada. It was therefore by no means certain that the refurbished section would actually fit even though it was correctly set up in the repair jig. As a consequence, it was several years before the tail section was joined and the anxious wait was over – the two married together without problem.

Following the loss of the first Blenheim and the approach of the post-restoration first flight of G-BPIV, it was decided that the aircraft's colour scheme should be as different as possible to that worn by G-MKIV. The scheme chosen was the dramatic semi-gloss all-black finish of Z5722, a Blenheim IV night intruder operated by 68 Squadron, RAF. In line with this colour scheme the aircraft was also fitted with two light-series bomb racks aft of the main bomb bay, as fitted to the original aircraft.

When the second restored Blenheim flew for the first time on 18th May 1993, with the late 'Hoof' Proudfoot at the controls, the quest to make the type more visible to the

British public was eased slightly. The aircraft was able to visit airshows and make itself available in different parts of the country and to thousands of people in one 'hit'. Additionally, the video *Forgotten Bomber* was screened on all the United Kingdom television networks as well as selling several thousand individual copies.

The Blenheim operated by the Aircraft Restoration Company today is some 5,000 lb (2,268kg) lighter than the original and when flown at airshows is normally crewed by one pilot plus the flight engineer, though for ordinary flying the aircraft can be flown by the pilot only. The nominal crew is three.

On 28th May 1993 the aircraft was rolled out and officially named at the Aircraft Restoration Company's base at Duxford. Viscount Rothermere, proprietor of the *Daily Mail* newspaper was invited to name the aircraft *Spirit of Britain First*, after his grandfather's executive Bristol 142 *Britain First*. Fittingly, Lady Violet Aitken, representing Wing Commander Max Aitken DFC RAF, the pilot of the original Z5722, accompanied Viscount Rothermere.

Ten years on from that first post-restoration flight, the aircraft continued to draw attention wherever and whenever it appeared during the 2003 airshow season – a fitting tribute to the dedication and fighting spirit of Graham Warner, John Romain and the small Aircraft Restoration Company restoration team. Now that same dedication and fighting spirit is needed again, for late on the evening of 18th August 2003 the Blenheim hit the headlines once again when it was involved in an accident whilst landing at its Duxford home. Damage to the airframe and engines is substantial and a survey is currently being undertaken to determine the feasibility of putting the aircraft back into airworthy trim once more. Surely nobody will bet against the Blenheim eventually returning to the skies – again!

3

North American P-51C Mustang
42-103831/N1204

Built on North American Aviation's production line in Dallas, Texas, P-51C-10-NT Mustang 42-103831 was declared surplus by the USAAF and stored at Stillwater AFB, Oklahoma, before being sold to Paul Mantz of Glendale, California, on 19th February 1946. Registered to Mantz as NX1204, it was raced during 1946 as Race 60 *Latin American*. Mantz further developed this aircraft into one of the hottest cross-country air racers.

Along with sister-ship P-51C-10-NT 44-10947/N1202 (now preserved as a static exhibit at the National Air & Space Museum in Washington, DC), NX1204 helped Paul Mantz dominate post-war air racing in the United States until 1950. Between them the two Mustangs won the Bendix Races in 1946, 1947 and 1948, in the process setting a new Bendix speed record – an average of 435.5mph (700.71km/h) – in 1946.

Mantz was the first and only winner of three consecutive air races. He retired the Mustang in 1950, two years after it had been reregistered as N1204 to Tallmantz Aviation

at the Movieland of the Air Museum within Orange County (now John Wayne) Airport, California. Displayed in front of the Museum hangar, the race-winning Mustang still took to the air with Mantz or Frank G Tallman at the controls. Both men made a living as pilots for the film studios and both died in flying accidents, Mantz in Buttercup Valley, Arizona, on 8th July 1965 during the filming of *Flight of the Phoenix*, Tallman in 1978.

Fortunately the Mustang had a brighter future. It remained on display until 1984 and was then purchased by Kermit Weeks in 1985 directly from the Tallmantz collection (along with several other aircraft), after which N1204 was put into storage to await its turn in the restoration queue. Two years later, Weeks contracted Cal Pacific Airmotive of Salinas, California, to rebuild the aircraft's wings. This was necessary because during the aircraft's career as an air racer the wings had been modified to a 'wet' configuration, to increase fuel capacity. This modification had necessitated the stripping-out

Kermit Weeks at the controls of his P-51C-10NT 42-103831/N1204 "Ina The Macon Belle". The immaculate rebuild and restoration work (see page 53 for detail shots) was carried out by Art Teeters at Cal Pacific Airmotive. Tom Smith

of the entire gun and ammunition bay sections, and the interior surface of the wings had been sealed to carry fuel.

Cal Pacific Airmotive found major corrosion throughout the wings that were completely disassembled. Several new wing ribs as well as new main and rear spar assemblies had to be fabricated. New gun bay ammunition webs were also fabricated and installed. All the gun mounts and castings had to be manufactured and installed. Essentially the wings were restored using a large jig fixture fabricated specifically to accommodate P-51C wings, to guarantee the correct flight characteristics once installed. New wing skins also had to be fabricated and fitted.

On completion of the basic wing structure, the mainplane was removed from the jig fixture and bolted together in a wing stand. The main landing gear had been overhauled and was then installed in the wings. It was also necessary to fabricate new stress doors for the wing fuel tanks. The gun doors were cleaned, restored and new outer skins spot-welded as per the original process at North American Aviation.

The next step was to commence restoration of the fuselage, which arrived at Cal Pacific Airmotive after the mainplane. Corrosion was again so severe that it was necessary to install four new fuselage longerons. New bulkheads and skins had to be fabricated as required. Due to extensive corrosion, 90 per cent of the cockpit enclosure mechanisms were manufactured as new. In addition, new wooden floorboards were made and a new heating and ventilation system manufactured to the original specifications. Coolant and oil tubes were made and installed and new hydraulic and oxygen lines were fabricated, marked with the appropriate coloured identification tapes and duly fitted.

Special material was ordered so Cal Pacific Airmotive could fabricate four new engine mount beams for the bearers that were installed; the Lord mounts were sent out for refurbishment with new rubber. The rare cowl formers were cleaned, stripped of paint, inspected and repaired as necessary before being attached to the new engine mount. The mount was then attached to the fuselage. The upper and lower cowlings were reworked to eradicate corrosion, and dents were removed. The side cowlings could not be saved so new units with stainless steel inserts were made, and all-new Dzus fasteners fitted as standard.

The tailcone assembly had to be stripped and new parts installed as required; these included new outer skins. The horizontal stabiliser, vertical fin, elevators, flaps and ailerons are basically of all-new construction as the originals were corroded beyond economical repair. However the rudder was fit for restoration. Once the subassemblies were complete the empennage was assembled and bolted to the fuselage.

The engine, a 1,490-hp (1,112-kW) Packard Merlin V1650-7, was overhauled by Dwight Thorne in Hollister, California. Following installation in the new 'motor mount', the whole unit was attached to the fuselage which was duly mated to the wing, exactly as the aircraft was originally assembled at North American Aviation. The forward scoop and 'dog house' also underwent major rework. New parts had to be fabricated, including new skins. To restore the original Harrison radiator, new upper and lower tanks were cast from aluminium, new side panels were manufactured and the radiator core simply overhauled. The oil cooler also was overhauled.

This particular P-51C model has a working fuselage fuel tank, which required extensive research and then refabrication of all the appropriate systems. One thing that is not evident to the outside observer is that the aircraft is equipped with original bulletproof self-sealing fuel tanks. All-new fairings were fabricated, assembled and adjusted to fit the aircraft. The inboard main gear doors had to be reworked, with the new outer skins spot-welded. The outboard main gear doors were reworked and the exterior skins of the inboard and outboard doors were polished.

Work on restoring the ammunition and gun bays required special detailing. The ammunition boxes, feeds and chutes had to be fabricated from drawings. Blank ammunition shells were marked at the tips as tracer, incendiary or armour-piercing incendiary and assembled into clips – a feature that was duly noted by EAA Judges when the aircraft was subsequently entered for competition. Replica .50-calibre guns were installed and an original gun camera was acquired, the latter to be installed for static display only. New bomb racks were cast from aluminium; all internal mechanisms for the shackles were machined and assembled as one unit.

A functional gunsight was fitted in the cockpit. Instrumentation is original, overhauled and even re-screened to resemble old radium dials. The only modern equipment installed (a transceiver, transponder and encoder) has been carefully concealed in the cockpit. Military radio equipment was refurbished and can be installed, but for static display only.

One of the final tasks in restoring the wings was to fabricate the new gun port leading edges, the originals having been removed when the wing was modified to a 'wet' configuration. Steel fixtures were fabricated, the gun ports hand-formed and then highly polished to match the finish on the rest of the aircraft. Art Teeters' team at Cal Pacific Airmotive even made a new lens for the port wing's leading-edge landing light.

During the restoration process, it was decided to install Type I cadmium-plated hardware and parts that have silver-colour plating, research having shown that this was originally done at North American Aviation. Since most hardware purchased today is Type II, which is gold in colour, this required extensive stripping of all the hardware followed by considerable replating work.

All of the Mustang's subassemblies were overhauled and restored to their original configuration. These included the hydraulics, oxygen bottles and all of the cockpit assemblies. Brass safety wire was used where safety wire was required. New electrical wiring was installed throughout the aircraft, with identification marked horizontally along the wire, again to original North American Aviation specifications. New surplus electrical switches and breakers were also installed.

Countless hours were spent researching the Mustang's internal and external markings. The real attention to detail came when water-transfer markings were manufactured and positioned on the aircraft, as per the originals, along with new phenolic and metal data plates. Even the propeller was stencilled, and the old-style Hartzell Propeller placards installed.

Prior to completion of the restoration, Kermit Weeks decided to have the aircraft finished in a 302nd FS, 332nd FG 'Tuskegee Airmen' colour scheme based on "INA The Macon Belle" flown by Lieutenant Colonel Lee Archer, the only 'Tuskegee Ace'. The Tuskegee Airmen (so named because they were trained at Tuskegee, Alabama) served as bomber escorts and became known as the 'Red Tail Angels' because they never lost a bomber under their care to enemy fighters.

During his military service, Lt Col Archer earned medals for bravery including the Distinguished Flying Cross, the Air Medal with 18 Oak Leaf Clusters, and the Legion of Merit. Lee Archer is still alive, and along with the Los Angeles, California, Chapter of the Tuskegee Airman organisation, was able to contribute greatly to the final restoration of the aircraft. Working closely with an artist, and studying old photos, the Zoot Suit character located on the aft port side of the fuselage was brought back to life. The nose art was then completed.

Restoration of the P-51C was interrupted on a few occasions, as work was undertaken to rebuild Kermit Weeks' P-51D-25-NT 45-11507/N921 (*see elsewhere in this book*), which was badly damaged by Hurricane 'Andrew' when it hit the Florida area on 24th August 1992.

The first post-restoration flight of N1204 took place on 30th November 2000. Early flights led to a few minor adjustments to set the rigging and all was well. Kermit Weeks returned to Salinas to put some more flighttime on the aircraft before flying it to its new base at Polk City, Florida. The aircraft left the Cal Pacific Airmotive facility on 31st March 2001 and headed to the EAA's Sun 'n Fun Fly-In event at Lakeland, Florida, where it won the Grand Champion Warbird award. Later that year, Weeks took the Mustang to Oshkosh where it was voted EAA Warbirds of America Grand Champion World War Two Warbird by the EAA Judges, and won a coveted Golden Wrench Award for the Cal Pacific Airmotive restoration team.

Photographs on the opposite page:

Art Teeters and crew at Cal Pacific Airmotive in Salinas restored Kermit Weeks' P-51C-10NT 42-103831/N1204 "Ina The Macon Belle", one of only four original P-51B/Cs, to exceptionally high standards. The attention to detail earned the company an EAA Golden Wrench award and the aircraft the coveted EAA Warbirds of America Grand Champion tag – hardly surprising when you look at the detail and workmanship both inside the cockpit and outside. All photos Tom Smith

4

Boeing B-29A Superfortress
44-62070/N529B

'Of all the aeroplanes we'd managed to locate and restore, we developed a special desire for the Superfort. It was not only the last word in World War Two aircraft design and performance; it was the only ship that would complete our collection.' So said Lloyd Nolen, Founder of the Confederate (now Commemorative) Air Force, when explaining the CAF hierarchy's decision that acquisition of a Boeing B-29 Superfortress was a must.

The CAF's search for a B-29 began as far back as 1966, but the early signs were not promising. When the CAF approached the USAF they were told that apart from a few museum examples, there were no B-29s still on inventory – either at disposal yards or storage facilities. However, such was the CAF founders' desire to have a Superfortress to restore, they refused to accept this apparent setback and began the search for their own airframe.

Not only was locating a B-29 proving to be problematic; it was believed that this would probably be the CAF's biggest restoration challenge, stretching the organisation's finances to the limit – cause for concern in some circles. That the quest would ultimately prove successful was in no small part down to the financial input and determination of one man, Victor N Agather. Incredibly, Agather had been closely associated with the development of the B-29 and spent many hours with Boeing engineers and flight test pilots. At war's end he was transferred to the United States, where he spent the final years of his military career training B-29 flight crews on post-war operations.

Following retirement and his new career as a businessman, Agather routinely contacted the Pentagon, enthusiastically outlining the CAF's plans to obtain and restore a B-29 to flying condition. The response was somewhat less than enthusiastic, the

A beautiful portrait of N529B "FIFI" with San Francisco's Golden Gate Bridge as a backdrop. Over a million people in the US get to see the aircraft each year thanks to its touring schedule from spring through autumn.
GHOSTS Phil Makanna

Department of Defense stating categorically that no B-29s extant were suitable for such resurrection and restoration.

Through aggressive networking the CAF spread the word that the search for a B-29 was on. Letters were written, phone calls made and weak leads followed up without success. The years passed by but nothing materialised. Yet, both Agather and his CAF cohorts simply refused to believe that there were no B-29s extant somewhere in the world. Then, one summer's day in 1966, word reached Agather that there were some 37 B-29s sat out in the open at the Aberdeen

Proving Ground in Maryland. It was quickly decided that Agather should fly up to Maryland and check the status of the aircraft. Frustratingly, Agather's hopes were dashed just as quickly as they had been raised, when his inspection confirmed that the aircraft were too corroded and none were a viable proposition for restoration to airworthiness.

Despite the fact that the B-29s in Maryland were virtually useless as restoration projects, their existence gave the CAF team new hope. If the USAF had managed to 'overlook' the 37 bombers at the Aberdeen Proving Ground, there was hope that other B-29s survived elsewhere and might be more suitable for restoration to flying condition.

The next lead came in the shape of information that one of the B-29s used by NACA as a 'mother ship' for the Bell X-1 test drops was held by the Allied Aircraft Museum in Tucson, Arizona. Agather made a phone call, established that the aircraft in question, NACA 137 *Fertile Myrtle* (built as B-29-95-BW 45-21787 and delivered to the US Navy as P2B-1S BuNo 84029) was attainable and backed up his interest with a down payment to the museum. Agather had his B-29 project! Except that he didn't, because in a

bizarre twist of events a letter containing the second promised payment was lost in the post and did not arrive at the Allied Aircraft Museum. Soon afterwards a company based in Oakland, California, acquired the B-29. Despite a hastily organised flight to California to try to rescue his acquisition bid, Agather could not secure ownership of the aircraft. It was now a case of back to the drawing board.

The next report of surviving B-29 airframes came from a scheduled airline pilot who had seen several of the aircraft apparently languishing in the Mojave Desert, California. Roger Baker, himself a CAF Colonel and aware of Agather's quest, was on a flight from New York to Los Angeles when he flew over the B-29s in question. One of the staff at the CAF's headquarters in Harlingen, Texas, contacted the Office of the Air Force in Washington, DC, to see if the USAF had any record of the aircraft. The reply was negative. Perhaps Baker had been mistaken.

Fortunately, Baker's insistence that he had not just imagined seeing several B-29s motivated the CAF staffer to investigate further. Baker was indeed correct. The Superfortresses were located at NWC China Lake, a sprawling US Navy installation. A tele-

phone call to the base confirmed that they had about 30 B-29s sat out in the desert, being used as gunnery targets. Apparently the aircraft were still under USAF control. After several more letters and phone calls and some friendly badgering, the USAF agreed to allow the CAF to have one of the B-29s. An added bonus was that they were prepared to allow the CAF access to all the other China Lake B-29s, so that they might pillage spares to help in the task of getting their selected airframe back to airworthiness.

The CAF elected to restore Renton-built B-29A-60-BN 44-62070 to fly, and the USAF and FAA deemed it possible to fly the aircraft out to Harlingen on a ferry permit – but only if the restoration work undertaken met with their approval.

Under the watchful eye of Colonel Duane Egli, many volunteers spent time removing the old wiring systems and installing new.

"FIFI" is currently the only airworthy example of some 50 surviving B-29. That she survived at all is down to the persistence of the CAF over many years as it sought to find a B-29 that could be restored to airworthy condition.
Warbird Index

The CAF restoration team arrived at China Lake on 31st March 1971. In a little over two months they rebuilt all the systems and replaced all the fuel, hydraulic and oil hoses. They installed and checked new instruments before running the engines, and testing the propellers. Control surfaces were re-covered after checking, and control cables carefully scrutinised. Several new parts were required and those not available via cannibalisation of the other B-29s were obtained from selected vendors. Jack Kern headed up the volunteers, having spent the previous months working on the B-29A as the main contractor.

By the summer of 1971 the restoration was complete and the engines had been ground tested. After inspections, the FAA was satisfied that the restoration work had been completed to its satisfaction and issued the promised ferry permit. CAF Colonels Randy Sohn and Lefty Gardner, both with relevant multi-engine experience, were selected as pilots for the flight to Harlingen. By 3rd August 44-62070 (now with the civilian identity N4249) was ready to take to the air again. Before the flight, the words 'Confederate Air Force' were stencilled on

both sides of the aircraft, 'Just in case this was the only time we ever flew her!' explained Captain Randy Sohn. While the crew carried out the necessary pre-flight checks a nosewheel tyre exploded and had to be quickly changed.

The crew loaded enough fuel to fly the 1,300 miles (2,092km) to CAF Headquarters and lifted off at exactly 0748hrs – just 12 minutes before the China Lake weapons range became active for the day! Crewmen for the seven-hour flight were Darrell Skurich, Roger Baker and Jim 'Mac' McCafferty. The flight, the first by a B-29 Superfortress for almost 20 years, went smoothly; minor problems encountered on the way included a small voltage regulator fire, and a split oil pressure line on the engineer's panel.

Following the jubilation of the successful flight came more stress and trauma for the CAF. Though the FAA had granted a single ferry permit to enable the crew to fly the aircraft to Harlingen, getting a full Certificate of Airworthiness was to be another story. Requests to the USAF seemingly fell on deaf ears. After considerable lobbying, Senator Barry Goldwater went into action to get the USAF to withdraw their 'no-flight' clause.

The USAF relented and, after one or two more political attempts to keep the aircraft on the ground, issued authorisation for it to be certified by the FAA.

The Commemorative Air Force B-29 Squadron is located at Midland, Texas, where N529B *"FIFI"* (named after chief sponsor Victor N Agather's wife) is maintained in flying condition with Consolidated LB-30A N12905 *Diamond Lil* as a partner. The CAF B-29 Squadron was formed to offer volunteer support for maintaining the aircraft in airworthy condition and as a means of concentrating B-29 expertise in one place. At the time of writing the Squadron has over 400 members around the world. *"FIFI"* is flown to airshows and taken on tour from spring to autumn (it is estimated that the aircraft is seen by over a million people a year in the United States), and returns to Midland each winter for essential maintenance. The aircraft is normally on public display in the CAF Hangar at Midland between November and May.

"FIFI" never looks more menacing than when photographed head-on. Bob Munro

5

Consolidated B-24J Liberator
44-44052/N224J

The world's only fully restored Consolidated B-24 Liberator is operated by the world-famous Collings Foundation of Stow, Massachusetts. A B-24J-85-CF, serial 44-44052, it was built at the Consolidated Aircraft Company's Fort Worth, Texas, plant in August 1944. The Liberator is a large aeroplane by any standards and the restoration of this ex-Indian Air Force bomber is documented as the world's biggest warbird restoration to fly (though Boeing's restoration of B-29-70-BW Superfortress 44-69972, under way as this book is being written, will probably take the title when complete).

B-24J 44-44052 was delivered initially to the USAAF but was soon transferred to the RAF in October 1944 and converted as a Liberator GR.VI. Serialled KH191 by the RAF, the aircraft was deployed to India in late 1944 and used by South East Air Command on maritime patrol and strike missions in the Pacific. It is believed to have seen some action against Japanese shipping.

The end of World War Two saw KH191 abandoned by the RAF at Khanpur. However, unlike many other aircraft classed as surplus to requirements when hostilities ceased, this Liberator eventually took to the air once again, in 1948, after it was selected as one of 36 such aircraft to be converted by the Indian Air Force to what they called B.VII status. It subsequently saw active service with the Indian Air Force for some 20 years, finally being retired in 1968. It was then put into storage for four years until its transfer to the Indian Air Force Technical College at Jalahalli where it served as instructional airframe T18.

In 1981 the Liberator was acquired by Doug Arnold of Warbirds of Great Britain, based at Blackbushe Airport, Hampshire. It was disassembled in India, packed aboard a Heavylift Shorts Belfast C.1 for transportation to the United Kingdom and then stored with Arnold's growing fleet of warbirds. The plan was to get the aircraft back in the air,

Complete, painted as All American, *registered N224J, and airworthy in May 1992. The rear fuselage carries a list of the individuals and companies that made donations to enable the restoration project to go ahead.* Patrick Bunce

but Arnold had a change of heart and the Liberator was advertised for sale 'as is' in 1984. After protracted negotiations, Robert F Collings acquired the Liberator and arranged to have it shipped by sea to the United States. Once again the big bomber was disassembled and this time packed in huge cradles aboard a freighter. One unit held the 64-ft (19.50-m) long fuselage, another the 55-ft (16.76-m) wide centre wing section; two 40-ft (12.19-m) containers held the balance of the aircraft parts. The sea journey to Boston, Massachusetts, took three weeks.

It was originally planned to restore the aircraft to static exhibition standard only, but

The scene at Warbirds of Great Britain shortly after ex-Indian Air Force Consolidated Liberator B.VII T18, in a less than desirable state, had been delivered. Patrick Bunce

The aircraft did not look any better on the inside and restoration must have been a most daunting prospect. The doubters did not reckon on the grit and determination of Bob Collings, Founder of the Collings Foundation, who masterminded the return of the B-24J to the air. Patrick Bunce

after considerable thought and a lot of 'input' from former World War Two Liberator crewmen, Bob Collings decided to have the aircraft restored to flying condition. 'We were totally convinced by the argument that said as a static aircraft only about 3,000 people [a year] may take the trouble to see her, but in flyable condition, and put on a nationwide tour, some three million might see her,' explained Bob.

Nate Mayo and Massachusetts-based volunteers had already started preliminary restoration work to static condition, but this work was halted. Tom Reilly Vintage Aircraft in Kissimmee, Florida, was contacted in order to evaluate the potential for an airworthy restoration. The company was tasked with restoring the airframe, systems and powerplants, although work on the latter would be subcontracted to a dedicated engine rebuilder. The project was to be supported by substantial volunteer labour, closely supervised, which would see the gun turrets, armament, radio equipment and the oxygen system restored as well as the addition of an incredible amount of detailing – especially important when the aircraft was to be seen by so many people.

Restoration of the Emerson Electric nose turret was sponsored by Emerson Electric of St Louis, Missouri. PPG Industries of Pittsburgh, Pennsylvania, supplied the turret

The scene at Tom Reilly Vintage Aircraft in Kissimmee, Florida, as the massive hulk of the Liberator is worked on. Jack Flinn

glass and United Technologies donated a genuine Norden bombsight. In June 1987 the wings, tail feathers and other parts were shipped to Tom Reilly Vintage Aircraft; the fuselage made the same journey a year later. Considering the amount of moving around the fuselage had undergone, it was in remarkably good shape. However, the results of close inspection and checks dictated that 20 per cent of the fuselage skin – and close on half a million rivets – had to be replaced.

The enormous restoration task meant the entire aircraft had to be disassembled component by component, each of which had to be accurately labelled prior to restoration and release to fly. Some 80 per cent of the B-24's components required some sort of attention, mainly due to minor damage and some surface corrosion.

Because the aircraft was to be once again airworthy, Bob Collings decided wisely to ensure that the engines, propellers, electrical and hydraulic systems were fully and properly restored. With this in mind, every single part of the huge hydraulic system was restored or replaced with new components. Vickers Hydraulics, Five Star Hydraulics and Aeroquip supported this part of the project, Loos & Co donated all the cables and hardware, and Ralmark supplied enough control wire pulleys to ensure that every one was new. Miami Avionics supplied the radio equipment and assisted with installation. As the restoration work progressed in Florida, the Collings Foundation monitored developments and ensured that the engineering task was not delayed due to lack of parts and hardware.

Steps were taken to ensure that whilst the engineering work was progressing, work on other items didn't just stand still. Huntington-based Fuel Safe agreed to assist in the fabrication of brand new fuel cells, and B.F. Goodrich donated new brake tubes. Goodyear came up with the tyres and a local company, Layzott Plastics, chipped in with moulded windows. Almost 100,000 man-hours were expended in the restoration process at a cost of $1.3 million. About one-third of the cost of restoration was offset by donations from 27 corporations and 1,500 individual donors. All in all, quite an effort!

Fortunately the Collings Foundation managed to save some funds as the four 1,200-hp (89.5-kW) Pratt & Whitney R-1830-65 engines and Hamilton Standard propellers could be overhauled, in spite of their extended periods of external storage over the years. Aviation Propeller of Opa Locka, Florida, donated the money necessary to overhaul all four propeller units. Pratt & Whitney of East Hartford, Connecticut, and Buick made donations towards the overhaul of one of the engines. Several of the other manufacturers originally involved in B-24 production stepped in with sponsorship of parts and services; these included Lord Corporation, Champion Spark Plug and Aero Kool.

After one last determined push, B-24J Liberator 44-44052 took to the air under its own power following the mammoth restoration on 8th August 1989, a fitting tribute to the determination of Bob Collings and the myriad of volunteers and donor companies. The restored aircraft was originally painted as *All American* in honour of the 15th Air Force B-24 that carried the same name. The original *All American* made the headlines when its gunners shot down no less than 14 enemy fighters during a single raid over Germany on 25th July 1944. Sadly, *All American* was shot down over Yugoslavia on 4th October 1944.

In 1998 the Liberator was renamed *The Dragon and His Tail* as a tribute to the USAAF veterans who served in the Pacific Theatre of Operations (PTO). A crew led by Joseph Pagoni flew the original *The Dragon and His Tail* (San Diego, California-built B-24J-190-CO 44-40973) on some 85 combat missions while assigned to the 64th BS, 43rd BG. Pagoni reported that the flamboyantly marked B-24 was always the focus of attention for Japanese fighter pilots attacking Allied bomber formations.

The original *The Dragon and His Tail* survived the war and later was stored, along with countless other surplus USAAF bombers, at Kingman, Arizona. Tragically, despite determined efforts to save the aircraft for preservation, *The Dragon and His*

Tail was the last B-24 to fall victim to the scrap man's cutting torch. Having decided to change 44-44052's markings by way of tribute to PTO veterans, Bob Collings commissioned Gary Norville of New Smyrna Beach, Florida-based American Aero Services to repaint the aircraft in the dramatic and flamboyant scheme with the dragon adorning the entire length of the fuselage.

Today *The Dragon and His Tail* flies on in tribute to those who built, flew and maintained the Consolidated B-24 Liberator bomber. The aircraft undertakes a national tour each year in company with the Collings Foundation's other four-engined bomber, B-17G-85-DL 44-83575/N93012 (*see elsewhere in this book*), thus enabling the maximum number of people to see the aircraft.

A dramatic study of All American *and, below and behind, its fellow Collings Foundation bomber, B-17G-85-DL 44-83575/N93012, while on tour in California.* Patrick Bunce

Although the original All American *was a 15th AF aircraft, the port fin and rudder of the Collings Foundation B-24J carried the marking of the 453rd BG, 8th AF, in recognition of the contribution made by its surviving personnel to help finance the restoration. The contribution of the 453rd BG, 15th AF, was similarly acknowledged on the starboard fin and rudder.* Patrick Bunce

Opposite page:
All-action shot of All American, *showing the aircraft's massive 110-ft (33.52-m) wing span to advantage.* Patrick Bunce

6

Gloster Gladiator I
L8032/G-AMRK

When the RAF received its first Gloster Gladiator I in February 1937, the type was already approaching obsolescence. The much faster Supermarine Spitfire and Hawker Hurricane monoplane fighters of markedly advanced design had already flown and were being developed urgently, with the eight-gun Hurricane scheduled to enter service by the end of 1937. However, the worsening political situation and the threat of conflict in Europe saw nine RAF squadrons re-equipped with the Gladiator – last of the RAF's biplane fighters – in the same year.

The Air Ministry had issued Specification F.7/30 for a new RAF fighter in 1930. The specification dictated a top speed of 250mph (402km/h) with a four-gun armament package and asked for a 20 per cent increase in speed and a doubling of guns carried over existing fighters then in RAF service. In addition to Gloster Aircraft's response, Bristol, Hawker and Supermarine all replied to the Air Ministry requirement, so it was decided to organise a competition to choose the winner. Gloster Aircraft were too tied up with manufacturing the Gauntlet fighter for the RAF to produce an all-new design to enter the contest, deciding at the last moment to offer instead their private-venture aircraft, designated S.S.37, as a serious contender. The design was based on the Gauntlet.

H.P. Folland had designed the S.S.37 that first took to the air in September 1934. Like the Gauntlet, the fuselage was of a steel-tubed space frame design. The wings were developed from steel tube spars and duralumin rib work. The airframe was entirely fabric-covered. Adjustments to its sister Gauntlet design included a more streamlined cantilever undercarriage with internally sprung wheels, new landing flaps and fewer wing struts. The proven and reliable Bristol Mercury 6S 530-hp (485-kW) radial engine was selected to drive the two-bladed, fixed-pitch, wooden propeller. To answer the Air Ministry armament requirement, two Vickers .303-in (7.7-mm) machine guns with 600rpg were installed in the forward fuselage and two drum-fed Lewis .303-in machine guns (97rpg) were carried beneath the lower wings. The Gladiator was duly announced as the winner of the competition.

Whilst the Gladiator's performance and armament were far better than those of the aircraft it superseded, and its handling characteristics were flawless, pilots were less enthusiastic about the aircraft's relatively heavy controls and the restricted visibility from the enclosed canopy. Soon after the first 71 Gladiator Is had been produced, the original armament of two Lewis and two Vickers guns was replaced by four belt-fed Browning .303-in machine guns with 400rpg for the two wing-mounted weapons and 600rpg for the two mounted in the forward fuselage.

Though outdated when it entered service in 1937, it is worth noting that the Gladiator was the mount of the RAF's (then) top-scoring fighter pilot, Squadron Leader Marmaduke Thomas St John 'Pat' Pattle, who

The Shuttleworth Collection's Gladiator I at rest before one of its many air displays at its Old Warden base. Bob Munro

Fresh out of restoration, this shot shows the quality of the fabric work to advantage. By now the Gladiator had been finished as N2308/HP-B of 247 Squadron, the only RAF Fighter Command unit to fly the Gladiator during the Battle of Britain when it was tasked with defending Plymouth naval dockyards. Bob Munro

With the throttle wide open, the air reverberates to the sound of the Gladiator's Mercury IX engine as the aircraft gets airborne from Old Warden. Bob Munro

flew the type for the majority of his distinguished career. His biplane tally was fifteen destroyed (plus one shared), three 'probable' (plus one shared 'probable') and three 'damaged' (plus two shared).

As well as sales to the RAF and Fleet Air Arm, the Gladiator was an export success story; sales of new-build aircraft, together with refurbished ex-RAF airframes, turned the Gladiator into one of the most utilised fighter aircraft of its era. Overseas air arms to use the type were: Belgium (22), China (36), Egypt (45), Eire (4), Finland (30), Greece (19), Iraq (14), Latvia (26), Lithuania (14), Norway (12), Portugal (15), South Africa (12) and Sweden (55).

The subject of this entry, Gladiator I L8032, was rolled out at the Gloster Aircraft Company works at Brockworth, Gloucestershire, on 4th October 1938, and was then prepared for service by 27 MU at RAF Shawbury, Shropshire. It was powered by an 840-hp (627-kW) Bristol Mercury IX air-cooled radial piston engine, sported a Watts two-bladed propeller and remained at Shawbury until 1941, at which point No.2 AACU, based at RAF Gosport, Hampshire, took it on strength. The aircraft's service life was spent being shuffled around Maintenance Units until it was sold back to the manufacturer in 1948. There was very little interest in maintaining any 'historic aviation relic' at that time and L8032 was duly despatched to Air Service Training Ltd at Hamble airfield, Hampshire, as a ground instructional airframe.

When Hamble closed, L8032 and one other Gladiator were sold to Flightways for the princely sum of £10. The proprietor of the company, one Vivian Bellamy, had flown Sea Gladiators in the Fleet Air Arm and was keen to buy both aircraft with the aim of putting them back in the air. The second aircraft (Gladiator II N5903 – at the time of writing being restored to airworthiness by The Fighter Collection at Duxford, Cambridgeshire) was used as a donor aircraft for L8032, with some parts simply being exchanged between the two aircraft. The 'rebuild's' engine used parts from both aircraft.

After a considerable amount of work L8032, registered G-AMRK, took to the air again on the evening of 13th June 1952. However, Bellamy's ownership was short-lived when Gloster Aircraft, having recognised the value of having an airworthy example of one of its own aircraft, purchased L8032 the following year. Bellamy later expressed the

opinion that it was simply too expensive for a private owner to maintain L8032 in airworthy condition. Glosters promised to work on it and keep it airworthy.

Just four years later, Glosters took the step of approving a complete restoration of the airframe, an idea promoted by Chief Test Pilot Dicky Martin, and undertaken by Gloster apprentices, working under close supervision. On completion of the work, L8032 was painted in 'B' Flight, 72 (Fighter) Squadron markings and took on the mantle of K8032, a move that received official sanction. Just as restorers today aim to represent aircraft in stock condition, the lengths to which the Gloster team went to ensure the aircraft was returned to its original configuration represented quite forward thinking

back then. As part of their task they installed four machine guns (it is not known if they had first been deactivated!) and a TR.9 radio. Apparently a fighter-type spade grip, with which the aircraft had previously been equipped, was added to the control column.

With the rapid amalgamation of companies within the British aviation industry and the bells tolling for the passing of the Gloster Aircraft Company as an individual entity, the Gladiator was subsequently donated to the Shuttleworth Trust on 7th November 1960. Air Commodore Alan Wheeler graciously accepted the aircraft on behalf of the Trust. The next ten years saw the aircraft flown and operated in a spirited fashion, becoming well known in the process and something of a flagship for its owners.

After ten years of operation, the Shuttleworth Trust determined that it was time to renew the fabric on the aircraft and in the process undertake a full check of the airframe. Flight One of Staverton, Gloucestershire, were commissioned to undertake the work in November 1971. Although the aircraft would retain its 72 Squadron colours until 1990, L8032, the correct serial, was reapplied 1974

The Gladiator demands an enormous amount of attention to keep it airworthy. Shuttleworth's Chief Engineer, Chris Morris oversees the maintenance programme, which is based on the aircraft flying between five and ten hours per year. The Bristol Mercury engine (a combination of N5903's 840-hp (627-kW) nine-cylinder Mercury VIII and the reduction gearing and wooden propeller from L8032's Mercury IX) has to be pre-oiled after three or four days of inactivity, this task taking up to four man-hours each time. The engine's exhaust ring was previously a critical item but is now made of stainless steel. The exhaust stubs have a finite life and are difficult to come by so if you know where there is a stash, Chris would be interested to hear from you!

7

Bell P-63 Kingcobra
42-69021/ N163FS

The Bell P-63 Kingcobra is a rare aeroplane indeed. In the summer of 1996 Colonel Frank Borman commissioned Elmer Ward's company, Square One Aviation, to restore a Bell P-63-6-BE to add to his growing collection of warbirds. Based in Chino, California, Square One Aviation is more closely associated with the P-51 Mustang, so this was a departure from their regular workload. However, it presented a new challenge and the company rose to meet it head-on. Simon Brown, then the manager at Square One Aviation, headed up the team and was directly responsible for reporting back to Frank Borman.

The aircraft, then registered N90805, was discovered at Van Nuys Airport, California. It had been stored there since 1947, having arrived to be modified to take part in the Thompson Trophy Races. The story related is that the Kingcobra had a bad centre of gravity problem due to the removal of the guns and ammunition from the nose section. Apparently, the pilot landed hard and blew all three tyres. The aircraft was simply pushed into the weeds where it stayed until 1973. Though a minimal attempt was made at restoration, this was subsequently abandoned and the aircraft put back into storage. Simon Brown said he first saw it in a T-hangar when he did the pre-buy inspection in June 1996.

Structurally the Kingcobra was complete and in overall good condition, but souvenir hunters had stolen many of the portable items from the cockpit. The flight instruments were missing and of course the armament had also been removed. All the magnesium skins (control surfaces) and castings were brittle and therefore unusable for the planned restoration programme. However, a large number of the original stock items were still installed in the airframe. Damage was limited to the areas of the aircraft where children had crawled over it during the years it was accessible.

I asked Simon how the structure of the P-63 compared to that of the P-51 Mustang. 'Both planes are rather simple in their design and much less complicated than a Grumman Bearcat or Vought Corsair,' he said. 'The P-51 is extremely well laid out. The P-63 is much more – in fact, very – cramped and difficult to work on. I understand that Bell's idea was to put the cannon in the nose and then figure out how to build the 'plane around it!'

My next question concerned spare parts: were they difficult to obtain for the P-63? Are there any that need to be fabricated? 'Yes and yes!' was Simon's reply. 'Spares that are peculiar to Bell are difficult – and some

The finished Kingcobra looks every inch a classic Bell fighter that has just rolled off the production line. Thierry Thomassin

really are impossible to obtain. We had to have missing parts made; indeed, we kept the machine shop busy for months. Jay Wisler found some very important stock pieces for us but I guess the hardest thing to find was the 37-mm cannon. After considerable research we made ours in the machine shop. We started from scratch – no documentation, etc. After spending two solid days at the National Air and Space Museum at Silver Hill in Maryland documenting their P-63, we had all the information required to proceed.'

From the start, Frank Borman was specific with his instructions, delivered with military precision: he wanted the Kingcobra to be the *best* warbird in the world! Work undertaken was to be completed to only the highest standard and the team's goal was to make the P-63 resemble an aircraft that had just rolled off Bell's wartime production line in Buffalo, New York. In order to achieve this, the detail work had to be exhaustive.

Square One Aviation acquired factory drawings that showed all the stencilling, decal and component locations. 'You name it,

it is in those blueprints; simply the best source we could wish for,' said Simon. 'We spent months going through the drawings, gleaning information and using knowledge to ensure the 'Cobra was as accurate as humanly possible. The mission was to try to make it look exactly as it was as it came off that line. To finish the airframe we painstakingly had the paint colours matched, and rubber stamps were made to stamp on the part numbers. Electrics specialist Chuck Cabe stamped the electrical wiring with the original World War Two markings – and routed the wires as per the original drawings.'

Mike Nixon's Vintage V-12's of Tehachapi, California, produced the only Allison engine that has the auxiliary supercharger hooked up and functioning. Though there is no strict TBO for the engine, it should easily run for between 750 and 1,000 hours before it needs major attention.

Who at Square One worked on the aircraft? The restoration was a team effort. Simon Brown, General Manager, oversaw the entire project and made all the important decisions, liaising directly with Colonel Borman as the project moved forward. Paul Marak, Shop Foreman, was responsible for actually building the Kingcobra. Ingo Moos was Project Leader. Tony 'Bocephus' Corbo took on the mantle of ensuring the historical accuracy of the rebuild. George Skoropos oversaw manufacture and provision of the armament. Jimmie New and Greg Laird were mainly responsible for the systems. Mechanics on the project included Randy Roy, Tom Michna, Art Jasso, Kirk Nelson, Concordio Allasada, Chris Convert, Bob Zeller, Don Smit, Wayne Tucker and Creel Carroll. Parts acquisition was the responsibility of Ken Smith and Mike Nightingale As mentioned earlier, Chuck Cabe tackled the electrics. Eric Jett, Jose Estrada, Dave Robbins and Rene Sauceda oversaw finishing and applied the paint.

The project took over 15,000 man-hours to complete from start to finish (the exact figure is secret), though much of this was spent ensuring the aircraft was exhaustively detailed. 'We spent a lot of time and maximum effort to put the Kingcobra in a class of its own, as perfect as possible – even to the point where we detailed areas where no one will ever see – and then more time ensuring it cuts the mustard historically,' explained Simon. 'It took a while to get all the information to make it accurate. We had to spend a lot of time either searching for the parts or making replacements.'

One thing that surprised the team was the sheer amount of work it took to research the material required to make the aircraft representative and accurate. If they were to undertake another restoration on the same type, such information would not have to be researched again.

US Propeller of California did the prop overhaul, and Jay Wisler of Warbirds Parts and Memorabilia in Florida supplied lots of original Bell material that made the difference and put this warbird in a class of its own. The National Air and Space Museum gave the team access to their P-63 for reference purposes and that proved to be an enormous help.

The first flight following rebuild took place on 11th February 1998, and the aircraft was test-flown for just ten hours by Frank Borman (who does all his own test flying). It took the Experimental Aircraft Association Warbirds of America Grand Champion World War Two Warbird award at Oshkosh in 1998 and also won a Golden Wrench Award for Square One Aviation at the same Convention. Frank Borman sold the Kingcobra to John K Bagley early in 2002 and the aircraft is now based in Idaho.

8

Avro Lancaster B.I
PA474

Of the 7,377 Avro Lancaster bombers built during World War Two, B.I PA474 is one of just two survivors that are airworthy. The other example, B.X FM213/C-GVRA (currently marked as KB726/VR-A of 419 Squadron, RCAF) is with the Canadian Warplane Heritage in Hamilton, Ontario.

Built at Avro's Chester plant in mid-1945, PA474 was assigned to the Far East-based 'Tiger Force', but the war against Japan ended before the aircraft could take part in any missions and so it was diverted to undertake photographic reconnaissance duties. It was while on assignment to 82 Squadron in Africa that PA474's upper dorsal turret was removed.

On return to the United Kingdom, PA474 was placed on loan to Flight Refuelling Ltd at Tarrant Rushton, Dorset, for trials as a pilotless drone. A change of plan meant the aircraft was instead transferred to Cranfield, Bedfordshire, for use by the College of Aeronautics. Its career as a flying testbed included trials of the Handley Page laminar-flow wing, and trial airfoil sections were mounted vertically on the spine of the upper rear fuselage.

In 1964 the Air Historical Branch 'adopted' PA474 for planned future display in the proposed RAF Museum at Hendon. Flown into RAF Wroughton, Wiltshire (where aircraft chosen for display in the planned RAF Museum at Hendon were being gathered), PA474 was subsequently painted in RAF Bomber Command wartime camouflage *sans* squadron markings. It was during this time that PA474 took part in two films, namely *Operation Crossbow* and *The Guns of Navarone*. Later that year, she was flown to RAF Henlow, Bedfordshire, in preparation for display at the planned RAF Museum.

However, before PA474 could be transported to her new home in north London, the then Commanding Officer of 44 Squadron (the first RAF unit to be equipped with Lancasters) sought permission from the Air Historical Branch to take PA474 on charge. Formal inspections at RAF Henlow had revealed the aircraft to be structurally sound and so permission was given for PA474 to make a single flight from RAF Henlow to 44 Squadron's home base RAF Waddington, Lincolnshire. Once at RAF Waddington, PA474 was painted in the markings of the

aircraft flown by Squadron Leader John Nettleton VC RAF on the Augsburg raid on the night of 17/18th April 1942.

Restoration of PA474 to flying condition began in 1964, a programme that would take several years to complete. After two years, work was progressing well and both the front and rear turrets had been replaced. Permission for PA474 to take to the air on a regular basis was granted in 1967, and gave new impetus to the restoration task. The aircraft joined the Battle of Britain Memorial Flight (BBMF) in November 1973. Much work has been done in the intervening years to improve the aircraft and make it ever more authentic, as well as allowing it to meet its many display commitments. A mid-upper gun turret was acquired in Argentina and shipped to the United Kingdom, being fitted in 1975 – the year that PA474 was formally adopted by the City of Lincoln.

Avro Lancaster B.I PA474 at the Great Warbirds Display in 1993 when the aircraft was finished in the markings of 103 Squadron. Eric Quenardel

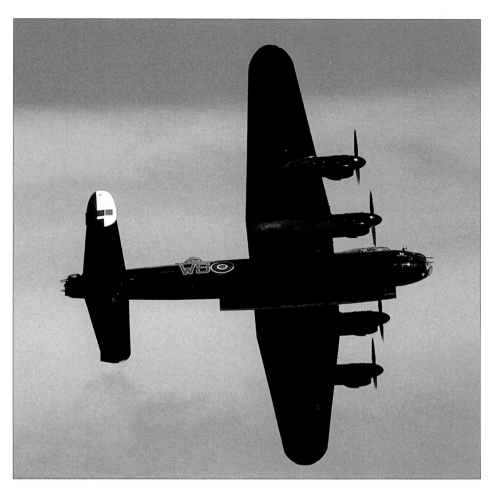

During the winter of 1995/96, PA474 received a newly fabricated main spar with assistance from British Aerospace, and this will extend the aircraft's airworthy career for at least the next ten years. From 1994 to 1999, PA474 was painted to represent W4964/WS-J *Johnnie Walker* (an aircraft originally with IX Squadron). The original W4964 took part in the first attack on the battleship *Tirpitz*, mounted from Russia, and flew over 100 operational missions during World War Two. Today, with its correct serial reapplied, the aircraft flies as QR-M *Mickey the Moocher* of 61 Squadron

The BBMF's 11 aircraft are maintained by a group of 18 technicians and mechanics led by a Warrant Officer engineer. Two electrical technicians look after instruments and ignition components and five other technicians oversee the acquisition of equipment and service specialist support equipment. The fleet is relatively simple compared to the modern RAF, but the aircraft demand the use of old skills that are no longer utilised on more modern RAF types.

The demand for spares to keep all 11 BBMF aircraft airworthy often requires close liaison and negotiation with specialist civilian companies operating within the vintage aircraft and warbird industries. As there are few Lancaster components available 'off the shelf', parts and components often have to be manufactured, making lead times difficult to establish and calling on the technicians' previous experience in many cases. The BBMF take their display commitments very seriously and all of the aircraft are considered to be as operationally important as regular RAF combat aircraft.

The BBMF works to a six-year plan for aircraft maintenance. At the end of its six-year period, the aircraft in question goes to a civilian contractor for a major overhaul. For the last 'Major' the Lancaster went to RAF St Athan, South Glamorgan. The vast majority of maintenance is carried out during the winter months, and the aircraft is signed off just before the commencement of the show season. In most cases the first bookings of the season come around early April.

The Lancaster is allocated 75 flying hours per year (give or take an hour or two), and has appeared at countless displays throughout the United Kingdom, being seen 'live' by millions of people. In between major overhauls the engineers try to concentrate on one particular aspect as a 'project' each year. For instance, one year the aircraft's Rolls-Royce Merlin engines received a lot of attention, including strip inspections of all the carburettors and the removal of several of the engine banks for routine maintenance. The basic philosophy is not that of merely keeping the aircraft serviceable and airworthy; it is one of constant improvement. Additionally, modern equip-ment is installed in such a way as to limit the visual impact in, for example, the cockpit area.

An internal tour of PA474 is a rare treat indeed. After scrambling up the crew ladder to enter via the rear crew hatch, it can be seen that the inside of the Lancaster looks stock. A large leather-cushioned area has been installed over the bolts that secure the tailplane spar. All the work to enhance the internal appearance of the aircraft is done using original drawings. It is obvious that the engineers have been innovative in their approach. For example, ammunition boxes have been converted to hold some tools in the aircraft; modification of the bunk-bed area over the oxygen-bottle bank was amended to house the modern VHF and UHF radio fit and to keep it dry (the 'Lanc' being renowned for leaking like a sieve). In the rear of the aircraft is the directional gyro that was used until it simply became unreliable. Further forward are the racks to hang the parachutes, which, if the situation demanded, would still be used!

The navigator's position looks very authentic and though modern navigational equipment is carried there is no visual evidence of such – until a unit is revealed which shows DME and VOR. This is another example of how the BBMF uses modern equipment to contribute to the overall safety of the crew without compromising the authenticity of the airframe. All the authentic radio gear is installed and on view, but it is seldom used due to its incompatibility with modern-day ATC communications.

Over the huge hydraulic flap-jack and spars and into the cockpit area, and it really is like stepping back in time. The flight engineer's station is next, with the main panel on the right-hand side. Most of the gauges are original but they are becoming more and more difficult to replace. The main instrument panel is stock, the only difference being the location of the flap indicator that is on the right-hand side.

By 1992 the BBMF was fairly sure that the rear mainplane spars on the Lancaster would become life-expired within the next few years. So the decision was taken to fly the Lancaster to RAF St Athan and have this major work done during the winter of 1995/96. It made sense to use the downtime to also renew two sections of fuselage spar that could be accessed as a result of the mainplane spars being removed.

During the winter of 2000/01, rewiring of the whole aircraft was undertaken. The original cabinet, which held 96 old-fashioned brass-ended fuses, was utilised to present a visually authentic fit. The fuses themselves were replaced with 40 E-T-A 483 circuit breakers, which offer the highest performance specification available today, in this case protecting circuits from 1A up to 20A. This is another example of modern technology being used to keep the RAF's only four-engined bomber flying today and on into the future.

9

Hawker Nimrod I
S1581/G-BWWK

Just a stone's throw away from the site of the Battle of Hastings, in a large workshop which it's owner jokingly refers to as a 'chicken shed', some serious engineering projects have been undertaken in support of the resurrection of some important Hawker aircraft. Among the aircraft to have passed through the workshop at Rye, East Sussex, is the subject of this entry, Hawker Nimrod I S1581.

These are the workshops of Aero Vintage Ltd, and they form an impressive and compact location for the small but dedicated team of engineers led by Guy Black. The drawing office overlooks the main workshop area where S1581 was painstakingly rebuilt. Its completion was the pinnacle of several years of innovative reverse engineering and thousands of hours of research into the original engineering techniques practised by Hawker Aircraft Ltd in the mid-1930s.

The original Nimrod specification was N.21/26, which outlined a requirement for a fleet fighter to replace the Fairey Flycatcher.

Formulated around the Hawker Kestrel-engined fleet fighter proposal outlined in Air Ministry Specification 16/30, the aircraft was unofficially christened 'Norn'. The original private-venture prototype first flew in 1930, and a sister machine was utilised for ground testing. Soon afterwards a contract was drawn up and the name Nimrod was officially chosen, both aircraft being taken on charge by the Air Ministry.

The Hawker Nimrod featured unswept, single-bay wings with a good stagger, permitting the pilot an excellent forward view from the cockpit. The complexly engineered all-metal tubular structure was fabric-covered and flotation boxes were constructed in the rear fuselage and top wing.

In March 1931 a Nimrod was put aboard HMS *Eagle* to participate in the British Empire Trade Exhibition in Buenos Aires, Argentina. On return to the United Kingdom the Nimrod was flown to A&AEE Martlesham Heath, Suffolk, for trials. An order for

Hawker Nimrod I S1581 was rolled out at Paddock Wood, Kent, following a trial fit of the wings. This view clearly reveals the excellent woodworking job and belies the investment required to see the Nimrod made airworthy. Author

35 Nimrods was placed subsequently with the Hawker Engineering Company; S1577, the first production Nimrod, took to the air on 14th October 1931 and was followed by S1578 on the last day of the month. Both aircraft completed flight trials at the Hawkers facility at Brooklands, Surrey, before being prepared for shipment to Japan aboard an aircraft carrier. When the two returned in February 1932, construction of the first batch of Nimrod Is had been completed.

All Hawker Nimrods had the ability to be configured for both float and wheel undercarriage and whilst S1577 was despatched to Martlesham Heath for trials, S1578 was

This detail shot shows the extensive wooden framework on the wing, the complex exhaust system and the wooden control wheel. Author

This detail shot shows the extensive wooden framework on the wing, the complex exhaust system and the wooden control wheel. Author

sent to the MAEU at Felixstowe, Suffolk, to be fitted with twin floats for waterborne handling trials. Deck-landing trials had already been conducted with a pre-production machine, and in April 1932 several landings aboard HMS *Eagle* were made by S1577. Early-production Nimrods were delivered aboard HMS *Glorious* (408 Fleet Fighter Flight) in 1932 as Fairey Flycatcher replacements and soon afterwards to 409 and 402 Fleet Fighter Flights aboard HMS *Eagle*.

A reorganisation of the Fleet Air Arm in 1933 saw the amalgamation of several shipboard squadrons. This entailed 800 Squadron (HMS *Courageous*), 801 Squadron (HMS *Furious*) and 802 Squadron (HMS *Glorious*) taking over the Nimrods, each of the squadrons being equipped with two flights of Nimrods and one of Hawker Ospreys.

Development of the type continued with the incorporation of arrester gear and headrest fairings. Nimrod I K2823 was used by Hawkers as a development aircraft and in February 1933 was re-engineered with swept-back upper and lower wings. These changes made way for the Nimrod II, production of which commenced in September 1933. The first Nimrod II was delivered in March 1934. The uprated and much-improved Kestrel V replaced the Kestrel II powerplant early in 1935.

The last Nimrods to serve with the Fleet Air Arm were in service with 802 Squadron aboard HMS *Glorious*, until Gloster Gladiators replaced them in 1939. The Hawker Nimrod was sold in limited numbers for export and recipients included Denmark, Japan, and Portugal; the latter two only had single examples with a view to licence production, which did not materialise.

As with all such restoration projects, the starting point for the Hawker Nimrod assignment was compilation of an archive of documentation, engineering information and technical drawings. Due to the often encountered legal problem of 'product liability', British Aerospace, though keen to assist Aero Vintage Ltd, were unable to do so. However, by making various appeals to all those who had been connected with Hawkers over the years, Guy Black was able to start filling in the gaps.

A large number of drawings came from pre-war employees and from government ministries in countries such as Spain, Australia, Canada and in particular, Denmark. Also at an early stage, Guy placed an advertisement in a local newspaper in Kingston,

Surrey, requesting that former Hawker employees come forward. Not only was this a good morale booster for the team to meet these people, it was also useful to hear of their personal experiences and their knowledge of the original engineering processes used at the factory. The response also yielded donations of many drawings, manuals and Air Publications. Guy had also been very active in scanning the various aeromarts and auctions of aeronautica and other memorabilia.

Les Jones became the full-time engineering draughtsman on the Nimrod project, forming and maintaining a drawings archive while at the same time keeping an eye on the subcontract work necessary to complete the aircraft within a reasonable period of time. Les made another significant contribution by originating drawings from parts

where the original Hawker drawings simply did not exist.

Though a lot of the original Nimrod parts could not be reused, Guy relates that about 30 per cent of the original components such as stainless steel plates, much of the aluminium components and some of the heavy steel parts would 'go again'. Hawkers used some very intricate engineered components and before any fabrication of new parts could be undertaken, Guy and the Aero Vintage team had to first produce some basic components to original specifications.

One such item that required an inordinate amount of time and a not insubstantial financial input was the now famous 'tubular rivet'. Prior to Guy's investigation into and production of these items, other companies had used nuts and bolts to replace the origi-

The Nimrod's massive radiator, wheels and brakes were all mini-projects within the pioneering restoration task. During flight trials the brake bags caused some problems, but these have now been resolved. Author

nal manufacturing methods. As a starting point the original material specifications were researched. Though this was quite easy using modern methods, the bad news was that there was no known suitable modern equivalent from which to manufacture the tubular rivets. After several approaches to British companies had proved fruitless, Guy found a company in France with the capability to manufacture the low-strength steel tube required for the rivets.

The riveted joints utilised in the construction of the Nimrod are, to some, 'over-engineered'. The joints include the main tubular shank, an aluminium spacer, and a pair of ferrules that insert at both ends. These have been manufactured in large quantities for Aero Vintage Ltd and this pioneering spirit means that the correct fittings can be used on all future biplane projects.

Another significant hurdle to overcome was the lack of the tubular spar material utilised by Hawkers; without it, the project would simply have come to a full stop. When the late Honourable Patrick Lindsay commissioned the manufacture of a Hawker Fury replica (K1930/G-BKBB), the engineers ended up making the spars from wood. To Guy this was an unacceptable compromise; he wanted total and exact engineering authenticity. Such a demand did not come cheap.

The Nimrod utilises a large steel spar shaped like a dumb-bell. Designed by Henry Chapman in 1926 and later patented by Syd-

ney Camm for the Hawker Engineering Company, the spar consists of two flanged polygonal booms folded from high-tensile strip, riveted to an interconnecting flange that is itself a complex rolled shape – and different for every spar! After locating supplies of the special steel spar it was essential to find a company that had a strip-rolling mill. After a great deal of searching the original machine used by Hawkers was found, but it was incomplete and in dreadful condition. Later, having found one functioning strip-rolling mill – and there are very few large ones still in use today – it was then another uphill struggle to persuade the owners to embark upon such small production runs.

Basically, the strip-rolling mill is a 60-ft (20.88m) long cast-iron table with a large number of powered 'stations' turning shaped rollers, each progressively forming the complex shapes required. Each pair of rollers is different, and there can be up to 30 or more pairs necessary to form any one section. Finding and executing such a solution was a major breakthrough for Aero Vintage Ltd; and the company's success was not lost on Tony Ditheridge at Hawker Restorations Ltd, who also needed similar material (centre-section spar booms) for his ongoing Hawker Hurricane projects.

The complex Hurricane centre section is similar to that of the biplane units, but is twice as big. It also has an identical enveloping section folded around it, all of which surrounds the tubular spar. Two of these boom

This view of S1581 reveals the pronounced stagger of the Nimrod I's unswept wings.
Bob Munro

assemblies are then riveted to a wide flange, stiffened vertically with stainless steel channels. The original units, now over 50 years old, are prone to corrosion and in some cases extreme hardening that renders them unserviceable for flight. So Aero Vintage Ltd was also contracted to produce these items for Hawker Restorations Ltd (*see elsewhere in this book*). The company was also able to help Tim Moore with his restoration of Hawker Demon I K8203/G-BTVE, which had been purchased from Guy Black a few years earlier. Aero Vintage Ltd also undertook the information management requirement and supplied drawings relevant to the Demon project.

Another essential investment required to get S1581 (and future Hawker biplanes) in the air was made in tooling. This in turn required much research and the acquisition of specialist steels. Hawker biplanes and the Hurricane rely on structures consisting of tubing that is squared at the ends. According to 'Hawker tradition' the tubes are not simply welded, but held together in a complex way using tubes with squared ends – stainless steel jointing plates with up to 80 separate items per joint – as well as making full use of the lightweight and effective tubular rivets mentioned earlier.

The Hawker Engineering Company had previously owned several of the tube-squaring machines, but only one survived and it was owned by British Aerospace who simply would not part with it. So Aero Vintage Ltd manufactured its own tube-squaring machine, using photographs of the original machine at Hawkers for reference. As part of his quest for relevant and necessary information, Guy Black had purchased the photographic archive of C.G. Grey, Editor of *Aero Engineering*, *Flight* and *Jane's All the World's Aircraft*, amongst others. This archive yielded a great deal of 'intelligence' and useful information, largely due to Guy's knowledge of engineering. Additional photographic reference material came from the Hawker Archive now held at the RAF Museum, Hendon.

The task of making the tube-squaring machine was made that much easier when Guy stumbled across a large number of squaring machine rollers in South Africa. It is believed they had been discarded from South African military stocks. At the time they were rescued they were being welded onto steel tubes for use as weight training equipment! Aero Vintage Ltd uses its tube-squaring machine to manufacture the new material required to continue the company's Hawker biplane quest.

Having overcome several major hurdles to get to the stage of working on the airframe, by late 1995 Nimrod I S1581 was sat on its wheels (which took over two years to research, draw and replicate) *sans* systems and fabric. The project was indeed moving forward.

Peter Hunt at Aero Vintage Ltd is responsible for panel beating and the production of radiators for the company's aircraft. He has been working with Guy Black for the past 20 years and has produced some marvellous structures, including the radiator for S1581 and all the metal panels. Some of the work on the Hawker biplane projects has been subcontracted to Steve Vizard's Airframe Assemblies on the Isle of Wight.

Restoration of the Rolls-Royce Kestrel V powerplant was entrusted to Mike Vaisey and Paul Sharman of Vintage Engine Technology Ltd (Vintech) at Little Gransden, Cambridgeshire, and they did a remarkable job. Clive and Linda Denney of Vintage Fabrics undertook all the fabric work on the Nimrod, with the wing sections being sent to their (then) premises at Earls Colne, Essex, for covering and finishing.

The next step was a trial assembly of the entire airframe and this took place in autumn 1999. Another three years passed before the work began to look anything like complete, with all the specialist systems and cockpit items having to be researched, sourced or manufactured, and fitted. By spring 2002 the Kestrel V powerplant had been installed and was being test run. All was shaping up nicely and the aircraft looked a picture.

Due to the location of the Historic Aircraft Collection's short airstrip in Kent, it was decided that RAF Henlow in Bedfordshire would be a more suitable location for the Nimrod's maiden flight. RAF pilot Flt Lt Charlie Brown was given the opportunity to undertake the first flight shortly after he had been invited to become Chief Pilot for the Historic Aircraft Collection. As the day of the first flight approached, Charlie gathered as much relevant information as possible, assisted by Guy Black who had been searching out original flight test reports. Meantime, Charlie had become closely acquainted with the people at Vintech in an effort to glean as much operating information on the Kestrel V as possible.

The aircraft was transported to RAF Henlow and properly assembled for the last time. Charlie then undertook extensive taxying trials. Vintech engineers were on site for final engine tuning and trials and on 11th July 2000, Nimrod I S1581 took to the air for the first time since its restoration. Following more flight trials and some feedback from former Hawker engineers, which resulted in a modification to the Kestrel V, the aircraft was declared fully fit.

It was always Guy Black's intention that the first Hawker biplane to be restored by Aero Vintage Ltd would pass to the Historic Aircraft Collection for trade with The Fighter Collection at Duxford, Cambridgeshire, for their Hawker Hurricane XII Z7381/G-HURI, and the exchange duly took place in August 2002. Several other Hawker biplanes are being restored at Aero Vintage Ltd at the time of writing, including a two-seat Audax.

S1581 wears the colourful markings of 802 Squadron, Fleet Air Arm, when it served in HMS Glorious during the 1930s. Bob Munro

10

Curtiss P-40E Warhawk
NZ3009/ZK-RMH

Built during 1941 at the Curtiss plant in Buffalo, New York, under a Defense Aid (Lease-Lend) contract, 41-25158 was one of 1,500 P-40E-1s produced for the RAF as Kittyhawk IAs, for whom it was serialled ET482. In fact the aircraft never made it to the United Kingdom; after delivery it was transferred to the RNZAF and shipped directly to New Zealand from the West Coast of the United States. After reassembly at Hobsonville Air Base, Auckland, the aircraft was brought on RNZAF charge as NZ3009 on 2nd April 1942. It was then assigned to 14 Squadron, which was forming at Masterton Airfield.

During this time it was flown by several famous 'aces' including Geoff Fisken, the top-scoring Commonwealth 'ace' against the Japanese. It has been suggested that during this time NZ3009 was extensively damaged in a forced landing due to carburettor icing and was allocated to Ohakea Air Base as a ground instructional airframe. If

so, it must have been repaired by 1943, as it was serving with 17 Squadron at Seagrove Airfield, Auckland, during their work-up period prior to the squadron moving to the combat area. NZ3009 next appeared at Ohakea in 1944, where it spent the remainder of the war with 2 OTU.

When huge numbers of RNZAF combat aircraft were declared surplus in 1946, scrap dealer Jack Larsen bought several of the P-40E-1s for scrapping along with Vought F4U-1 Corsairs, Lockheed Hudsons and Lockheed Venturas. The aircraft were stored and gradually 'processed' at the now famous scrap yard in Rukuhia. When approached, Jack Larsen said he wanted £250 for a P-40E hulk.

As a young aviation enthusiast, Charles Darby became aware of the massive scrap yard and persuaded his mother to drive him to the site, where he looked at the P-40s and made notes as to their markings and

condition. In 1958 Derek Woodhall in Christchurch formed the Aviation Historical Society of New Zealand (AHSNZ). Charles Darby helped form the Auckland branch soon afterwards. Over the years, Darby made several more trips to Rukuhia in company with Bob McGarry. Darby and McGarry didn't have the £250 asking price for one of the P-40s, so they did a deal to swap the aircraft for an equivalent amount of scrap that they eventually managed to put together. Larsen agreed that their acquisition could be left in his yard.

Darby and McGarry selected NZ3072 as their P-40. However, when Larsen contacted the pair to say the scrap yard site had

The fuselage of NZ3009 in the early stages of restoration by Pacific Fighters in New Zealand in March 1996. The restoration work was undertaken for the Duxford-based Old Flying Machine Company. Jim Winchester

The stabiliser for NZ3009 under restoration.
Jim Winchester

The restored cockpit of NZ3009 shows the stock finish. Thierry Thomassin

to be cleared and they should remove their prize, both men were away on business. Volunteers from the AHSNZ prepared to dismantle the aircraft and make it ready for transportation to its new home, but due to a breakdown in communication, NZ3009 was dismantled instead, and a set of wings from another P-40E (NZ3202) were also readied to leave the yard.

Using a Museum of Transport & Technology truck, the airframe of NZ3009 was prepared for the trip to the museum's site in Auckland, an agreement having been reached whereby Darby and McGarry maintained ownership of the P-40E but the Museum could loan it for display purposes. It had always been the intention of the two owners to restore the aircraft to flying condition. Signed in July 1970, this short-term agreement was initially renewed once and then again for a further 15 years. When the contracted time frame expired, the Museum claimed they had been given the aircraft and were therefore the owners. Darby and McGarry disputed this and litigation was followed by more litigation. Finally, after lengthy and complex arbitration, NZ3009 was released to its two owners on condition that they supplied another P-40, restored to static exhibition standard, for the Museum to display.

The next part of NZ3009's life was even more complicated. Charles Darby and Jim Pavitt decided to form a specialist P-40 restoration company to be called Pacific Aircraft. One of the plans was to restore NZ3009 and use the funds generated by its sale to produce tooling and facilities to restore other P-40s. Pacific Aircraft would also build the static P-40 for the Museum of Transport & Technology. Meantime, Charles Darby had agreed the sale of NZ3009 with Ray Hanna of the Old Flying Machine Company and signed a contract to rebuild NZ3009 for him; this would be Pacific Aircraft's second project. Work commenced and the Museum received their static exhibit, a composite aircraft displayed as NZ3039. Next in line for attention was NZ3009.

Garth Hogan was introduced to Charles Darby via a third party as someone with a keen interest in owning or part-owning a P-40. Whilst there was a syndicate aeroplane in progress, Hogan was too late to participate and approached Charles Darby with a view to mounting a joint effort to get another P-40 airworthy, this time ex-RAAF P-40N A29-448 which had been recovered from Papua New Guinea.

The New Zealand Civil Aviation Authority confirmed the identity of the P-40E as NZ3009 by comparing original photos taken at the storage facility with actual repairs and marks on the fuselage. The sequence num-

ber on the lower longeron also confirmed its identity as NZ3009.

The restoration and repair of NZ3009 was carried out in accordance with. the structural repair manual and original specifications. The work commenced with the wings. Like many warbirds, the temptation is to start with the fuselage. However, the major work on the P-40 is in the mainplane, which is very labour intensive. The wings were completely disassembled and rebuilt, but most of the original components were used. Only some skins and stringers were replaced.

The age-hardened and perished fuel tanks in the wings had to be replaced, and it was decided on this occasion to depart from originality and use fibreglass and fuel-resistant vinyl ester resin, moulded to the original pattern but utilising the original fittings, including the direct-reading fuel gauges. The tanks were installed in the correct location, in the wing centre section below the cockpit.

Most of the metal structure in the wing is of original manufacture, including the multiple spars. The fuselage was basically in good shape despite the aircraft being stored externally for a number of years. It was stripped and cleaned, patched and repaired where necessary and the belly skin replaced. All fairings were replaced except for the under-carriage fairings and doors, which were rebuilt original items. The unique original Curtiss rivets with their 78° angle heads were utilised for the original structure, but standard, modern 100° rivets were used in the modern structure. One nice touch was the use of modern wiring, 'overlaid' with period braiding to make it look authentic.

Numerous forgings were produced and used by Curtiss and whilst the team located a large percentage of them, some new forgings had to be cast. As with all 'deep' restorations, every subassembly was dismantled to its smallest size, checked and tested as required and replaced or refurbished as necessary, before being reassembled.

Over 200 instructional placards were made for the aircraft; based on originals, documentation and drawings, all of them were researched, checked and passed by Charles Darby. Some 150 instructional decals were also produced and printed on clear adhesive acrylic, which is more resistant to distortion and wrinkling during application than the original material.

JRS Enterprises of Minneapolis, Minnesota, overhauled the 1,360-hp (1,015-kW) Allison V-1710-115 engine that is installed in NZ3009 (the original was a 1,150-hp (858-kW) V-1710-39). The propeller is a Curtis Electric C-532D unit with 'toothpick' blades. There were no significant modifications or deviations from the original aircraft, apart from the fuel tanks and the -115 engine.

In the summer of 1997, Pacific Aircraft ceased trading and it was decided that all of the company's assets, including the P-40 tooling and associated equipment, would be sold. Realising that the tooling would be needed to complete A29-448, Garth Hogan purchased what was necessary and launched a new company, Pioneer Aero Restorations. Pioneer is staffed by a majority of the old Pacific Aircraft workers. By combining much of the information and detail from Charles Darby's personal P-40 collection, the tooling built up during the restoration of the two P-40s and purchased from Pacific, and Garth Hogan's business ideas and acumen, the new company was in a position to enter the restoration business. The staff brought with them a wealth of engineering experience, and Pioneer quickly made an excellent name for itself.

The work to restore NZ3009 to airworthiness was almost complete, and Pioneer staff were tasked with completing the project. After an intensive six-year rebuild, P-40E NZ3009/ZK-RMH took to the air on 19th December 1997, the first time it had flown since 1945. In February 1999 the aircraft was shipped to the Old Flying Machine Company at Duxford, Cambridgeshire, arriving on 19th March. Today the aircraft flies as part of the Breitling Fighters team, its latest scheme being that of a sharkmouthed AVG aircraft. Registered as G-CCBE in March 2003, it rejoined the New Zealand civil register as ZK-RMH after the disbandment of the Breitling Fighters team at the end of the 2003 airshow season.

NZ3009 breaks formation from the other members of the Duxford-based Breitling Fighters team. Uwe Glaser

11

Goodyear F2G-1 Super Corsair
BuNo 88457/N5588N

When the F2G Corsair emerged, World War Two was nearing its end and consequently only a small number of F2Gs were manufactured. The gigantic four-row Pratt & Whitney R-4360 28-cylinder Wasp Major radial engine gave the aircraft a top speed of around 450mph (724km/h) – enough for it to outperform any early jet fighter. In the famous air races of the late 1940s, that power was put to good use when F2Gs won two Thompson Trophies. Half a century later, in 1999, N5588N won the Rolls-Royce Trophy at Reno, Nevada, for excellence in aircraft restoration. Today, only three F2Gs survive.

Considered by Corsair aficionados to be the ultimate Corsair restoration for years, Goodyear F2G-1 Super Corsair N5588N attracts maximum attention wherever it goes. Bob Odegaard acquired the aircraft in 1996, then spent many hours researching its manufacture and history, and physically restoring the aircraft to award-winning condition as his own tribute to this rare fighter.

The restoration of Bob and Donna Odegaard's rare F2G Super Corsair is an example of the time, dedication and money required to restore a warbird to award-winning standards. When I asked Bob for infor-

mation on the project he very kindly sent me the following story that says it all.

'The F2G Super Corsair was designed as a "Kamikaze killer". The F2G-1 Corsair was land-based with no catapult hook, no tail-wheel hook, a longer propeller and wings that you manually removed the lower bolt to swing the outer panel up. The F2G-2 was like a standard F4U. By the time the Navy got through with the new air scoop, the performance was considerably better than the Goodyear specifications you read about, according to test pilot Don Armstrong.

'My airplane's Bureau Number, 88457, was one of the four that Cook Cleland bought from the Navy. This was a test airplane assigned to Pax River and they didn't want him to fly it, only to use the parts. Well, when 88457 crashed, those parts from 88458 were used to rebuild 88457; they just used all of them at the same time and didn't bother to disassemble them first! This airplane, 88457 (*Race 57*), won the Tinnerman Trophy in 1949, and came in third in the Thompson Trophy Race that same year.

'After that it was left to rot. I was the seventh person who tried to rebuild it. Every place it went, some parts disappeared. By the time I got the aircraft, virtually the whole

The first engine runs for the huge Pratt & Whitney R-4360-20WD Wasp Major in the F2G-1. Donna Odegaard

firewall forward was missing. I knew the Crawford Transportation Museum (Cleveland, Ohio) had the engine mount from Cook's *Race 94* (F2G-1 N5590N), and hoped I could somehow make a deal and buy it from them. They were very helpful and we made a trade. I couldn't find a nose bowl and ended up with the closest replacement. John Lane of Airpower Unlimited suggested a Harpoon nose bowl, which he had for me to try. It worked. We made the rest of the cowling, which was composed of compound-curved stainless steel exhaust chutes, and the works. The wing root fairings were a major problem. Again, friends came to the rescue. The Crawford Transportation Museum had recently acquired *Race 74* (F2G-2 NX5577N) from Walter Soplata. They loaned me the fairings and Bill Yoak formed them on his *Yoto Hammer*.

'The whole canopy and frame was missing. The Crawford Transportation Museum also needed new glass for their F2G, so we shared the cost of having Dick Evans make the tooling. We each had two canopies made.

I cleaned the Crawford frame and in the process duplicated all the parts. Prior to this, I tried to get a P-47 canopy to work, because the prototype supposedly had a modified P-47 unit installed. Butch Schroeder loaned me one to try but it didn't come close to fitting. When I finally got the sides formed, which is a ribbed compound curve, I heat-treated them and they curled like pretzels. I learned I had to heat-treat them vertically. I made a second set and it worked.

'The rest of the rebuild was straightforward. I was really concerned about getting the right colour, red. None of the colour pictures I had [of the aircraft] were the same. I knew the look I wanted. Too much red would make it look like a model toy, and too much orange would make it look like a pumpkin. My eye was attracted to the lettering on a magazine that was perfect. I took it to the paint dealer for a match.

'Finding the right propeller wasn't too hard. The F2G-1 Corsair had a different blade than the F2G-2. The F2G-1 was a land-based interceptor and had a longer blade

and different profile. It just so happens that the Curtiss C-46 Commando airscrew (with three Hamilton Standard blades on it) is the same, but even longer yet. I was hoping to find some blades not meeting airworthiness standards for a C-46 that could be shortened to meet my needs. The most likely place would be Miami, Florida. Sure enough, Miami Propeller had some, along with a hub from a Howard 500.

'The engine was another story. One engine guy told me to get a C-124 engine because it would "fit right in". One could be purchased – as a fresh overhaul (1965) in the can – for $4,000. So I bought one and sent it out to have the bearings replated and assembled. I also wanted to incorporate a front bearing modification developed by the late Frank Sanders of *Dreadnought* (Super Sea Fury N20SF) fame. This supposedly keeps the front main from moving into the cam drive under high G loads. Well, I finished the airframe but was still without an engine. After talking with Gene Powers, who has probably run more canned engines than anybody, he suggested I re-oil it, run it, and make sure it didn't "make metal". I added a commercial filtering system and ran the heck out of it. All was okay!

'When I tried to install the engine, the R-4360-20WD (used in the C-124) had a 4-inch (102-mm) longer blower than the original R-4360-4 engine. So I took the blower off the engine it raced with in 1949, checked it out, installed it and everything ran fine, except the propeller would not cycle. Then we learned the R-4360-20WD didn't have the transfer collars on the shaft to make the Hamilton Standard props work. Again, I robbed parts from *Race 57*'s original engine and we were off.

'I was always told that the rear cylinders were harder to cool and I wanted to put a lot of ground time on the airplane first. This Corsair really surprised me. You can tie the tail down, aim it into the wind and run it all day at cruise power with no trouble cooling the engine. On the ground you get about a 25°C split between the front and rear cylinders. However, at cruise, it will be 10°C at the most.

'The oil system returns about 42 gallons (159 litres) a minute and has two 20-inch

(51-cm) oil radiators in the wing roots. At low cruise with the oil doors closed, you have trouble keeping the oil temperature in the green and both cylinder temperatures (it has a dual gauge in it; like a twin, with one probe in the front cylinder and one in the rear) will ride right at the bottom of the green range. The airplane doesn't have inter-coolers like the F4U's so the temperatures come up pretty fast with boosted power. For power in the range 54-63 inches, it has water injection.

'I installed an exit oil temperature gauge to monitor normal oil temperature as an inlet temperature. You can learn a lot from that. If you have a ring, guide or bearing problem, the extra heat they generate is temporarily masked by the cooler's ability and the tank's reserve before the inlet temperature rises. This way you see the problem earlier. When the engines are test run after production or overhaul, oil exit temperature is monitored and has to meet certain limits and then is forgotten. I believe adding this feature to a warbird can add to the safety of operating the aircraft.

'I also added exit oil filters with bypass lights. This is also a must for safety as well as saving money on engine repairs. If you change oil and filters at 25-hour intervals and notice metal in the screens, in which one of those 25 hours did it start? These filters are a little sensitive and after engine work the light will probably come on because of gasket material and carbon getting knocked loose. However, I feel this is a minor problem to put up with considering the gain. If you start the engine with a little too much rpm, the lights flicker some and that's when I feel they are set just where I want them.

'The F2G's original emergency gear blow-down system was a marginal (volume-wise) CO_2 bottle. The only way to make sure it was charged was to remove it and weigh it. I replaced it with a high-pressure nitrogen system with a gauge in the cockpit for an easier pre-flight check. I also replaced the small round bladder hydraulic accumulator with a larger-piston B-25 cylinder accumulator with a pre-charge gauge in the cockpit. I decided to install a second seat with dual controls. This was easier than a standard Corsair because of the bubble canopy.

'Flying the F2G is an absolute dream! I had the chance to spend a weekend with Don Armstrong, who was Goodyear's Chief Flight Test Pilot for the F2G programme. It was by far his favourite out of some 160 models of the aircraft that he flew. In his inspiring book *I Flew Them First*, he calls it his "homesick angel", which I feel is properly named.

'The military specification for the F2G on take-off was 420ft (128m) of runway at 15,000 lb (6,804kg) and 20-knot wind. The F2G's Pratt & Whitney R-4360-4 engine

Bob Odegaard, accompanied by the legendary Cook Cleland, receives the Rolls-Royce Heritage Trophy at Reno in 1999. Tom Smith

had 3,000hp (2,239kW) dry and 3,500hp (2,612kW) wet. My R-4360-20WD has 3,850hp (2,873kW) wet.

'The F2G-1D has two rudders, one normal and an auxiliary rudder actuated by a hydraulic cylinder. It has only two positions: straight back and 12° right. When the flaps come down to 30°, the auxiliary rudder moves to the right, which is the take-off position. If you want the auxiliary rudder over, you have to use flaps for take-off. The take-off rolls are very short. I just hold the brakes, add power and as the tail comes off the ground, I release the brakes as it comes up to take-off power. With the auxiliary rudder over, it goes absolutely straight. Fun! When you break ground, gear up, flaps up, you can feel the auxiliary rudder straighten out because the airplane wants to fly sideways. Exit oil temperature will go to 90-95°C easy on take-off and climb, while the inlet [temperature] stays around 65°C. Cylinder temperatures will go to about 200-210°C at cowl flaps. Maximum cruise is 2,000 turns at 30 inches, with exit oil temperature coming down to 85°C. Cylinder head temperature settles at 175°C; inlet oil temperature stays at 65°C.

'Aerobatics are very easy at cruise power, even vertical manoeuvres. The ailerons and elevators are very smooth and easy, even

with airspeeds of around 400mph (644km/h) indicated. Landings are also pleasant. The long oleo struts remind me of an old 7AC Champ. But once the airspeed bleeds off and rudder effectiveness is lost, you'd better have the tailwheel locked. I have forgotten twice and what a ride!

'Taxying is probably the hardest. With the R-4360 up front, there is more weight than the F4U and it wants to over-control on the "S" taxi. The R-4360 in the F2G has seven dual mags, or 14 sets of points and coils. The magneto switch allows you to check all the lefts and all the rights like a normal switch. If you have a problem, you can check the seven individually, and by listening outside,

you can quickly find the problem. On a B-36 or KC-97 with six or four engines running, this would be difficult, so they added an oscilloscope at the flight engineer's station for checking the magnetos.

'This airplane is the most fun I have ever had flying – and I have had a *lot* of fun!'

This beautiful air-to-air study emphasises the huge Goodyear airframe: a 40ft 12in (12.49m) wing span coupled to a 33ft 10in (10.31m) fuselage. Note the 'passenger' taking full advantage of the back seat Bob Odegaard installed in the aircraft. Scott Germain (www.warbiraeropress.com)

12

Hawker Hurricane IIa
P3351/ZK-TPL

On 12th January 2000, some 60 years after its construction, a survivor of the Battle of Britain took to the air at Christchurch, New Zealand. The unmistakable shape of Hawker Hurricane IIa P3351 represented the fruits of a six-year labour of love undertaken by Air New Zealand Engineering Services in New Zealand and Hawker Restorations Ltd in the United Kingdom.

Uniquely for a warbird, P3351 is a survivor of four battle campaigns. Manufactured and assembled at Brooklands, Surrey, in 1940, the aircraft was deployed to France on 1st June of that year as an attrition replacement for 73 Squadron, at that time based at Le Mans. With the Battle for France coming to an end and the Allies hastily being evacuated from Dunkirk, 73 Squadron were active, as they had been since the start of the war, wrestling frequently with the enemy.

Hurricane P3351 was flown out of Rouen on 3rd June bound for 73 Squadron's ALG at Echemines. The ground crews quickly adorned the aircraft with the code letter 'K'. Flown as a component of 'A' Flight, P3351 carried out defensive patrols over northern France, witnessing the savage retreat of the British Expeditionary Force.

The aircraft continued to fly operationally, including bomber escorts and patrols as further retreats took place, and by 18th June the squadron was based at Nantes, flying sorties over the withdrawal of British troops retreating from Brest and St Nazaire. Early in the afternoon on that day, the ground crews were making their escape via whatever exits were still open, and the Hurricanes were conducting defensive sorties. The Germans were advancing on the base and in a frenzied action all remaining Hurricanes were refuelled, some 20 getting airborne to escape back to England. One of the last to leave was P3351, with Pilot Officer Peter Carter at the controls.

With the Battle of Britain in full swing, 73 Squadron was allocated R&R following the trauma of the withdrawal from France. As for P3351, she received some routine maintenance and the codes 'TP' were painted on her fabric sides. On 7th July 1940, 73 Squadron, now based at RAF Church Fenton, Yorkshire, was flagged as operational again.

On 19th July 'A' Flight embarked for Prestwick, Scotland, having been assigned to night flying patrols. All was proceeding normally until, on 21st July 1940, Alf Scott, airborne in P3351, misjudged his approach and

was forced to undershoot, which resulted in a heavy landing and undercarriage collapse. The Hurricane ended up on its nose. Three other Hurricanes were damaged that night. All were duly hangared, awaiting collection by the repair unit.

As the Battle of Britain gained momentum, P3351 was sent for repairs. By early September, and with a new Merlin engine installed, she was posted to 32 Squadron based at RAF Acklington, Northumberland. In the 12 weeks that followed, P3351 was flown intensively by Pilot Officer Rose on training sorties involving patrols of the north-eastern coast of the United Kingdom. The aircraft moved with 32 Squadron to RAF Middle Wallop, Hampshire, on 16th December, where she became part of 10 Group. However, just five days later P3351 was sent to pastures new to start a career with American pilots.

Many Americans had already volunteered for service with the RAF and RCAF before the United States officially entered World War Two. RAF pilot casualties in 1940 meant that such volunteers were welcomed with open arms, resulting in the formation of three American 'Eagle' squadrons. Though thousands volunteered, just 244 American pilots were to fly for 71, 121 and 133 Squadrons of the RAF, eagerly giving up their liberty to join the fight.

Hurricane P3351 arrived at RAF Kirton-in-Lindsey, Lincolnshire, on 21st December 1940 but the first recorded operational flight with 71 Squadron did not take place until 16th February the following year. On 10th March two Hurricanes flew a patrol out over the Humber Estuary. This sortie was also to end in disaster when, during a twilight landing, Pilot Officer Sampson-Taylor crash-landed, damaging P3351.

In just four weeks the Hurricane was back to full health, rejoining 71 Squadron which by now was stationed at RAF Martlesham Heath, Suffolk. With hostilities approaching a peak, P3351 would see substantial combat flying over the next five weeks with countless patrols and scrambles.

As the Hurricane IIa began to replace the Hurricane I in May, P3351 was sent to 55 OTU at RAF Usworth, by the Scottish Borders. Here she was painted with 55 OTU's 'PA' code letters, but her individual letter remains undetermined at this time.

Soon after the aircraft's arrival at Usworth, the actions of a Polish Flying Instructor, Sgt

Stanislaw Karubin, resulted in P3351 being despatched yet again for repairs after he flew into high-tension wires on 13th May. Though Karubin managed to nurse the Hurricane to RAF Ouston, Northumberland, the wing leading edge had to be repaired on site, and once again the engine was replaced.

When P3351 returned to active duty, two events occurred which, though seemingly irrelevant at the time, would in later years reveal an amazing coincidence of timing. The events in question saw Pilot Officer William 'Dusty' Miller, from Invercargill, New Zealand, fly P3351 twice on training sorties. Remarkably, 'Dusty' Miller now lives in Wanaka, New Zealand, and proudly shows 'his' Hurricane to those who visit the New Zealand Fighter Pilot's Museum.

On 9th September 1941, Sergeant Polson's liaison with P3351 ended in misery. Whilst undertaking an evening training sortie, P3351's Merlin engine began to overheat and then seized. Polson bellied the stricken Hurricane into a field near Headingley, Yorkshire. Post-war, the true story emerged: Polson was 'tail-chasing' with a mate, the two having a competition to see how low they could get. Polson got *too* low and in the process took out a hedge, after which he was very quickly forced to 'land' P3351!

The badly damaged P3351 was collected, repaired and upgraded to Mk IIa series I status before being put into storage to await allocation to a unit. A new serial number, DR393, was allocated on account of her modified status. January 1942 saw DR393 flown to Hawkers for another upgrade, this time to Mk II series II. In fact, this particular Hurricane's RAF squadron career had ended with the crash-landing in Yorkshire. Her next assignment would be to a much colder clime and a torrid battle followed by almost 50 years lain dormant, unloved and in inhospitable conditions.

On 26th March 1942 DR393 was transported to Glasgow, having been selected for delivery to Russia under the Lend-Lease Agreement. Crated in preparation for shipping to the vast wasteland of northern Russia, DR393 left the United Kingdom on 3rd May 1942 along with another 23 Hurricanes aboard the merchantman SS *Ocean Voice*. Forming part of convoy PQ16, this was to be a most dangerous assignment, but one for which DR393 would not even have to get airworthy. The German Navy, fully aware of the convoy, made every conceivable effort to

The Merlin engine installed in Hurricane IIa P3351/ZK-TPK. ANZ Engineering

November 1997 and the Hurricane fuselage has been re-covered with fabric. ANZ Engineering

With the wings installed, work now centres on systems installation as the project approaches airworthiness. ANZ Engineering

ensure that this vital supply of Hurricanes never reached their destination.

Following safe passage to Iceland, convoy PQ16 set course for Murmansk and over the next week was attacked from all angles by German U-boats. Despite several attempts to sink her, the SS *Ocean Voice* managed to reach her destination on 30th May. The Hurricanes were swiftly assembled and DR393 spent the following year flying with the Russians. Sadly, no records have been discovered that detail her operational career in Russia, but it is known that she was refitted with Russian cannon armament. Undoubtedly she saw extensive action against the Luftwaffe.

It is believed that DR393 crashed in the winter of 1943. (During the later restoration process the radiator yielded a 20mm cannon shell lodged deep inside the aircraft.) Recovered from Russia in 1991, a year later DR393 was purchased by Sir Tim Wallis for his Alpine Fighter Collection in Wanaka, New Zealand. It was his intention to see the Hurricane restored as P3351 and for her to fly again. Following negotiations with Air New Zealand, keen to bring an important part of aviation history to New Zealand, an agreement was reached whereby the national airline would restore the Hurricane to airworthiness. Duly transported to ANZ Engineering Services in Christchurch, the remains of P3351 were unloaded and inventoried. Under the overall control of AFC Chief Engineer Ray Mulqueen, the long and complex restoration project was off and running.

Compared to an aircraft of monocoque construction such as the Spitfire or P-51 Mustang, the Hawker Hurricane is very different, based around a complex tubular structure. Put simply, each joint comprises mechanical joints, squared at each end and requiring special equipment to roll the special T50 steel.

As outlined in the story of Sea Hurricane AE977/N33TF (*see elsewhere in this book*), Tony Ditheridge's AJD Engineering at Milden, Suffolk, had to undertake considerable research into the complexities of Hurricane construction and assembly. Sir Tim Wallis, realising it would be vital to have access to this technology for the restoration of P3351, had already held meetings with Tony with a view to forming a joint venture company called Hawker Restorations Ltd. It was soon agreed that Hawker Restorations would undertake the rebuild of P3351's tubular

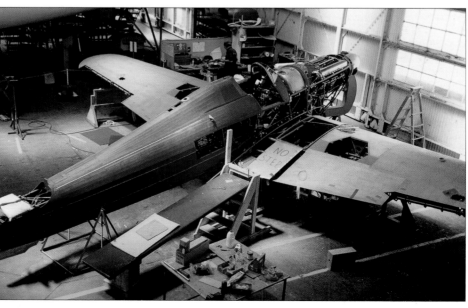

structure, empennage and woodwork; work on the mainplane would be subcontracted to Airframe Assemblies on the Isle of Wight. ANZ Engineering Services salvaged a substantial number of the original parts and these were shipped to Hawker Restorations for incorporation into the new structure.

In late 1995 the Hurricane's fuselage framework, now completed and signed off, was exported from the United Kingdom so the project could progress at Christchurch. Meanwhile, ANZ Engineering Services volunteers had been gainfully employed refurbishing the myriad of parts they had access to.

A propeller hub acquired by the Alpine Fighter Collection and wooden propeller blades manufactured by Hoffman in West Germany (and approved by Dowty Rotol) were all assembled by Skycraft in the United Kingdom. Skycraft also manufactured the missing parts, then assembled and tested the completed unit.

A late-model Merlin engine, with engine logs, was discovered in the United Kingdom. and overhauled in the United States. An inspection by the overhaul shop revealed that the unit had new pistons, cylinders, cylinder head and supercharger units. After a smooth overhaul process and bench testing, the Merlin arrived in Christchurch in November 1997, and was installed soon afterwards.

The worldwide search for all the components necessary to complete the restoration had also borne fruit. In addition, New Zealand industry was approached to assist with the project, and the response was heartening. The radiator was made by Replicore in Whangarei and the casing was manufactured by Auto Restorations in Christchurch.

The assembled components were looking most Hurricane like when ANZ Engineering Services contracted the Croydon Aircraft Company of Mandeville to apply fabric to the fuselage and other areas requiring such treatment. The newly rebuilt wings, imported from Airframe Assemblies, were permanently attached early the following year. Over the next eleven months, components were added to the airframe in short order. By December 1998, P3351 was being prepared for painting.

Meantime, the complex radiator had been causing some headaches for the subcontractor tasked with refurbishing the unit. The hexagonal tube cores are traditionally made of either pure copper or 80/20 copper/nickel compound. Several attempts at replicating the construction had ended in tears and much gnashing of teeth, due to the material crushing during forming. However, the manufacturers persevered and after two years, made and utilised a simple rolling tool. This proved to be the answer and the radiator was then made to the same specifications as when it was originally manufactured. Some 6,000 individual tubes were cut to length, formed and cut for radiator and oil cooler cores. Auto Restorations then spent

two months finishing and testing the unit that was duly installed on the Hurricane in September 1999.

In late 1999 the Merlin engine once again barked into life at Christchurch Airport, singing out loud and clear, to the joy of onlookers, many of whom had laboured long and hard on the restoration. At last the Hurricane was approaching airworthiness. Finishing touches were applied to the original Battle of France paint scheme, including the codes TP-K, and by January 2000 Hawker Hurricane IIa P3351 was ready to take to the air again, this time on fresh soil.

On 12th January 2000, summer-time in the southern hemisphere, P3351 flew for the first time in 60 years, performing flawlessly; a fitting tribute to all those who had contributed to its restoration and a testament to Sir Tim Wallis' foresight and determination.

Hurricane Pilot's Notes by Keith Skilling
From the moment you walk towards the Hurricane and notice its fabric-covered fuselage and large wing and tail sections, until the final dying crackle of the Merlin, it oozes nostalgia and character. As well, it is large and sits surprisingly high off the ground, high enough that it requires assistance in the form of a retractable strap, aft of the trailing edge, to mount it. Then again another step is embedded in the side of the fuselage above the wing to prevent a final indignity.

After checking undercarriage locked down, switches off etc, the walk around is typical, apart from a few peculiarities. The wheels sit at an unusual angle; normal, I'm assured. The radiator is a work of art and is checked carefully for leaks, a coolant leak being the demise of many of these fine aeroplanes. A tap on those beautiful exhaust stubs for the reassuring 'ting' and the rest is pretty typical for this type of aeroplane. Remount the beast again – and it is difficult to do with dignity – and settle into the cockpit.

The cockpit sides are about chin high, giving a surprisingly snug feel of security – until you realise that there are only a few millimetres of plywood between you and the 20mm bullet! The cockpit is a bit of a mishmash, with bits and pieces attached wherever a space could be found on the tubular framework, and it certainly reflects the period when little thought was given to who would fly it. The electrics are on both the left and right side panels and the instrument panel, and the rpm lever is on a different quadrant to the throttle and mixture, which in turn are close together and of a similar, confusing size. The undercarriage and flap selector is the same lever, an 'H' pattern operated in similar fashion to a car gear lever, and that in itself is a marvel of design or a masterpiece of confusion.

A prominent large brass switch, 1920s vintage, operates the landing lights, which in turn are pilot adjustable up or down, by means of a cable and lever arrangement. I'm not sure how one would manage to find the time or even manage to operate this

adjustment on finals to land at night. However, this is all part of the character, and is certainly a refinement on the Polikarpov [I-16 Rata] that was designed during a similar period.

The standard of workmanship on this Hurricane is simply superb and everything works exactly as advertised; surprising for an aircraft of this vintage, but it certainly adds to the pilot's confidence.

After strapping in, things generally flow from left to right until it is time to start the engine. Fuel ON, on the left side of the cockpit, battery switch ON, right side of the cockpit, the DC Master ON, left side, the start master and booster ON, right side, fuel pump ON, right side, front instrument panel and then back to the left for the start and prime switches. You get the picture.

The starting procedure adopted by the Alpine Fighter Collection is a little different to the way I have started Merlins in the past, and on the other Hurricane that I have flown. I am assured it prevents stack fires, and has something to do with 'top dead centre' and saving the starter motor! From cold this Merlin requires six good one-second primes; when hot, no primes. Brakes parked, and with the left leg holding the control column hard back, press the start button. The engine fires almost instantaneously, a quick dab of prime keeping it running as the magneto switches are turned on; a few more dabs of prime as the mixture is opened to auto rich with your third hand, and it should settle down to idle at about 800rpm. This sequence does take some practice, to assure a good clean start, but it works, and my attempts at the more common procedure have produced some wonderful fireworks and delightful expressions of momentary horror from the faces of the assembled spectators.

After start, the normal tidying up is done: temperatures and pressures, flaps checked, start master off, radio etc. As the power is increased for taxi, one of the distinct characteristics of the Hurricane becomes apparent: vibration, and a loud engine harmonic. Without prior warning of this the novice would probably return to dispersal and request some severe remedial actions. However, it is normal and one soon gets used to it, but it is harsh and unlike all other Merlin installations. Taxying presents the normal problem of reduced visibility over the nose although it is better than most other World War Two fighters, but the required weave is easily managed by the hand-operated pneumatic brakes. On concrete it wants to bound away at idle.

With the oil temperatures at 15°C and the radiator at 40°C, it is time to commence the run-up. The Hurricane will tip on its nose if care is not taken with the application of power. Never use the park brake, of course; and slowly increase boost to -2 pounds of the +12 available; any more and the tail will start to lift off the ground. Check the prop CSU a couple of times and the magnetos,

An atmospheric air-to-air study of P3351 prior to its first appearance at the bi-annual Warbirds Over Wanaka show on South Island, New Zealand. GHOSTS: Philip Makanna

looking for around a 100rpm drop, but as with all these old gauges, fluctuations of the mechanical drives are a problem, and a fair bit of information is transmitted by feel and noise!

Normal pre-take-off checks are completed, with particular emphasis on the rudder trim (full right), the temperatures and pressures, and setting of the radiator flap fully open. I open the throttle reasonably slowly, checking that all is stable and set at +8 inches and 3,000rpm. This power setting is ample at the light weight we are flying and allows for a much more controlled affair.

By this time the tail has come up and the swing to the left is easily held with right rudder. At 80mph (129km/h) she wants to fly and accelerates quite quickly. Care must be taken not to exceed the gear limiting speed of 120mph (193km/h), so quite a steep climb out is required; none of the 'hold it down' airshow stuff. At the same time the left hand is taken off the throttle and crossed to the control column and returned rapidly if the throttle friction has not been adjusted firmly enough. The right hand is then used to release the gear safety latch and select first gear, on the gear/flap selector quadrant. This raises the undercarriage.

The hands are then reversed to select climb power: 2,650rpm and +6 for a climb rate of around 2,500ft/min (12.70m/sec) at 150mph (241km/h). After checking the all-important temperatures and resetting the radiator, it is time to initially notice some of the characteristics of the Hurricane. Vibration levels are reasonably high and it is noisy, not that nice V-12 sound you hear from the outside but, as you are sitting 6ft (1.82m) directly behind an unsilenced Merlin, more of an earth-shattering roar.

As well, it is getting warm as the pipes carrying the engine oil and the radiator glycol between the engine and the radiator pass down the outside of your legs. This heat can become a real problem on a very hot day, but what a blessing during the English winter. This Hurricane is fitted with louvres and vents, thanks to the thoughtful Air New Zealand engineers. The coolant pipes are lagged and of course they give off an appropriate odour, and when mixed with the various fumes from the engine it all becomes a very distinctive concoction! Very soon a slight haze has appeared. Yes, I am definitely in a Hurricane!

At cruise power, 2,000rpm and +0, she gets along nicely at around 180mph (290km/h); max lean cruise of around 2,150rpm and +4 gives a healthy 235mph (378km/h). The flight controls are lovely and light and reasonably well harmonised, and it is surprising stable, making for a good gun platform!

The elevators lack a bit of feel as they are still quite tight on this aeroplane, making formation flying difficult, but it is a known problem with the Hurricane and they will free up. Power up for some manoeuvring to, say, 2,650/+6 and it really comes alive. The large, thick wing allows good tight turns – good enough to out-turn all the contemporaries – and there is a characteristic tightening and tuck-in pitch to watch and control as things tighten up. However, drag is relatively high and she runs out of steam a little quicker compared to other World War Two fighters. The ailerons are light but rate of roll is relatively poor, slightly better than the P-51, but behind the Spitfire. Loops and rolls are fine but acceleration is slow.

At VNE of 390mph (627.5km/h) it is perfectly trimmed, but care must be taken with the lightness of the controls; even changing the radiator gills at this speed provides a marked pitch change.

In the previous Hurricane that I have flown, as the nose was lowered to accelerate to around 250mph (402km/h) for a loop, the cockpit became noticeably warmer and the haze increased. Through the inverted portion of the loop it got cooler and clearer, and down the other side, warmer and smellier again. This aeroplane is just starting to develop these tendencies as flying hours build up; yes, it sure has character.

Stalling presents no problems, with the usual wing drop; vicious with the undercarriage and flaps down, but it is easily controlled. Stalling speeds are surprisingly slow, varying from 75mph (120km/h) clean to 55mph (88.5km/h) in the landing configuration. Spinning is for a maximum of two turns only and exit is rapid with standard recovery technique. There is little else to do but get on with savouring the delights.

The only problem with the landing is slowing it down to 120mph (193km/h) limiting speed for both flap and undercarriage

lowering. It is surprisingly slick and as the throttle should not be fully closed, it takes most of the downwind to slow after breaking at even a modest speed of around 250mph (402km/h). Landing presents few problems into wind. First of all, select second gear for undercarriage down, then fourth gear for a few moments, for half flap. A curved base turn almost onto the ground is recommend to ensure good visibility over the nose. A speed of 100mph (161km/h) around base with half flap is comfortable, reducing to 95mph (153km/h) with full flap crossing the fence; a slight flare and hold-off gives a reliable three-point landing.

On the ground there is a tendency for the Hurricane to wander a little, but it is quite easily controlled. Crosswinds provide the normal interest associated with a 'tail-dragger' but I prefer a three-point landing because the flare required is less, generally, than any other aircraft of this type. Remember, however, these aeroplanes were designed to operate off big square grass fields into wind!

Every flight in this type of aircraft is something to savour and remember, but somehow there is something special to me about the Hurricane. Sure, it lacks the charisma of the Spitfire and some later World War Two fighters, but it did win the Battle of Britain. It also lacks the handling qualities of the Spitfire and others, but it was designed a lot earlier than all of them, and then not developed to the same extent. Compare it to designs of a similar era – Polikarpov I-16, Spitfire I, the very early Bf109s – and it could certainly hold its own. Remarkably, it then went through World War Two being used successfully in every conceivable role and theatre, still virtually as a 1936 model, while all the rest were subject to huge modification. So as I step out of the cockpit with a huge satisfied grin, am I dismounting the most capable of them all?

13

Mitsubishi A6M5 Zero
5347/N46770

This aircraft is the only authentic, airworthy example of the Mitsubishi A6M5 Zero Model 52 in existence today. Built by Nakajima in May 1943, it was the 2,357th aircraft off the production line and served with 261 Naval Air Corps, one of two such Imperial Japanese Navy units, with whom it flew on Operation 'Pogo' (air defence of the Japanese homeland). In March 1944, it was reassigned to the air defence of Saipan, Tinian and the Palau Islands, and based at Asilito airfield. Captured at Asilito in June 1944 during Operation 'Foraged', the aircraft (bearing the serial 61-120 on its tail) was shipped to the United States for evaluation purposes aboard the aircraft carrier USS *Copahee* bound for San Diego, California.

Overhauled at NAS North Island, California, the Zero was flown for the first time in the United States soil on 5th August 1944. On 22nd August the Zero was transferred across country to NAS Anacostia, Virginia, before being flown on to NAS Patuxent River, Maryland, the following day.

Wearing the code TAIC 5 (for Technical Air Intelligence Center), the Zero played a vital part in the evaluation process of this important enemy aircraft, being flown for over 20 hours during the months of September and October 1944. The pilot for the majority of these trials was Clyde C Andrews, his task being to compare the Japanese fighter's performance and handling with that of the P-38 Lightning, P-47 Thunderbolt, P-51 Mustang, P-63 Kingcobra, F4U Corsair, F7F Tigercat and the British Seafire.

Interestingly, Andrews checked out Charles Lindbergh in the aircraft and Lindbergh continued with the evaluation programme. As the flight evaluations continued, several other distinguished test pilots flew the aircraft, including R.H. Burroughs and C.L. Sharp (Vought), C.H. Meyers (Grumman) and Jack Woolhams (Bell).

Following the evaluation trials, the Zero returned to NAS Anacostia on 30th November 1944. Just one week later, the aircraft (still marked as TAIC 5) departed on the return trip to NAS North Island, where it was used to fly sorties against pilots about to be deployed to the Pacific Theatre of Operations in February and March 1945.

By September 1945 the aircraft had accumulated almost 200 hours of test and evaluation flights for the TAIC. It was then flown north to NAS Alameda, California, where it was effectively struck off charge a few weeks later.

This recovered Zero fuselage, seen in October 1991, was used in the Flight Magic Zero project.
Thierry Thomassin

In 1950 the aircraft was acquired by Ed Maloney's Air Museum in Claremont, California, where it was painted as 'V101'. Transferred to nearby Ontario in 1965, the aircraft was again put on static exhibition until a decision was made in the early 1970s to restore it to airworthiness; a project that culminated in a post-restoration first flight on 28th June 1978. Steve Hinton (Ed Maloney's son-in-law and well-known warbird pilot and engineer) takes up the story:

'The Zero restoration came about back in the early 1970s. We had taken our Ki-84 'Frank' to Japan for a big airshow. That's another story, but what came from this is the fact that the Japanese people really loved it. This made us think seriously about restoring the Zero and taking it to Japan.

'Ed Maloney worked hard to find a sponsor for the project but was not able to put it together. Instead, we were able to find help from many people and companies. The restoration business was much different back then. We officially started the restoration in 1975. The aircraft was complete but in poor condition. The wing spars were rotten and the rest of the airframe and engine were in need of a complete overhaul.

'We disassembled the Zero and a company in Long Beach, California, started the job of replacing the wing spars. The engine was sent to another company where we could work on it with their help. We did not have much of a budget so what we relied on was a lot of good-hearted volunteer help. Because of the uniqueness of this project, we were able to pull it off. Ed was able to get many companies to supply hardware and some materials; others helped supervise volunteers. We did this with the goal of tak-

ing the Zero to Japan and a target completion date of summer 1978. The wing centre section spars were replaced and the airframe shell finished by 1976.

'We moved the shell back to Chino where Jim Maloney, myself and a couple of other dedicated, part-time guys started to assemble the airframe for flight. The engine was overhauled over a two-year period and installed in early 1978.

'It all came together and the aircraft was ready to fly on 28th June 1978. Don Lykins flew it first. Don was part of the Zero restoration effort, helping arrange support from the donor companies and vendors. Don is on The Air Museum Board of Directors – he has been with the Museum since the beginning. We flew the Zero around Chino for about 20 hours, painted it [as 61-120], loaded it on a ship and sent it to Japan. We flew it in Japan for three months, attending nine different airshow events before shipping it back to California. It was a big hit and was seen by thousands and thousands of enthusiastic Japanese.

'Some of the challenges of the restoration were the airframe, because it was constructed using the then new Duralumin and the spars had since completely rotted out. The inter-granular corrosion made them look like wood. We replaced them with modern- alloy aluminium, had them machined and reinstalled them. All the systems had to be rebuilt including the fuel tanks, pumps, control surfaces, electrical and hydraulics; even the seat had to be modified so a 6-ft American could at least sit in it! I don't know how Charles Lindbergh flew our Zero back in 1945 with his long legs.

'The engine was also a challenge. It was

The Planes of Fame A6M5 Model 52 Zero is an original War Prize, captured on Asilito airfield, Saipan, in June 1944. Thierry Thomassin

suffering from rust and corrosion and needed to be completely restored. We were able to save most of the engine, and with overhaul techniques *à la* Pratt and Whitney, that is chrome cylinders, valve guide and bearing rework, the engine ran perfectly. By the way, in spite of what you may read, this Sakae engine is not a Pratt. It has 14 cylinders and that is where the similarity ends. Different piston designs, rods, oil system, bearings, supercharger and gear designs make it very different.

'The propeller was exactly like a Hamilton Standard unit. The overhaul shop used a lot of Hamilton Standard parts on it. Though we tried to keep it pretty original we did not have the network that is in place today to find information and parts, so we modified and replaced a few things to make it airworthy and better suited for its new life. I think we spent about four years, thousands of man-hours and blood, sweat and a few tears to rebuild this one.

'As I said before, things were different in the warbird business 25 years ago. We had different standards then. Having said that, I don't know if it would have turned out much different [today] though. The Zero is a simple aircraft and is easy to fly and maintain. It has a great engine and is a very important aircraft for our collection.'

Today the Zero flies regularly out of the Planes of Fame Museum base at Chino, California, and has starred in several films including the recent blockbuster *Pearl Harbor*.

14

Hawker Sea Hurricane
AE977/N33TF

The wreckage of Hawker Sea Hurricane AE977, originally built as a Hurricane X by the Canadian Car and Foundry Corporation, was recovered from a crash site at Godney, Somerset, in 1988. The aircraft had crashed on 5th December 1942 after colliding with another Sea Hurricane, Z4702, whilst serving with 749 Squadron, Royal Navy. Ownership of the remains was transferred to the Alpine Fighter Collection of Wanaka, New Zealand, in 1994. The airframe was appropriately registered G-TWTD to Sir Tim Wallis and Tony Ditheridge of Hawker Restorations Ltd of Milden, Suffolk, on 21st April 1994. Following an exhaustive rebuild, the first post-restoration flight took place at RAF Wattisham, Suffolk, on 7th June 2000. In October 2001 the aircraft was sold to Chino Warbirds Inc of Chino, California, where it arrived in January 2002 and was subsequently registered N33TF.

The uneventful (some might say uninteresting) history of this particular Sea Hurricane in fact hides a remarkable story – that of one man's vision and determination to resurrect, restore and rebuild this particular aircraft to flying condition.

Moat Farm in Milden, Suffolk, is the home of Hawker Restorations – and the place where Tony Ditheridge, the man in question, has lived for the past 20 years. The sprawling buildings of Hawker Restorations disguise an efficient organisation that houses several rare and unique warbird projects plus a compact and, for the pilot, challenging farm strip at the rear, which adjoins the company's workshops.

Over the past six years a remarkable operation has taken place at Moat Farm that has seen the restoration of several Hawker Hurricanes for customers around the world. Though this book is generally about the restoration of warbirds to flying condition, the resurrection of the Hawker Hurricane, perhaps more than any other warbird type operational today, is down to the drive and determination of Tony Ditheridge, making this a relevant part of the story.

Tony Ditheridge is a colourful and intense individual whose enthusiasm for pure engineering and old aeroplanes, from World War One types through to their World War Two successors, is boundless. Tony is a true evangelist of Hawker engineering and I suspect that if he had ever been acquainted with Sir Sidney Camm, they would have been the best of friends.

In the annals of aviation history the Supermarine Spitfire has always overshadowed the Hawker Hurricane. Despite the fact that the Hurricane fought on more fronts, was able to withstand more battle damage than any other fighter of its day and was, along with the brave pilots that flew it, responsible in large part for the preservation of the United Kingdom's freedom during the Battle of Britain, there always seems to be more interest in the Spitfire.

Though there will never be as many flyable Hurricanes as there are Spitfires, the former, as a rarer warbird, most certainly represents a better long-term investment for the warbird owner. A chat with Tony over a beer or cup of coffee will quickly leave no doubt in your mind as to which is the best of the two!

The Hawker Hurricane is a complexly engineered piece of aviation construction. Whilst there are many 'long-term' Spitfire rebuild projects being undertaken across the world by individuals (albeit supported by a real industry in this new millennium, able to supply parts and components on an 'as required' basis), the Hurricane is a very different proposition. Short term, a do-it-yourself Hurricane project might seem more attractive; long term, it is more cost-effective to have an aircraft rebuilt by Hawker Restorations, taking advantage of the expertise that is backed up by a wealth of knowledge and approval from the CAA to fly. There simply is no 'cheap rebuild' option. An individual could spend hundreds of thousands of pounds properly rebuilding a Hurricane only to get part way through the project and wish he hadn't started it.

Like so many other warbird people, Tony's interest in old aeroplanes was fuelled by his interest in old motor cars. As a youngster his interest revolved around model-making and collecting, as Tony puts it, '…anything old, rusty, mechanical…anything dilapidated and overpriced, I'd buy it! I was a sucker for them.' This led, much later, to Tony's passion for rebuilding vintage cars. In the late 1970s Tony saw a TV programme about flying de Havilland Moths and became enthusiastic enough to get involved himself. He kept a Tiger Moth until the early 1990s, learned to fly and progressed onto Stampes, Stearmans, Zlins, Chipmunks and a broad range of other vintage aeroplanes.

Tony's real move into aeronautical engineering and aircraft restoration came after Desmond St Cyrien (purchaser of two Sop-

with Pups and a Camel from a landowner in Lincolnshire) suggested that Tony form a company specialising in the rebuilding of World War One aeroplanes. This idea led to the establishment of AJD Engineering.

Desmond St Cyrien had two British Caledonian airline engineers working on his Sopwith aeroplanes at the time British Airways took over the airline. Tony offered the pair new jobs, and thus Richard Watson and Graham Self became part of AJD Engineering. The team of three rebuilt a Boeing Stearman (the first aeroplane to emerge from the new company) and finished the St Cyrien airframes as well.

It was during this initial period that Tony was introduced to the late John 'Jeff' Hawke, who calmly told the fledgling AJD team that they were the right people to undertake a commission he had from the Chilean Air Force to build a 1916 Bristol M.1C shoulder-wing monoplane. The catch? Just 12 weeks to complete the task! That time frame was unrealistic, but AJD Engineering did it in a highly creditable 20 weeks, with Tony and Richard Watson accompanying the airframe to Chile where it was assembled and flown. The Chileans were so impressed with the work that they commissioned the company to build an Avro 504K, an RAF S.E.5a and a Bleriot XI. 'So that was our introduction to World War One aeroplanes,' remembers Tony.

Since then, AJD Engineering has built several more Avros; the Southampton Hall of Aviation, Hampshire, houses an Avro 504J, an Avro 504K is airworthy and another Avro 504K was rebuilt for Sir Tim Wallis in New Zealand. The company has also built a Sopwith Camel for the US Army Aviation Museum at Fort Rucker, Alabama, a Sopwith Pup for another collector in the United States, and a Bleriot Monoplane for the Aviodome at Amsterdam, Holland.

What happened next was a turning point in AJD Engineering's history and saw the formation of Hawker Restorations Ltd. When AJD Engineering supplied an S.E.5a to Sir Tim Wallis, conversation between Sir Tim and Tony revealed that Sir Tim had recovered some ex-Soviet Air Force Hawker Hurricanes from Russia and was looking for someone to restore them. By sheer coincidence, Tony was at that time looking at a Hurricane rebuild project, having recovered some airframes from Canada four years previously.

The first Hurricane to be completely assembled by Hawker Restorations Ltd, AE977 was based on the remains of a crashed Sea Hurricane recovered in 1988. The aircraft was finished as LF-D, the codes worn by Douglas Bader's personal mount (V7467) during his time with 242 Squadron, RAF Fighter Command. Author

'I was certainly keen to rebuild a Hurricane,' recalls Tony. 'Essentially at AJD, though we are a small team, we are first and foremost pure engineers – toolmakers, millers and turners. However, I explained to Tim that during my investigations four years previously, I had examined the logistics of restoring a Hurricane and had come to the conclusion that I did not have enough money to invest in tooling to even start the venture or to commence what would be a very expensive tooling exercise. Tim replied by asking me for a proposal to rebuild a Hurricane. I submitted this to him – he sent me a ticket and just four days later I was in New Zealand, just before Christmas. The typically impetuous Tim Wallis!

'I was in New Zealand for just four days and as a sign of good faith he gave me a cheque for a lot of money – basically, I made a commitment to supply the Alpine Fighter Collection with a completed airframe ready for systems, engine, etc [which was to be completed by Air New Zealand]. In fact we achieved this in 20 months and since then we have become very good friends with the people in New Zealand.' Hawker Restorations was off and running.

From the start, Hawker Restoration's primary aim was to focus on Hurricanes. The company invested in metallurgy, tooling and personnel, grasping the learning curve and protecting the investment by capturing the intellectual rights to achieve it. The Hurricane is certainly a phenomenally complex aeroplane and, says Tony, 'a very expensive aeroplane to rebuild.' The new Hurricane rebuilding programme has certainly worked for Hawker Restorations. The funding for tooling, the manufacture of spars, metallurgical investigation work, the sheds full of machining, intensive research tasks and subcontracting made it all possible.

Tony had accurately calculated that to produce a single Hurricane, properly rebuilt with correct new engineering, would cost over £1.5 million. To be able to produce materials in multiples would lower the unit price to less than £1 million. Considerable investment was involved, and a considerable amount of research was required to ensure that the project was viable.

One vital ingredient was the range of skills already available at AJD Engineering. Just as with the original Hawker Aircraft Company, there was a discernible natural progression from building complete World War One aircraft through to the Hurricane, as was the case back in the 1930s. Hawker Restorations was the product of the development of these skills. The addition of key personnel such as Chief Engineer Paul Mercer, Bob Young and Phil Parish (who between them have over 40 years of warbird experience) has enabled the company to develop and cope with the systems side – complex aspects like engine installation, propellers, etc. The workshops at Moat Farm were able to concentrate on pure engineering.

To achieve its goals, Hawker Restorations had to attain the CAA's A8-20 approval and the Moat Farm company was the first to be awarded it, by a year. The company also gained M5 and E4 CAA engineering approvals that allow them to seriously engineer pretty much anything required and, just as importantly, get it certificated and quality 'stamped'. To facilitate the completion of the Hurricane for Sir Tim Wallis, Air New Zealand engineering approval was also obtained.

The attainment of the various engineering approvals from the CAA enforced a new discipline at the company, raising the quality of the restoration work and vastly improving the supporting documentation. Though this would increase the price to the end user, it was seen as added value by those with the foresight to recognise it. The first Hawker Restorations Hurricane, Mk IIc P3351, was delivered to Air New Zealand in November 1995. Just eight months later there were two more airframes in a similar state at Moat Farm. The learning curve was steep.

Due to the huge investment in having all the materials specially manufactured, Hawker Restorations became the sole suppliers of specially made centre section and tailplane spars and all the appropriate major Hurricane structural parts that go with them. The company supplied the centre section and tailplane spars for the rebuild of the MoD Hurricane IIc LF363, which had suffered severe fire damage after crashlanding at RAF Wittering, Cambridgeshire, on 11th September 1991 following engine failure.

The Hurricane is certainly for the serious warbird collector. It is not a cheap acquisition. Why, I asked Tony, is the Hurricane more expensive to build than the Spitfire? His explanation and comparison were uncomplicated: '...the construction of the Spitfire is a monocoque in form, basically a series of pressed formers with sheet metal riveted to them in a jig. So, really, this is a complex sheet metal exercise.

'Conversely, the Hurricane is a round, tubular structure where every bay is squared at one end. Then at that junction there is a machined component or several machined components, two side plates, ferrules that have, typically, two-tenths of a thou fit with a spacer in between all that. To give you some idea, I can show you one joint on a Hurri-

cane and there are about 180 pieces in it – and that is one joint on one side!

'So there are literally hundreds of thousands of components in a Hurricane, and they are all precision components where the fits and clearances are incredibly tight. So add the components, the engineering skill, the machining it takes to do it and it starts to become clear what is required.'

In the early days of the Hurricane projects the company subcontracted a machine shop to work some 300 hours a month just to machine Hurricane components. The Hurricane also has some fairly complex sheet metal work in the cowling area, and a complex and impressive-looking wooden structure (known as a 'dog kennel') in the cockpit and canopy area that has to be hand crafted. Each project also requires a fair amount of traditional fabric work to be undertaken.

One interesting fact is that while 'basket case' Hurricanes look externally complete, typically there are only about four boxes of stainless steel fittings remaining once all the corroded tubes have been extricated! Consequently the Hurricane is very much an in-depth restoration job. The cost of the work is driven by the availability of machine components and thus the number of man-hours required. As noted earlier, Hawker Restorations is the sole supplier of spars and other vital components for rebuilding Hurricanes, having developed the materials et al in conjunction with Guy Black and his company, Aero Vintage Ltd.

One thing that is hidden when you look over a Hawker Restorations Hurricane is the sheer amount of research that was required to back up the engineering ability at the company. In the formative years, through AJD Engineering, Tony began examining the specifications for materials and processes, liaising closely with Guy Black. The pair worked together to determine what the orig-

Hawker Sea Hurricane AE977 under restoration at the Hawker Restorations workshops at Milden, Suffolk. The airframe is seen here with the Packard Merlin 224 engine installed but still awaiting its wings. Author

inal material was, what the modern equivalent was (if it existed), and whether the CAA would permit them to use it. They then had to find someone to manufacture it, heat-treat it and slit it and then design 120 rollers to roll-form it to the correct shape. That 'little' exercise cost a fortune and took over a year to accomplish. Hawker Restorations received the finished materials three months before they delivered Hurricane IIc P3351 to Air New Zealand. A similar process had to be established for the tailplane spars; and then the company had to go to Austria and Germany to source and purchase seven tons of specially made material. All of this had to be approved by the CAA.

Another mammoth task concerned the gathering of basic data for the Hurricane. At the outset the company had no drawings. Extensive searching enabled them to build their own archive of design information. The workforce rose to the enormous challenge and within a relatively short period of time was properly equipped to tackle the task of rebuilding a Hurricane to the highest standard. Tony points out that none of this would have been possible without the support, financial investment and enthusiasm of Sir Tim Wallis – a man who, says Tony, 'runs at a thousand miles per hour'.

I left Moat Farm feeling that I had been a privileged witness to the rebirth of one of the world's most underrated warbirds. There will never be as many rebuilt and restored Hurricanes as there are Spitfires or Mustangs, but thanks to Hawker Restorations the existing Hurricanes – and future restorations – are set to fly well into the 21st century.

15

Hawker Sea Fury FB.11
VR930

In 1994 a decision was made to restore Sea Fury FB.11 VR930, then a static exhibit, back to airworthy condition to replace FB.11 TF956, which had been ditched in the waters of the Firth of Clyde, Scotland, on 10th June 1989 while performing at the Prestwick Airshow.

The Sea Fury selected for restoration first flew on 23rd February 1948 from the Hawker plant at Kingston, Surrey, and entered Royal Navy service on 8th March 1948 at RNAS Culham, Oxfordshire. Between May and September 1948, VR930 (coded 110/Q) served with 802 NAS at RNAS Eglinton, Northern Ireland, before being put into storage. From December 1948 to August 1953, VR930 was stored in reserve at various Royal Navy Aircraft Holding Units including Anthorn, Abbotsinch and later Fleetlands, where she was overhauled before returning to service with 801 NAS.

The aircraft logged a further 280 flying hours before detachment, in July 1954, to Fleetlands for refurbishment. Following time spent held in reserve at Anthorn and RNAS Lossiemouth, VR930's next assignment was in November 1959 with the Fleet Requirements Unit based at Hurn Airport, Dorset. Struck off Royal Navy charge on 5th November 1962, VR930 was then put up for disposal with a grand total of 1,280 flying hours. Her next journey was to the Colerne Collection near Swindon, Wiltshire, where she remained until 1976 when the airfield closed and the collection was dispersed. Following this, VR930 was acquired once again by the Royal Navy for use as a spares source for Sea Furies TF956 and WG655, and officially as a reserve exhibition aircraft for the Fleet Air Arm Museum at RNAS Yeovilton, Somerset.

Following storage at both RNAY Wroughton, Wiltshire, and RNAS Lee-On-Solent, Hampshire, and the loss of both TF956 (as related earlier) and WG655 (forced-landed after engine failure on 14th July 1990), VR930 became the target for a rebuild to flying condition. With the Royal Navy Historic Flight (RNHF) so obviously lacking a Sea Fury, and desperately searching for one, they were fortunate when British Aerospace (BAe) responded to calls for assistance. The company arranged to have the Sea Fury restored to flying condition

Below and overleaf: The bulk of Hawker Sea Fury FB.11 VR930 being hoisted aboard a low-loader for the road journey to RNAS Yeovilton, home of the Royal Navy Historic Flight. courtesy British Aerospace

alongside Harriers being produced at its Military Aircraft Division, located on the site of the historic Blackburn Aircraft Works at Brough, Humberside.

Early in 1994, BAe Chief Executive Sir Richard Evans had informal talks with the site director at Brough, Bob Fox, about the feasibility of BAe taking on another historic aircraft project for the RNHF. BAe Brough had already completed the restoration of Fairey Swordfish II W5856 for the Flight. Initially, three aircraft were inspected: Sea Fury FB.11 VR930, Sea Fury T.20 VZ345 and Hawker Sea Hawk FGA.6 WV908. In January a team from BAe Brough had visited RNAS Yeovilton to undertake surveys and hold in-depth discussions with personnel at the RNHF. After much research and cost analysis, it was decided that the RNHF's first-choice airframe, VR930, would be rebuilt to flying condition. In June 1994 Dick Evans officially sanctioned the project.

The Sea Fury appeared to be in poor condition but in fact it had been properly stored and had only superficial damage However, although all of the major structure was available, surveys undertaken by BAe showed that some parts had been robbed to keep Sea Furies TF956 and WG655 airworthy. All major parts would require a full strip, inspection and non-destructive testing and then repair as required.

By January 1995 work was already well under way. With the major inspection and surveys already completed, work on the significant structures and the drawing up of the all-important 'wants' list was progressing well. Though as much of the original aircraft as practical would be utilised in the restoration it was decided that the electrical, pneumatic and hydraulic systems would be replaced in their entirety. To help the aircraft better operate in today's modern ATC environment, it was also decided to modernise the radio and IFF systems. Much of the original instrumentation in the cockpit had been plundered and robbed for other aircraft. The five fuel tanks would also have to be refurbished or replaced.

BAe's brief was to refurbish the airframe only; it was the RNHF's brief to both provide and have the 2,480-hp (1,850-kW) Bristol Centaurus 18 radial engine overhauled. The engine selected for the project was transported to Ricardo Consulting Engineers for a full strip, inspection and certification. Refurbishment of the aircraft's propeller unit was also to be the responsibility of the Royal Navy.

Thanks to the intervention of BAe, which canvassed the involvement of the entire British aviation industry in the project, Dowty Engineering agreed to handle the refurbishment of the hydraulics system and Hi-Matic took on the pneumatics. SERC agreed to look after the oil cooler. With all this in hand, a formal contract was drawn up between Rear Admiral T.W. Loughran, FONAC (the controlling authority in the Royal Navy) and British Aerospace.

The restoration of VR930 to flying condition was completed in April 1997, after which the aircraft was painted as 110/O in a carefully researched colour scheme representing her service with 802 NAS aboard HMS *Vengeance* in 1952 during the Korean War. She was officially handed back to the RNHF on 21st May 1997 at a ceremony held at BAe Brough. The project as a whole had taken some 30,000 man-hours to complete. During that time, the RAF sportingly allowed access to Sea Fury T.20 VZ345 (actually on inventory with the RAF) for reference purposes and critical spares support.

From the outset, BAe said that VR930 would be built to modern military aircraft standards and at the end of the project a military F700 (Form 700) would be presented to the RNHF with the aircraft. The restoration work was also carried out to BAe Brough-approved design and quality standards.

Following the handover the finishing touches were applied at BAe Brough, and VR930 was delivered back to RNAS Yeovilton by road on 12th September 1997. After two months of preparations and engine installation, the first ground runs were carried out in November 1997. However, in March 1998 the Centaurus 18 engine developed a major problem that necessitated significant additional repair work. The work took time and it was over two years later, in June 2000, when the engine was returned to RNAS Yeovilton for reinstallation in VR930. Not surprisingly, VR930 was the star of the static line-up at RNAS Yeovilton's 2000 Air Day. More successful engine runs commenced later that year.

After all the final work had been completed and the new F700 duly signed off, Sea Fury FB.11 VR930 sped down the runway at RNAS Yeovilton and took to the air on 1st March 2001 for her first flight in almost 40 years. The pilot on this historic occasion was Steve Noujaim, a civilian who was well qualified to fly the type, having regularly displayed the late Paul Morgan's Sea Fury FB.11 WH588/G-EEMV *Baby Gorilla* on the UK airshow circuit. The first flight was a success and VR930 subsequently underwent test flying during April 2001.

The public debut of the RNHF's latest addition came at the Biggin Hill Air Fair on 2nd June 2001, flown by RNHF boss Commander Phil Shaw RN. The aircraft is now based at RNAS Yeovilton and is expected to make many more airshow appearances. Though engine problems have plagued the aircraft, it is all set to serve the RNHF very well over the coming years.

Bristol F.2B Fighter
D8096/G-AEPH

Designed by Captain Frank Barnwell of the British & Colonial Aeroplane Company to replace the obsolete BE.2s that were becoming easy meat for German fighters during World War One, the Bristol F.2 was intended to be powered by the 120-hp (89-kW) Beardmore engine. However, coincidental with Barnwell's early design work in 1916 was the emergence of the Rolls-Royce Falcon I, capable of developing a more useful 190hp (142kW). It was quickly recognised that the extra power offered by the Falcon I would allow the F.2 to be transformed into a two-seat fighter, as opposed to the reconnaissance aircraft originally envisaged.

On 9th September 1916 the Bristol F.2A made its first flight, and by March the following year the aircraft was being pressed into service with front-line Royal Flying Corps (RFC) units. The F.2A was swiftly succeeded by the F.2B, which featured improved visibility from the cockpit, some structural changes to accept a higher-rated powerplant, and modifications to the wings and tailplane. The F.2B utilised an uprated version of the Rolls-Royce Falcon I. This engine was the subject of substantial development due to the pressures of war and the Falcon II developed 220hp (164kW), but this improvement was in turn quickly superseded by the 275-hp (205-kW) Falcon III. With this engine and some changes to their fighting tactics, RFC pilots flying the F.2B saw an immediate transformation in the aircraft's performance and effectiveness.

The Bristol F.2B's introduction to battle had been nothing short of calamitous – a tactical error closely watched by none other than Freiherr Manfred von Richthofen. Unsurprisingly, the famous German ace had concluded that the Albatros D.III was 'undoubtedly superior' to the F.2B in all aspects of its performance. This evaluation was quickly conveyed to other German pilots in the form of the purest intelligence, but it had the adverse effect of putting them off their guard.

The 'Brisfit' was essentially an excellent fighter, sturdy and manoeuvrable. It was the RFC's tactics that were at fault. The .303-in (7.7-mm) Lewis machine gun mounted on a Scarff ring in the rear cockpit was being used as the main attack weapon, not the forward-mounted .303-in Vickers synchronised machine gun. Once the crews changed tactics, the pilot attacking enemy

The Shuttleworth Collection's Bristol F.2B Fighter did not see service during World War One, but it did see post-war service with 208 Squadron before being disposed of. Bob Munro

aircraft with the forward-mounted gun and the rear gunner using the Lewis gun to provide defensive fire, the tables were turned. The 'Brisfit' was transformed into a deadly weapon of aerial combat.

Some crews became very proficient, such as Canadian pilot Lieutenant A McKeever and gunner Sergeant L Powell, who destroyed 30 German aircraft in six months whilst flying 'Brisfits'. Such was the success of the new tactics that some German fighter pilots would avoid Bristol Fighter formations of three or more aircraft, whatever their advantage in number.

The introduction of the Falcon III powerplant also brought unsurpassed reliability. However, because production of F.2B airframes exceeded the number of Falcon IIIs available, several hundred airframes were fitted with the 200-hp (149-kW) Sunbeam Arab engine in an attempt to satisfy the demand for attrition replacements. Unfortunately these Bristol Fighters were generally not as successful or reliable as their Falcon-engined counterparts.

The Bristol Fighter proved such a success in RFC service that it eventually equipped 14 squadrons. When the RAF was formed on 1st April 1918, 'Brisfits' of 22 Squadron flew the new Service's first sortie. The type remained in post-war RAF service, mainly in the army cooperation role, until 1932. The last F.2Bs in service, those of New Zealand, were phased out in 1936. When production

ceased in 1927, over 5,250 Bristol Fighters had been built.

Built by the British & Colonial Aeroplane Company at Brislington in Bristol in 1918, the Shuttleworth Collection's Bristol Fighter, D8096 (c/n 3746) is an original airframe but it did not see any wartime operational service. It was manufactured as a Mk I Fighter version and retrofitted in 1924 as a Mk II, at which time it was allocated a new c/n, 6848. The aircraft underwent further modifications at the Brislington factory in 1931, emerging as a Mk III 'Brisfit' with yet another new c/n, 7575!

In 1936 Captain C.P.B. Olgilvy purchased the airframe and registered it as G-AEPH with the ultimate aim of flying it. However, for reasons unknown it was placed in storage until 1949. The Shuttleworth Collection then acquired it, and it was restored to airworthiness by the Bristol Aeroplane Company. Its first flight following rebuild was made in early 1951, and the aircraft was soon performing at air displays. It took a minor part in the film *Reach For The Sky* and except for downtime for restoration and regular maintenance, it has been a stalwart of the Shuttleworth Collection at Old Warden ever since.

Martin B-26 Marauder
40-1464/N4297J

Martin B-26-MA Marauder 40-1464 was one of three such aircraft that were forced-landed at Smith River in British Columbia, Canada, on 16th January 1942 after running low on fuel. Nearly three decades later, in September 1971, an expedition led by warbird collector and restaurateur David Tallichet retrieved the aircraft from an area more famously known as 'Million Dollar Valley', for his Yesterday's Air Force collection.

Transported to Chino, California, the twin-engined warbird was gradually rebuilt and restored to flying condition and later registered N4297J to Tallichet in June 1991. Post-restoration test flying commenced with the first flight on 18th April 1992. The next 23 hours of flying were made with both David Tallichet and Roscoe Diehl at the controls. The aircraft then spent some time as part of the USAF Museum Collection at March AFB, California, and out on loan between 1992-93.

Following the loan period, it was back to Chino on 28th April 1994 for attention by Tony Ritzman and Carl Scholl at Aero Trader. Thorough and careful inspection work led to the aircraft being scheduled for repair as necessary to enable it to make a safe transcontinental flight to Polk City, Florida, for its new owner, Kermit Weeks (to whom it was re-registered on 7th September 1994). The repairs were quite extensive in some areas but cosmetically the aircraft was left 'as is'.

The two main problems found during the inspection were the mounting of the horizontal and vertical stabilisers and the condition of the entire hydraulic system. On examination, it was discovered that all the bolts in the tail assembly were suffering from corrosion; many were worn and loose in their holes. This necessitated the removal of the complete tail assembly, so as to enable rebushing and reaming of the holes and the installation of new bolts.

Because most of the systems on the B-26 are controlled by hydraulics (including the landing gear, brakes, flaps, cowl flaps, oil shutters and bomb doors), the hydraulic system had to be completely rebuilt, and this was the job that took the most time. Problems with the rigging and plumbing of the landing gear required extensive research before the necessary rectification work could be undertaken. Standard B-26 Marauder wheels and brakes were also installed on the aircraft at this time.

All of the control surfaces were re-covered and balanced. This work was completed on 22nd March 1997, and the aircraft was test-flown just three days later. Over the following 12 months the bomber was periodically flown out of Chino by Kermit Weeks, Carl and Tony.

On 10th March 1998 the Marauder left for Florida with Kermit, Tony, Jack McCloy, Ken Kellett and Jay Wisler on board as crew. The chosen route was Chino to Falcon Field in Mesa, Arizona, then on to Las Cruces, New Mexico, and Denton, Texas. On the 11th the B-26 departed Denton with a fuel stop

Photographed at Chino, California, in 1991, B-26-MA 40-1464/N4297J was then owned by the Military Aircraft Restoration Corporation headed up by collector David Tallichet.
Warbird Index

scheduled in Hattiesburg, Missouri, en route to its new home as part of Kermit Weeks' Fantasy of Flight visitor attraction in Polk City.

After displays at several airshows in Florida during 1998, Weeks took the Marauder to the EAA Fly-in at Oshkosh, Wisconsin, where I found the starboard Pratt & Whitney R-2800 Double Wasp radial powerplant 'making metal'. The R-2800 was removed, overhauled and reinstalled in April 1999, and the aircraft flown back to Florida. The Fantasy of Flight crew put a total of 49 flying hours on the aircraft, a significant portion of its 125 hours total flying time.

Above and Below: *The Marauder at Chino in January 1995 when it was being prepared for the ferry flight to Kermit Weeks' facility in Polk City, Florida.* Thierry Thommasin

18

Boeing B-17G Flying Fortress
44-83575/N93012

The Collings Foundation's B-17G-85-DL Flying Fortress 44-83575 was built by the Douglas Aircraft Company at Long Beach, California, and accepted by the USAAF on 7th April 1945. Pressed into service too late to see any combat operations, the aircraft was modified as a TB-17H and SB-17H for air-sea rescue duties and assigned to the 1st Rescue Squadron, Military Air Transport Service, based at Borenquin, Puerto Rico.

In early 1952 the aircraft was passed to the Special Weapons Center at Kirtland AFB, New Mexico. Later it was ferried to Yucca Flats, Nevada, rigged with instrumentation and then exposed to the effects of three different atomic explosions. These tests were conducted in an effort to determine actual damage patterns to aircraft.

Following these tests, '575 was examined by specialists who certified that the aircraft would require several thousand hours of rectification work if it was ever going to fly again. After 13 years of decreasing radiation the aircraft was sold, as part of a job lot, to Valley Scrap Metal. However Aircraft Specialties did not intend to scrap the aircraft, instead commencing a restoration to flying condition. Damaged skins were used as patterns for new skins and these were fitted before the engines and propellers were cleaned up, inspected and tested.

Despite the assessment of the experts, '575 was to soldier on as water bomber No.99 for the next 20 or so years until ownership passed to the Collings Foundation in January 1986. Tom Reilly Vintage Aircraft in Kissimmee, Florida, took on the lengthy restoration task and the company's work paid off when the restored aircraft was adjudged an award-winner, collecting several accolades early in its new career as a warbird.

It was always planned, as with all Collings Foundation bombers, to make the aircraft as available to the American public as possible. This is best achieved by undertaking a tour, and this is accomplished every year in company with the Collings Foundation's B-24J-85-CF Liberator 44-44052/N224J (*see pages 57 to 61 in this book*). Each tour includes flying the bombers thousands of miles, during which the B-17G has been unlucky enough to suffer two major mishaps.

The first occurred in August 1987 when *Nine-O-Nine* was caught by severe crosswinds seconds after touchdown after a display at Beaver County, Pennsylvania, and was forced to settle way down the active runway to make a safe landing. The bomber rolled off the end of the runway, bellied through a chain-link fence, ripped up a power-line pole and slewed into a large ravine. Not surprisingly, this resulted in extensive damage; the main landing gear units were sheared off and the bomb bay doors, ball turret, chin turret, wings and fuselage were all badly smashed. To make matters worse, two engines and their propellers were ripped from the aircraft on its wild ride.

There were no major injuries to the crew or others on board, but despite the valiant efforts of the crew *Nine-O-Nine* looked very sorry sight. Thanks to donations from corporations and individuals, thousands of hours of work went into lovingly restoring the aircraft for a second time. The time, money and effort paid off and *Nine-O-Nine* once again undertook tours of the United States – until 1995, when the aircraft suffered a major main landing gear problem and had to belly-land at Sioux City, Iowa.

While on approach for a normal landing, pilots Jon Rising and Scott Johnson, with Patrick Bunce as crew, selected gear down and heard a loud, disconcerting thud. The gear was switched off as the crew evaluated the problem. They soon realised that while the port main landing gear unit had come down, the starboard unit was barely out of its wheel well. The starboard landing gear was the cause of the loud noise. Patrick was duly despatched to hand-crank the undercarriage but the emergency hand crank turned freely in both directions. After considering all the options, a decision was made to fly the 60 miles (96km) to Sioux City MAP at a high power setting to burn off some of the 1,200 gallons (4,542 litres) of fuel onboard.

The reason for choosing to head for Sioux City MAP was because it offered a wider runway than the original destination and had more support facilities for aircraft like the B-17. After further consultations with the operations people at the Collings Foundation, the airport manager agreed to foam the runway. Jon and Scott reviewed procedures for landing on one main wheel; their major concern was that the deployed wheel would fold back under the wing and push the turbocharger into the No.2 fuel cell – fire was a real possibility.

As the aircraft approached the airfield, Jon, Scott and Patrick were informed that the decision to foam the runway had been reversed – but they had been running the engines at high power settings to burn off fuel and were thus committed to a landing. The lumbering, stricken B-17 was close to the airfield and so ATC gave permission for her to land. As the aircraft rolled out on finals the batteries were shut off and the magnetos, mixtures and master bar were shut down as she flared for touchdown. The port wing began to drop; this forced the landing gear unit to take the strain and then collapse. As it did so, the drag link knuckle joint folded out instead of in. *Nine-O-Nine* protested as her weight put pressure on the drag link, delaying the impact of the wing on the runway surface. Finally the drag link gave way and *Nine-O-Nine* yawed to the left, pulling toward the grass. Jon Rising stood on the right brakes in a valiant attempt to stop a huge ground loop; it worked and the aircraft came to a halt at the intersection of the two main runways having turned through 90°.

Scott had the cockpit window open and the two pilots egressed the flightdeck area and headed towards the rear of the aircraft. Not one of the crew had as much as a scratch. The recovery process began quickly and less than three weeks later *Nine-O-Nine* was airborne on her first post-crash test flight before departing Sioux City en route to Valparaiso to join her B-24J sister-ship.

After each year's US tour, *Nine-O-Nine* flies south to New Smyrna Beach, Florida, for essential winter maintenance, conducted by Gary Norville and his team at American Aero Services. Gary and his team have maintained the B-17G since 1991. Maintenance is conducted over a two to three-month period, usually commencing in November. Whilst the bomber is 'grounded' it receives everything from routine maintenance to engine changes, sheet metal repairs and complete systems checks and overhaul. Major work has included the removal of the wings for inspection of the wing spars for cracks and corrosion as the result of a well-publicised Airworthiness Directive issued by the FAA in 1994.

Many people ask how much the big bomber costs to operate, but calculating an accurate figure is becoming increasingly difficult due to the rising price of fuel, insurance and other maintenance costs.

For example, at February 2000 prices, overhaul of the aircraft's four 1,200-hp (895-kW) R-1820-97 engines cost between $30,000 and $35,000 plus $5,000 to change each engine and its accessories. Each engine will normally run for 1,000 hours before an overhaul is required.

Fuel consumption is 200 US gallons (757 litres) per hour at cruise and this figure more than doubles at higher power settings. Oil consumption is also relevant, coming in at up to 2 US gallons (7.6 litres) per hour per engine. An oil change con-

sumes 35 US gallons (132 litres). Each year the aircraft undergoes 25, 50 and 100-hour routine inspections. The major check and annual maintenance programme involves up to seven mechanics for a period of six weeks and can cost as much as $200,000 depending on how much work is required.

Based on a calculated figure of 30 hours' maintenance for each hour of flight, the overall operating cost comes to more than $2,000 per flying hour. This puts into perspective the financial input required to keep this historic bomber in the air.

The B-17G is finished as 42-31909/OR-R of the 323rd BS, 91st BG 'The Ragged Irregulars'. Based at Bassingbourn in Cambridgeshire, the original '909 flew 140 consecutive missions over Europe without an abort. Patrick Bunce

19

Supermarine Spitfire LF.Vb
BM597/G-MKVB

The final months of 1940 saw the Luftwaffe despatching the new Messerschmitt Bf 109F on attack profiles over southern England. This aircraft flew higher – up to 38,000ft (11,582m) according to combat reports – and faster than any of its predecessors. Bearing in mind that the Hawker Hurricane could only reach 20,000ft (6,096m) for combat operations and the Supermarine Spitfire I and IIs had difficulty reaching 36,000ft (10,973m), the Bf 109F's altitude advantage posed a real problem for RAF Fighter Command.

Several meetings involving senior RAF officers followed and it was noted that modifications to the Spitfire airframe would be unlikely to have any effect on the performance of the aircraft at higher altitudes. The answer lay in the development of the Rolls-Royce Merlin powerplant and in particular the supercharger.

Rolls-Royce was already testing and developing a two-stage supercharger for the Merlin. The unit was fitted to the Merlin XX

engine that had been produced in small numbers, mainly for installation in the Spitfire III. After further discussions and analysis of flight test results, Rolls-Royce agreed that the engine's high-altitude performance should be further developed. What resulted was the Merlin RM5S, or Merlin 45, which would increase the Spitfire's service ceiling by 2,000ft (609m).

As the Merlin III was already in production, orders were issued that these engines should be modified as soon as possible. Three development Spitfires were quickly fitted with the 1,440-hp (1,074-kW) Merlin 45 and testing commenced at A&AEE Boscombe Down, Wiltshire. With the new engine the Spitfire could climb to 20,000ft (6,096m) in 6.2 minutes and reach 38,000ft (11,582m) in order to meet the challenge from the Bf 109F. It was soon established that the modified Merlin 45-equipped Spitfire was a success and the Air Ministry urged Supermarine and Rolls-Royce to expedite the new

model into service without undue delay.

Following trials, a decision was made to marry the Merlin 45 to a strengthened Spitfire Mk I fuselage, and install a larger radiator. The new aircraft would be designated Spitfire V, generally accepted to be the most successful variant of the Spitfire family. After some initial problems with oil coolers, some 23 Spitfires were converted at the Rolls-Royce factory at Hucknall near Nottingham.

By spring 1941 many converted Spitfire Mk Is and Vs were being delivered to RAF Fighter Command squadrons, enabling them to meet the Bf 109F threat head-on. By the following May, when the Spitfire V was officially unveiled, it was already in full production.

Built in 1942, Spitfire Vb BM597 was amongst a batch of 1,000 aircraft assembled at the Supermarine factory at Castle

Charlie Brown flies BM597 close to the camera-ship for a beautiful air-to-air study. Richard Paver

Bromwich, Birmingham, under contract B981687/39 and delivered to 5 MU at RAF Burtonwood, near Manchester in April 1942. In May the aircraft was assigned to 315 (Polish) Squadron at RAF Woodvale, Merseyside, followed by a further assignment on 5th September to the co-located 317 (Polish) Squadron with whom it wore the codes JH-C. Whilst in service with this unit the aircraft suffered Cat B damage in combat on 13th February 1943. It required extensive repairs by de Havillands and further modifications were made by Vickers Armstrong before it was allocated to 33 MU.

In June 1943 BM597 returned to Vickers Armstrong, possibly for engineering modifications before it was transferred to 39 MU at RAF Colerne, Wiltshire. January 1944 saw BM597 transferred to RAF High Ercall, Shropshire, for close on a year's storage with 222 MU, after which it was issued to 58 OTU in 1945, the aircraft's last military assignment. On 16th October 1945, BM597 was relegated to instructional airframe status and moved to 4 School of Technical Training at RAF St Athan, South Glamorgan, and allocated maintenance serial 5713M.

After use as a training aid at St Athan, BM597 was moved to RAF Hednesford as a gate guard, followed by postings to Bridgnorth and eventually RAF Church Fenton in

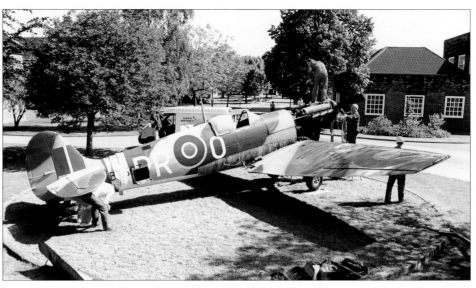

BM597 patriotically guarded the gate at RAF Church Fenton until it was removed following the now famous exchange between businessman Tim Routsis and the Ministry of Defence. Author

BM597 as 'valuable cargo' being secured ready for the trip down the A1 from RAF Church Fenton and into temporary storage at Braintree, Essex. Author

BM597 in temporary storage, following its removal from the gate at RAF Church Fenton. Author

Yorkshire, where it was once again sat on the gate and exposed to the elements.

In 1967 the aircraft was removed from its position on the gate and transported to RAF Henlow, Bedfordshire, for possible use in the film *Battle of Britain*. However, the Spitfire did not fly during the filming; instead, in October 1967, it was used as the master aircraft from which the moulds for fibreglass Spitfires (for destruction and set dressing in the film) were produced. This work took place at Pinewood Studios, Hertfordshire, where the aircraft remained until 1968, after which it was transported back to RAF Henlow by road for checking prior to its return to RAF Church Fenton. It served as a gate guard at RAF Linton-on-Ouse, Yorkshire, from

1975 until 1979 before being assigned back to RAF Church Fenton where it was again placed on the gate following basic refurbishment from 1979 until 1988.

In 1985, British businessman Tim Routsis began negotiations with the Ministry of Defence's Historic Aircraft Committee with a view to obtaining five gate guard aircraft: Spitfire XVIs TE476 (RAF Northolt), TD248 (RAF Sealand), RW382 (RAF Uxbridge), TB252 (RAF Bentley Priory) and the subject of this story, Spitfire V BM597, from the gate at RAF Church Fenton. In exchange, the RAF Museum at Hendon would receive a Curtiss P-40 and a Bristol Beaufort VIII. Routsis also contracted London-based Feggans Brown to manufacture and supply a mixture of 12

Above left: Restoration of BM597 commences at Audley End. This aircraft was always considered to be the jewel in the crown by Tim Routsis and it was originally his intention to have it restored for himself. Author

Above: Despite its long-term exposure to the often less than hospitable English climate, internally BM597 was in reasonable condition, probably as a result of the care and attention administered to it by its RAF inventory holder. Author

Having been stripped down to virtually nothing, Spitfire LF Vb BM597 comes 'back up' at the hands of the original Historic Flying restoration team at Audley End. The engine bearers had just been installed when this photograph was taken. Author

Spitfire and Hurricane GRP 'dummies' to replace the real aircraft.

At the same time, the Ministry of Defence decided that the surviving historic Hurricane and Spitfire 'gate guards' should indeed be removed and offered for exchange to boost the RAF Museum collection. This was not the first time such an arrangement had been made. The late Doug Arnold of Warbirds of Great Britain had struck a similar deal with the Ministry of Defence, which saw three Spitfire XVIs transferred to his ownership in exchange for aircraft supplied to the RAF Museum at Hendon.

Over a period of several months, all five Spitfires left their posts at the RAF Stations. In June 1988 BM597 was unceremoniously removed from the gate at RAF Church Fenton and transported to a storage shed where it awaited its turn in the queue for rebuild to fly. Nearly a year later, on 2nd May 1989, the aircraft was appropriately registered G-MKVB to Historic Flying Ltd (the name of the company founded by Tim Routsis, Clive Denney and Ian Warren).

Once Historic Flying had taken up residence at Audley End airfield in Essex, BM597 was transported to the new premises where it remained in storage for the best part of five years. The aircraft was duly sold on to The Historic Aircraft Collection Jersey, Channel Islands, on 4th November 1993, and Historic Flying was commissioned to undertake a full rebuild to airworthy status.

The Rolls-Royce Merlin 35 engine was removed from the fuselage engine mount and sent for rebuild by Rolls-Royce specialists Paul and Andy Wood at Great Easton, Essex. Meantime the fuselage was placed in a custom-built jig and checked for alignment, before being dismantled right down to the stringers and frames. Many of these had to be replaced and new skins cut and formed. Every rivet in the aircraft was replaced. The wings were bolted leading edge down in a special jig and completely refurbished with new wing spars and extrusions; the majority of wing skin panels were also replaced with new.

The stripped-out and completely reskinned fuselage was painted internally and externally and 'baked' in the special unit held by the company. The fuselage and wings were duly mated upon completion of the work. Individual systems components were overhauled or replaced before being reassembled and repositioned into the restored aircraft's fuselage. On the Spitfire, systems installation takes many hours before the engine can be 'plumbed in'. Additionally, all-new hardware was used throughout BM597, which is also equipped with a new electrical wiring loom, new coolant pipes and all-new hydraulics systems.

Historic Flying Ltd is the main commercial Spitfire restoration company in the world. Work on BM597, their third Spitfire V, followed restoration of EP120 for The

Flight Lieutenant Charlie Brown, RAF in BM597 shows off the upper wing camouflage pattern to advantage. Uwe Glaser

Fighter Collection and AR614 for the Alpine Fighter Collection in New Zealand (this aircraft has since been sold to Flying Heritage Inc in Seattle, Washington). The company was able to make BM597 their best-ever restoration by using the knowledge they had gained from restoring the previous two airframes. It flew for the first time after restoration on 20th July 1997.

In an emotional reunion in July 1999, BM597 was reacquainted with two of its former World War Two Polish pilots, Squadron Leader Ludwik Martel and Squadron Leader Tadeuz Anderz. The restored aircraft had been finished as JH-C of 317 (Polish) Squadron, complete with a prominent Polish Air Force insignia beneath the exhaust stubs and the squadron badge immediately aft of the cockpit.

For several months in the summer of 2000 the aircraft took part in the filming of *Pearl Harbor*, where it represented a Spitfire (AR352/RF-C) of the 'Eagle' Squadron. A further film appearance came the following year when BM597 was painted for use in *Dark Blue World*. The aircraft is currently based at Duxford, Cambridgeshire, from where it is operated by the Historic Aircraft Collection.

20

North American P-51D Mustang
45-11507/N921

One of an initial batch of 30 of a planned 370 P-51D Mustangs ordered by New Zealand to replace Vought F4U-1 Corsairs in service with the RNZAF's 12 operational fighter squadrons, P-51D-2-NT 45-11507 arrived in New Zealand on 6th September 1945. The war having ended, the New Zealand Government cancelled the bulk of the 370-aircraft contract, but it was committed to acceptance of the first batch of 30 Mustangs, which had already been shipped.

On arrival in New Zealand the Mustangs were immediately transferred to the RNZAF base at Hobsonville, covered in a rubberised Plastiphane coating to help prevent corrosion, and placed into storage. In February 1947 barges and tank transporters were used to move the redundant aircraft to Ardmore, where they sat for a further four and a half years. In August 1951 a decision was taken to activate a trial batch of six aircraft to

evaluate them for Territorial Air Force use. The TAF had been reformed in 1948 and comprised 1 Squadron (Auckland), 2 Squadron (Wellington), 3 Squadron (Canterbury) and 4 Squadron (Otago).

In June 1952 45-11507 was delivered to 3 Squadron at Woodbourne and allocated serial NZ2417. After an uneventful career with the TAF the aircraft was officially retired from service on 11th August 1955 and put into storage at Woodbourne the following day. By June 1957 the last of the RNZAF Mustangs had been retired from service and the airframes passed to the Government Stores board for 'disposal'. A batch of 19 airframes, one of which was NZ2417, was offered for disposal in April 1958.

The following month, farmer Ron Fetchney purchased NZ2417 for the sum of NZ $75. To enable transportation to Fetchney's Aylesbury property the aircraft's wings were

torched off just outboard of the main undercarriage bays. However, a new mainplane was acquired from Melvin Grooby at the ANSA company and the Mustang, by now registered ZK-CCG, was restored to flying condition. The aircraft took to the air for the first time in November 1964, complete with the mainplane from NZ2409.

Despite the aircraft's excellent condition the New Zealand Aviation Authority insisted that it be maintained to airliner standards. Furthermore, because the aircraft was not certificated as a civilian aircraft in New Zealand and there were no civilian maintenance records, NZ2417 had to be completely taken apart, thoroughly inspected and signed off down to the smallest component.

By this time Captain Jack MacDonald, a pilot with New Zealand National Airways Corporation, had become involved with the project and through his offices the rigorous inspection of the aircraft was carried out in the airline's workshops, with Jack himself carrying out the majority of the work. The task was made easier by the fact that a large spares holding had been made available when the aircraft was purchased. This included two zero-time Rolls-Royce Merlin engines, radiators, a propeller, main landing gears, ailerons and several other miscellaneous bits and pieces.

The aircraft was finally certified in November 1964 (it flew for the first time following restoration on 29th November) and both MacDonald and Fetchney displayed the aircraft at several airshows before it was once again put into storage in Fetchney's barn in 1968, due to lack of funds. The Mobil Oil Company had agreed to provide funding in exchange for prominent display of their logo on the side of the Mustang.

Five years later, John J Schafhausen visited Fetchney's farm to view the aircraft. Schafhausen's father was a personal friend of Jack MacDonald and had asked him to bear him in mind if ever the aircraft came up for sale. Negotiations went on for a year and eventually the aircraft was sold to Schafhausen. On 4th April 1974 ZK-CCG was flown to Christchurch where it was dismantled for shipment to the United States. Packed into a standard-size shipping container along with the spares holding, the Mustang arrived safely at Seattle, Washington, successfully cleared US Customs, and then was despatched to Spokane, Washington, by road.

In late 1974, with assistance from personnel stationed at Fairchild AFB, Bob Shockley supervised the reassembly of the Mustang. John Herlihy, well known for his work with the Grumman F8F Bearcat, flew to Spokane in early 1975 to test-fly the aircraft, which by then had been registered N921.

John Schafhausen was very keen to see the Mustang dressed in an authentic colour scheme at a time when it was perfectly acceptable for warbirds to wear civilian colour schemes. After examining several books on the 8th AF, he decided the Mustang should be painted to represent the personal mount of Major George 'Ratsy' Preddy, who flew with the 352nd FG when it was based at Bodney, Norfolk (and later in Belgium) during World War Two.

Following reassembly the aircraft was test-flown and then ferried to Aero Paint Systems at Renton, Washington, where painter Jerry Lindberg took on the challenge of recreating the paint scheme for Preddy's Mustang which was *named Cripes A'Mighty 3rd*. After studying available photographs of Preddy's aircraft, N921's old white paint was stripped off. The aircraft was then etched and primed before the new colours were applied over a period of six weeks.

John Schafhausen flew the aircraft weekly over the next few years before Gene Stocker of State College, Pennsylvania, purchased it in 1978. Stocker's ownership of N921 was brief and in 1979 the aircraft was acquired by

Kermit Weeks for his Weeks Air Museum, then located at Tamiami, Florida. In 1982 the aircraft was the subject of significant restoration work. Some ten years later, in August 1992, Hurricane 'Andrew' swept through Florida and caused immense damage to several areas, including the Weeks Air Museum. One of the aircraft damaged during the storm was N921. Some months later the aircraft was shipped to Cal Pacific Airmotive in Salinas, California, where it was completely restored, to much the same very high standards as Kermit Weeks' beautiful P-51C-10-NT 42-103831/N1204 (*see pages 51 to 53 in this book*).

21

Goodyear FG-1D Corsair
BuNo 92471/N773RD

The Vought F4U Corsair (and those built by Goodyear as the FG and F2G) is a somewhat neglected fighter type, but one that is at last gaining recognition in the warbird community, with a record amount of restoration activity now being invested in surviving members of the Corsair family. At the time of writing some 15 of the 52 survivors are being restored, the majority to flying condition.

When they designed the Corsair, Vought created the most outstanding naval fighter of World War Two, and undoubtedly one of the best piston-engined fighters ever manufactured. Designer Rex Beisel had actually started design work on the type in 1936, striving to develop a high-performance fighter based around the Pratt & Whitney R-2800 Double Wasp, the most powerful engine then available and also in the early stages of its development. In February 1938 Beisel submitted two designs in response to the US Bureau of Aeronautics' requirement for a new single-seat, high-performance monoplane armed with at least four machine guns, the V-166A and V-166B. On 30th June 1938 a prototype was ordered under the designation

XF4U-1; the aircraft flew for the first time on 29th May 1940. The rest, as they say, is history.

In addition to production of the F4U-1D fighter bomber by Vought and Brewster, Goodyear built a total of 2,302 FG-1Ds powered by the 2,250-hp (1,679-kW) water-injected Pratt & Whitney R-2800-8W Double Wasp. Ray Dieckman acquired his FG-1D, BuNo 92471, from Dianne Tope in March 1995, and soon afterwards began the monumental task of rebuilding the airframe to flying condition.

The late Harry Tope had started to rebuild the Corsair from scratch, so it had first been completely dismantled. Some work was undertaken by Kal-Aero in Kalamazoo, Michigan. However, Ray wasn't happy with just getting the aircraft back in the air. He wanted to achieve only the highest standards and make the aircraft an award-winner in every respect, so he chose to ensure that the aircraft was totally original, with just a few 'compromises' he felt were necessary to ensure safety during flight.

The first task was to move the aircraft from its former home in Michigan to Chino

Airport, California, where Ray has his hangar. On arrival the aircraft and all the spare parts were duly unloaded. Though Ray was no stranger to warbird restoration, having both seen and assisted the workers at Chino-based Fighter Rebuilders on various projects, he was filled with trepidation as he considered how he would turn the large pile of components into a living, breathing FG-1D Corsair. Based on the knowledge he had gained working on other projects, Ray first made an inventory of all the parts and began preparing himself and the hangar for the restoration task ahead. Ray knew that he had the makings of a very interesting project.

The dismantled Corsair had been stripped of all internal parts and the ailerons were missing – and that was just for starters. Early on, it was discovered that the engine mount would need significant work. Roger Lamb of Lamb Components (specialists in supplying

An excellent air-to-air study showing the now famous two-tone blue, flat finish paint on Ray Dieckman's FG-1D. Frank Mormillo

Right: *Structural work was well advanced on the centre section of Ray Dieckman's FG-1D Corsair N733RD in August 1995.* Warbird Index

Centre: *March 1997 and N733RD was on its main gear.* Thierry Thomassin

Bottom and overleaf: *With yellow zinc paint on the wings and fuselage, national insignia applied and the giant R-2800-79 Double Wasp engine installed, the project begins to resemble a real Corsair.* Frank Mormillo

components for drag racing vehicles) took on the task of rebuilding the engine mount. To construct the ailerons, Ray acquired original drawings and was loaned a set of ailerons from Richard Bertea, the (then) owner of Chino-based F4U-5NL Corsair BuNo 124486/N49068. Tony Fuicama took on the task of constructing the new ailerons.

Meantime, so as not to have the venture awaiting parts, Ray trawled the aviation parts and spares sources across the United States, and even made it known that he was prepared to travel overseas to obtain the missing parts required to restore his aircraft. One of the first parts to be made from scratch was an accessory cowling as this was also missing from the original package. It took almost three years for the project to give the appearance of moving forward, although anyone closely associated with any restoration project will tell you that it is more difficult to see such progress when you are working on the aircraft yourself.

When Harry Tope commenced his restoration of the aircraft, he elected to paint the cockpit light grey, but this was not what Ray Dieckman wanted and so the cockpit was stripped of grey paint and refinished using an imron green that gives the appearance of zinc chromate. Preservation Instruments donated the original instruments required to make the cockpit area as representative of a World War Two FG-1D Corsair as possible, and much research was done to establish the original cockpit layout, colours and finishes. The airframe was void of all hydraulic pipes and equipment, so all of these items had to be manufactured, trial-fitted, removed, finished in a yellow zinc colour and then permanently installed with new couplings and fittings.

At an early stage in the project, Ray decided that he wanted a rear seat installed. The seat had to be custom-made and rear windows had to be manufactured to fit the airframe. The windows had to be jettisonable to facilitate rear passenger egress in the event of an emergency. Now, if the need should ever arise, the back-seater can bale out of the aircraft.

A Pratt & Whitney R-2800-79 was obtained and installed by Day Air of Stockton, California. This version of the engine would allow the fitting of a non-standard (but worthwhile) pre-oiler to help guarantee the longevity of the powerplant. Sun Air Parts donated a large number of components for

the engine rebuild. The huge, three-bladed Hamilton Standard propeller unit was over-hauled by Golden State Propeller and fin-ished in the correct markings and stencils before it was attached to the aircraft.

As the project continued to advance, Ray's search for Corsair parts took on renewed vigour. His travels took him as far afield as New Zealand, where he was able to tap into a small treasure trove of parts and other 'bits and pieces' from ex-RNZAF Cor-sairs. The parts included new but original firewall linings and many others that would prove very useful.

Jim Morin fitted a GPS system and new King Gold Crown radios into the Corsair. Bill Mix took on a lot of the detailing work that contributed significantly to the quest to make this aircraft an award-winner. Very often it is this accurate detailing that scores the extra points necessary to beat the oppo-sition. Roger Sperber supplied a lot of the hardware and contributed towards the mechanical aspects of the restoration. L&L Anodizing is credited with undertaking the enormous amount of anodizing and metal-plating of components throughout the air-craft. EFS Hydraulics provided a complete overhaul of the hydraulic systems. Standard Aircraft Parts supplied the copper conduit for the aircraft, with Sherri Dieckman work-ing on the large amounts of wiring bundles on her dining-room table!

The Corsair really started to take shape in mid-1999. The *Marine's Dream* colour scheme, in the colours of Corsair ace Major Ken Walsh, was applied using paint donated by the Deft Paint Company, and stunning it looks too in its authentic two-tone blue fin-ish. The US Marine Corps was renowned for its fighting spirit and many pilots achieved 'acedom' flying the Corsair, including VMF-214's Colonel Gregory 'Pappy' Boying-ton (28 victories), Major Joe Foss (26) and the aforementioned Major Ken Walsh (21).

By early 2000 the project had made sev-eral more major advances and the engine was ground-run and systems tweaked ready for the first flight, the day of which was approaching rapidly. As an added bonus, the aircraft's Goodyear data plate was taken into space aboard the Space Shuttle by cel-ebrated Marine John Glenn and Kurt Brown.

After five years of determined effort, sourcing parts around the globe, long hours in the workshop and meticulous attention to detail, *Marine's Dream*, registered N773RD, took to the air for its first post-restoration test flight on 26th May 2000. Just two months later, Ray attended the EAA Oshkosh Con-vention with the aircraft and was awarded Reserve Grand Champion by the discerning EAA Judges at the event. Ray Dieckman him-self was rewarded with the Golden Wrench Award for his valiant efforts in restoring to its former military glory what was once little more than a stripped-out hulk.

The cockpit of N733RD in September 2000 as the project approached completion. Frank Mormillo

22

Hawker Hind
K5414/G-AENP

Developed to meet Air Ministry Specification G.7/34, the Hawker Hind was a replacement for the Hawker Hart; basically, a stopgap fighter prior to the introduction into RAF service of the Bristol Blenheim and Fairey Battle. However, if one took a snapshot of the RAF in the early 1930s, it would not be difficult to imagine Hart and Hind domination, for the RAF was equipped almost exclusively with both.

The main differences between the Hind and the earlier Hart were the powerplant (a Rolls-Royce Kestrel V) and the incorporation of refinements such as the cut-down rear cockpit developed for the Hawker Demon. The Hind prototype (K2915) was constructed in haste due to Hawker's development work, and made its first flight on 12th September 1934. Subsequent to the first flight, many other refinements were made and other engine options proposed. The first production Hind (K4636) was flown on 4th September 1935, with the type entering RAF service just two months later. As aircraft were delivered they equipped some 20 RAF bomber squadrons. Foreign air arms that acquired the Hind included

This shot of K5414 shows the aircraft looking all the more authentic thanks to the addition of four dummy bombs on the underwing shackles. Bob Munro

The Shuttleworth Collection's Afghan Hind in its original Afghan Air Force colours. Worthy of note are the external ballast weights visible just behind the Afghan roundel. James Kightly

Afghanistan, Latvia, Persia (later Iran), Portugal, Switzerland and Yugoslavia.

Just two years later, in 1937, the Hind was phased out of front-line service with the RAF, finding a new niche as a trainer; a number were also supplied to Commonwealth countries, including New Zealand. No wonder then that the Shuttleworth Trust at Old Warden, Bedfordshire, began a search for a Hind to add to the Shuttleworth Collection. The catalyst was the retirement from flying duties of Hawker's very own Hart biplane, which was destined to enter the RAF Museum at Hendon, London.

Fill her up, sir? The almost bizarre sight of K5414 being refuelled at Old Warden.

K5414 getting airborne on a test flight from Old Warden following rectification work. The aircraft has worn the markings of XV Squadron for a number of years. Both Bob Munro

When the Shuttleworth Trust began its search for a Hind in the late 1960s, it soon discovered that the last few remaining examples were to be found in Afghanistan. Some eight new-build Hinds had been delivered to the Afghan Air Force in 1938; later they were joined by another 12 examples from RAF stocks. The 20 Hinds remained in Afghan service until 1956 when, remarkably, they were simply put into storage at Bagram, north of the capital Kabul, and forgotten about!

When the Shuttleworth Trust contacted the authorities in Afghanistan to enquire about the possible donation of a Hind, the reaction was positive. The Afghan Government imposed few conditions, one of which was that the aircraft should be exhibited in an Afghan Air Force paint scheme following its rebuild to fly. In late 1970 the Commander-in-Chief Afghan Air Force, General Gulbahar, presented the aircraft to the Shuttleworth Collection and plans were made to recover the bare airframe to Old Warden, where it would be rebuilt to fly.

Following the offer of logistical support from the Ford Motor Company, plans were made to undertake the 6,000-mile (9,654-km) road trip to repatriate the rare biplane fighter. The long and arduous recovery operation was fraught with difficulties, but eventually the aircraft arrived at Old Warden for the start of an equally difficult restoration. Stripping of the airframe revealed some interesting and makeshift repairs that had been carried out in Afghanistan in a desperate attempt to extend the aircraft's useful service life, which came to an end when

the Afghan Air Force ran out of spare parts.

The first problem occurred when both the radiator and oil cooler were duly despatched to SERC for restoration. Though the oil cooler could be repaired and overhauled, the radiator was in too poor condition to restore. As luck would have it, Hawker Siddeley offered a swap with the Hart's radiator, as the latter aircraft was about to be incarcerated in the RAF Museum – but fate duly scuppered that plan when it was discovered that the Hart's radiator was beyond economical repair. Enter Cambridge Radiators, who until this time had specialised in car units. After some discussions, the drawing up of well-laid plans and the cutting and placement of 4,000 tubes, a new radiator for the Hind was ready.

Essentially, the framework of the Hind is a combination of Hawker square-ended, custom-made tubing and a complex crafted series of wooden sections, stringers and other structures, completed with the addition of fabric. When it came to restoring the framework, fate intervened again – this time favourably – because the spar and fuselage metal framework were deemed to be recoverable. (It is interesting to note that this was many years before Guy Black commissioned the manufacture of spar material to restore his Hawker biplanes.) However, every piece of the woodwork had to be replaced. The original airframe was fitted with a Palmer brake system but this was beyond economical repair and deemed a hazard, so a pneumatic system from a Hawker Hart was fitted instead.

The aircraft's Hawker lineage and the immaculate fabric work on the upper and lower wings and tailplane are clear to see. Bob Munro

Though it looks every inch a fighter, the Hind is a labour-intensive aeroplane to keep airworthy. The Rolls-Royce Kestrel V-12 in-line engine is lifed at a mere 30 to 40 flying hours, with the Afghan-type engine leaded main bearings costing up to £7,000 each time they need to be replaced. The Hind is now equipped with a set of lead bronze bearings with an 'unknown' life span. The cylinder liners are now permanent, with a set costing £6,000. The engine has to be pre-oiled after just three to four days of inactivity; this job takes three to four man-hours each time it has to be performed. The Annual CAA Permit renewal takes 40 man-hours. Routine tasks, like pre-flight checks, take about three man-hours. The engine requires an oil change (10 gallons; 45 litres) each year and similarly consumes 10 gallons of glycol. In flight the engine drinks a cool 10 gallons of fuel an hour; five gallons (23 litres) of oil are consumed in a year of normal operation.

With commercial engineering rates currently at £30 per hour, the cost of insurance, CAA fees (display licences), Annual Permit renewal costs as well as fixed staff costs, it can be seen that the Shuttleworth Collection's appearance fees don't even cover the Hind's basic annual costs. Nevertheless, its spirited performances make K5414 a firm favourite with airshow crowds.

23

Northrop N9M-B
N9MB

First flown in 1942, the N9M was a one-third scale prototypes for the B-35/B-49 'Flying Wing' bombers, its primary role being to test the fully powered irreversible hydraulic flight control system used in the B-35.

The N9M-1, the first of the four N9Ms built, was lost after 30 hours' flying time. The N9M-2 and N9M-A, respectively the second and third aircraft, suffered powerplant problems, that is a lack of power, and were retired early. Both utilised 260-hp (194-kW) Menasco air-cooled engines, inferior to the 315-hp (235-kW) eight-cylinder Franklin X0540-7s used by the N9M-B, the fourth and final example to be built. The latter aircraft first flew in 1944 and made its last flight for Northrop in May 1949. Though the Menasco-powered aircraft were simply written off and scrapped, the N9M-B was more fortunate in that one of the original warbird pioneers, Ed Maloney, acquired it in the early 1950s for the nascent Planes of Fame Museum.

It was some 30 years later that fate took a hand in proceedings when one of the original team who worked for Jack Northrop on the 'Flying Wing' Programme, Bion Provost, visited the Planes of Fame Museum at Chino, California, and saw the remains of the N9M-B. Due to his involvement with the original programme and his specialist knowledge, he realised that what he was looking at could be the sole survivor of the XB-35 and YB-49 bomber projects.

Highly motivated, Provost immediately talked to Planes of Fame Museum officials, at the same time offering his own services to help get the N9M-B back in the air. Undaunted by the huge challenge the restoration presented, Planes of Fame reacted favourably and a series of meetings was held, with Provost present, in order to see how the project could be advanced to fruition.

It was early 1981 when work commenced at two sites in Southern California, Chino Airport and Hawthorne Airport, and by the summer all available components were moved to a permanent site at Signal Hill, California. The work was split into two major parts: the wooden wings and control surfaces; and the tubing of the aircraft's centre section, which included the engines, landing gear and cockpit section.

At the outset, efforts were concentrated on the aircraft's centre section. All the components were carefully stripped out and recorded. The undercarriage and the Franklin engines were contracted out for specialist overhaul. The tubular centre section was painstakingly stripped, sandblasted and then all the welds checked for corrosion, cracks and other damage. Oil was then flushed through the tubular framework before it was prepared for painting. Completion of work on this all-important centre section framework was an indication that real progress was being made.

Sadly, due to product liability considerations, the Northrop Corporation – consulted early on in the project – had declined to offer any assistance due to the fact that the Planes of Fame Museum intended that the restored N9M-B would fly on completion of the restoration work. This lack of access to any drawings or other documentation proved to be a major obstacle to the museum staff and volunteers working on the project. However a series of glossy photographs, taken by Northrop during the original construction process, proved to be most useful. These precious items were originally used by Northrop to illustrate progress reports demanded by the USAAF. Fortunately, copies of the photographs were obtained from aviation historian Gary Blazer's photographic collection. They say a picture is worth a thousand words and in this particular case it was indeed so, for the photographs enabled the team to undertake some intricate reverse engineering.

Like many projects involving rare and unique aircraft, Project N9M widely utilised this reverse-engineering process. First, each of the project volunteers would take a particular component or area of the aircraft and investigate what was located there originally. This in turn enabled the team to establish what materials and tools would be required to complete the restoration (or in some cases, reconstruction) of that particular part or area. Very often, tooling and jigs had to be manufactured from scratch to accomplish the task. Any parts that were obtainable 'off the shelf' would be ordered along with the required tools. On arrival the parts would be checked, painted (if required) and then installed. Writing about the process is a lot simpler than accomplishing any of the actual tasks!

During the gradual refurbishment of the fuselage centre section the restoration team's attention also turned to the construction of the wooden wing. As the raw materials arrived – spruce, aircraft mahogany plywood and preg-wood – plans were being made to start work on the wing itself. The dedicated team worked tirelessly every weekend for some 12 years. As the remaining original wing sections were in such a poor state and continuing to deteriorate, none of the original material could be utilised in the restoration project. The result was that the entire wing structure had to be constructed from scratch – reverse engineering at its finest.

Fortunately, the lofted drawings for the NACA airfoils were documented. Utilising this information and measurements taken from the original wings, a master drawing of the outer mould line for each rib was produced. These drawings provided the final wing shape at each station. By using the remnants of the old wing ribs as patterns, new ribs could be constructed using the same materials as in the original.

To assist in assembling the valuable new wing structures, a lofting platform measuring some 12 x 25ft (3.65 x 7.62m) was manufactured. The surface was painted white and the entire wing loft profile was transferred to the surface. The leading edge, trailing edge, spars and ribs were all located. The root rib was clamped in place, the spars built outwards and the ribs fitted. This entire process – again sounding simple on paper – took five years to accomplish and certainly tested the will of the team to see Project N9M through to completion.

One problem that quickly became apparent was the lack of information on where the stringers actually passed through the ribs. The solution was to 'dry fit' the ribs and hold them in place on the spar until all of the wing ribs were completed. Chalk lines were made on the top and bottom to indicate the position of the stringers, enabling the wing ribs to be removed, and stringer supports, vertical on one side of the rib and diagonal on the other, were glued into position. The completed, marked ribs were then permanently installed and the stringers carefully cut in. The completed structure was then covered in a beautiful hand-made aircraft mahogany skin. The plywood had to be steam-bent over the leading edge, tragically covering all of the hard work previously accomplished to such high standards!

By early 1990 the entire structure began to resemble a Northrop N9M as both wings and the centre section were assembled for a trial fit. On checking, the entire geometry, wing-tip-to-wing-tip, was a mere 3/16in (4.76mm) across the entire 60-ft (18.28-m) wing span.

Stepping back a few years, the entire project had been moved again from Signal Hill to space at Wiggin's Connectors in the nearby city of Commerce. As work on the aircraft progressed, perhaps to the untrained eye painfully slowly, the team remained pretty much the same in number (25 seemed to be the most stable number of workers at any one time), with new people coming on board as others left. Many of the new volunteers had heard of the project through the publicity material issued at the annual Planes of Fame Airshow at Chino. The average Saturday work party numbered between eight and twelve. As if by magic, various specialists – aircraft instrumentation, radio equipment, electrical, propeller, fire suppression – arrived, seemingly at just the right moment. Fate is the hunter!

Suppliers also had an important part to play. Well over 100 companies donated materials, tools and expertise, many in no small measure. Without such donations the project simply would not – could not – have been completed.

Two views of work under way on the N9M-B that show to good effect the high standard of restoration and rebuild work inherent in the project, especially in the woodwork of the wing structure. From start of work to first flight, restoration of the N9M-B took nearly 14 years to complete. Thierry Thomassin

Following the 'dry' assembly process, the wings were removed from the centre section and finished. This meant contouring, installation of flying controls and hydraulic systems, and the skinning and cutting out of numerous access doors. At the same time, work proceeded on the centre section: the radios and flight instrumentation were installed in the cockpit and the complicated hydraulics system was fitted, connected up

and tested. A major milestone was achieved when the undercarriage, sat on jacks, was retracted and extended for the first time.

While the wings were being skinned with mahogany ply, work commenced on the control surfaces. Dave Murray and a small band of helpers built the inboard and outboard flaps and elevons (the latter are in fact ailerons that work together for pitch control). Over a five-year period, Ken Lehmer

also received their final tweaks before being assembled.

In October 1993 the entire N9M-B, with airfoils on one trailer and the centre section on another, was taken back to Chino aboard Daryl Bond's All Coast Lumber trucks (Daryl is a warbird enthusiast, perhaps best known for his two-seater TF-51D-25-NT 44-84860/N327DB *Lady Jo*). Upon arrival, the trucks were unloaded at the Planes of Fame Jet Museum site and the components reassembled and rigged, ready for test flying. The canopy sections were assembled and installed on the cockpit and sealed with mastic. Several airlocs had been removed from the airframe for painting and finishing and now had to be fitted individually.

The aircraft appeared ready to take to the air. The tension mounted. During the taxi tests it was noted that oil was leaking from the cylinder head of one of the Franklin engines. The spare was installed to save time, but then both of the engines began to show the same problem. Franklin had built just 13 powerplants for the N9M project, and the three units held for the Planes of Fame N9M-B are the only such units known to have survived, so this was a time of great tension for the team. Fortunately, in the nick of time, one of the restoration team located someone who had worked on these engines for many years. It was quickly discovered that a common problem was a crushed gasket between the aluminium head and the steel cylinder. Replacement of the gaskets solved the problem.

As the permanent final assembly was completed and the connections made, they were torqued and wired. Late December 1993 saw the final weight and balance check being undertaken and signed off, after which the FAA issued a Special Airworthiness Certificate. On 29th December 1993 the Franklin engines were run for the first time on the aircraft since 1949. Over the following months, engine run-up and slow-speed taxi trials were undertaken, final adjustments were made to the airframe and minor glitches eliminated. The cylinders from both airframe engines and the spare had to be removed, and the newly manufactured gaskets installed following checks for damage to the powerplants. It was a slow process and exasperating for the team, especially as there were other projects requiring attention at the Planes of Fame Museum. So it wasn't until 11th November 1994 that the fourth and final N9M built took to the air for the first time with Don Lykins at the controls. Since then the aircraft has been flown several times and holds people's attention wherever it goes.

produced the complex rudder system. Constructed from an aerodynamically shaped box which holds two split flaps, the rudder system (controlled by hand wheels in the cockpit) can be pivoted about the leading edge, providing both pitch and roll trim. As an example, when the pilot wants the aircraft to turn he steps on the rudder pedal. A hydraulic actuator inside the box deploys the split flap to provide drag on the inside of the turn.

One of the most difficult tasks facing the team was the rigging of the control cables that had to be routed through the enclosed spaces in the centre section and wings. As cables were strung and tensioned, standoffs had to be built and installed every 3-5ft (0.91-1.52m) to hold the cables in place, thus keeping the whole system aligned. This was one of the tasks accomplished by a team led by Bion Provost. When this part of the construction was finished, the hydraulic system was activated and the controls

tested and adjusted where necessary. Pilots Steve Hinton and Don Lykins were then able to sit in the cockpit of the N9M-B and get a 'feel' for the controls. It had been 40 years since a member of the Northrop 'Flying Wing' family had been in such an advanced state of construction and both pilots liked the feel of the controls.

The next step was to paint and finish the entire craft. Most of this work was completed early in the morning and out in the open. All of the wooden surfaces were masked and sanded several times to provide a good key for the final coatings of finish. Two coats of polymide paint were applied. The aircraft was painted in its original scheme of bright yellow with primary blue undersides. On completion of the painting, portions of the centre section – rudders, access doors and landing gear doors – underwent final assembly. Some 1,200 operations were required to attach the air baffles and counter-balance weights to each elevon. The propeller units

24

Republic P-47D Thunderbolt
44-90460/N9246B

The P-47D was the most produced version of Republic's Thunderbolt fighter with a total of 12,602 being constructed. Of these, 6,093 -RAs were built at Evansville, Indiana, and a further 6,509 -REs at Farmingdale, New York. Although design of the P-47 Thunderbolt was completed after World War Two had begun, a grand total 15,683 were built, in 13 different versions, making the P-47 the most produced American fighter of the period.

On 6th May 1941, some eight months after an order for the Thunderbolt had been placed by the US Government, the prototype XP-47B took to the air from Farmingdale, New York, flown by Lowry Brabham. Though the first flight had to be cut short when the pilot declared an emergency due to fumes in the cockpit, the omens bode well. Initial performance figures showed that designer Alexander Kartveli had done a good job.

With the war in mainland Europe hotting up, deliveries of production fighters made the European Theatre of Operations a priority for operational deployments. Although the 56th FG, based near New York, were the recipients of the first P-47Bs to roll off the Farmingdale production line in May 1942, the first P-47Cs began arriving in the United Kingdom in December of that year and were immediately pressed into service with the 4th, 78th and the newly deployed 56th FGs. Whilst performance against the enemy at medium and low level left something to be desired, at high altitude the 'Jug' gave a good account of itself. Tactics were developed accordingly. The P-47 also served as an escort fighter until it was replaced by the North American P-51 Mustang.

After World War Two the P-47 went on to serve with the Air National Guard. Aircraft declared surplus by the USAF were eagerly snapped up by various air arms including those of Bolivia, Brazil, Chile, Colombia, Dominican Republic, Ecuador, Guatemala, Honduras, Iran, Italy, Nationalist China, Nicaragua, Peru, Portugal, Turkey, Venezuela and Yugoslavia.

Bill Klaers and Alan Wojciak's Westpac Restorations are the P-47 restoration specialists. The fuselage of Neal Melton's P-47D-40-RA is seen at the company's workshops in June 1998, early on in the restoration process. Thierry Thomassin

As the statistics of World War Two were compiled, the magnificent contribution that the P-47 had made to the war effort became clear for all to see. It had flown over half a million missions in just two years of operations from March 1943 to August 1945. It had also accumulated almost 2 million combat flying hours, with an additional 2½ million training hours being flown in the United States. Another incredible statistic: the firing of almost 60,000 rockets and the unleashing of 135 million ammunition belts.

In the warbird stakes the P-47 Thunderbolt, in contrast to the P-51 Mustang, is still quite a rare and underrated aeroplane. There are, according to the author's own *Warbird Index*, 57 surviving Thunderbolts (compared to 311 Mustangs), of which just 12 are airworthy aircraft with another five in the process of being rebuilt to fly.

One of the countries that utilised the Thunderbolt during World War Two and beyond was Brazil, 136 P-47Ds being supplied to the Força Aérea Brasileira (FAB) up to 1952. Gloster Meteor F.8s replaced the surviving P-47Ds from 1953 onwards, the last examples soldiering on until 1960. When Neal Melton, owner of several airworthy piston and jet warbirds and founder of the Tennessee Air Museum, began his search for a P-47 in 1994, several ex-FAB P-47Ds remained extant in Brazil along with a substantial amount of spares. After some research, Neal quickly discovered that

almost all the surviving Thunderbolt warbirds had been sourced in South America.

The Thunderbolt that Melton eventually purchased was built as P-47D-40-RA 44-90460 and, after US service, was assigned to the FAB as 4175/F-47 on 30th October 1953. It was eventually withdrawn from use and stripped for spares, and was surplussed by March 1958. Following transfer to Recife AB, 4175 was put on display between 1970 and 1978, painted as 226450/A1. It was transferred to the prestigious Museu Aeroespacial at Campo dos Afoncos, Rio de Janeiro, in 1987. Later that year, it was returned to the United States, where it subsequently led a shadowy existence.

In September 1988 the aircraft went into storage along with another three ex-FAB P-47Ds, its future uncertain. By August 1991 the Thunderbolt had been acquired by Airplane Sales International and was registered to them as N9246B in September 1995. On 2nd October 1996 Neal Melton acquired the Thunderbolt and handed it over to Alan Wojciak and Bill Klaers of Westpac Restorations in Rialto, California, for many years the acknowledged Thunderbolt specialists. There the aircraft was taken apart down to the last screw and then completely rebuilt. A lot of parts had to be remanufactured because they were no longer available on the market. Alan Wojciak takes up the story: 'This Thunderbolt restoration was fairly groundbreaking in some areas. The wing

spars were probably the biggest job of all. The later D models and the N models were fitted for rockets, and so Republic added a ¼-inch (6.35-mm) steel strap to the lower leg of the main spar and the rear spar in the areas where the rocket mounting's would be fitted on the bottom of the wing surface. Years of moisture will start corrosion in these areas. There is no repair permitted by Republic (in the Structural Repair Manual) to these wing spar caps. Merely trying to figure out how Republic built up the sub-assemblies for the wing was the challenge.

'After studying many factory photos we commenced disassembly to permit access to the spar assemblies. Once the spars were removed we had to manufacture new spar caps from 4-in x 4-in x 18-ft (10-cm x 10-cm x 5.48-m) long extruded aluminium stock. All of the machine work on the new spar caps was basically done by hand on a 12-ft (3.65-m) bed mill. As far as I know, at that time, no one else had undertaken that process with a P-47 wing before.

'Other things that stand out in my mind as fairly difficult were the tail surfaces, engine cowls and fuselage longerons, in addition to the flight controls. All these items are very intense sheet metal projects and it really tested our abilities. Thanks are due to Neal, who invested in the fabrication of all of the fix-

tures and tooling needed to disassemble, fab-ricate and reassemble all those items, which had not been done before on other aircraft.

'There really aren't too many Thunderbolt projects out there to pick from. Some are better than others but the ones that have been around awhile are now actually viable projects to start with, now that we can get access to rebuild the larger items that before would scare people away. The engine over-haul was done by Jeff Blakey in Texas and the propeller was restored by Golden State Propeller in San Luis Obispo, California. The majority of the engine accessories were refurbished by Thunder Airmotive.

'Even after you go through all of the prob-lems and get the airframe and systems up to speed, a whole new set of problems come into play when you reach the point of getting the aircraft in the air again. Neal's Thunder-bolt was no exception. We had problems with the prop governor, oil leaks on the engine that were all challenging, plus diffi-culties with some of the other accessories.

'On one of the later time-building flights, I had the engine quit on me after being air-borne for about an hour and a half and had to dead-stick it at Rialto. For some reason, fuel was getting to the carburettor but not through it to the discharge nozzle. I had fuel pressure but no noise from the Pratt & Whitney – and

Restoration of the cockpit was undertaken by Westpac Restorations using another P-47D rescued from Brazil several years earlier as a 'donor' aircraft. Uwe Glaser

Engine overhaul was undertaken by Jeff Blakey in Texas; the Curtis Electric Propeller was overhauled by Golden State Propeller in San Luis Obispo, California. Uwe Glaser

that definitely gets your attention, let me tell you! It all worked out in the end, but it seems that we always go through this period of gremlins that we have no control over.

'I must say that Neal is a great man for tak-ing a chance with us and giving us the opportunity to figure out some of the big mysteries with the Thunderbolt. He loves fly-ing it and I'm just glad that he does. It's all about the future generations being able to see aircraft like Neal's Thunderbolt and other warbirds to remember what all those young men did long ago so we could have the freedom we enjoy today.'

Three years' restoration by Westpac, funded by Neal Melton, was needed before the Thunderbolt took to the air again. It was painted in the colours of Lieutenant Colonel Gilbert O Wymond's *Hun Hunter XVI* of the 65th FS, 57th FG. In preparation for taking the Thunderbolt aloft, Neal completed 60

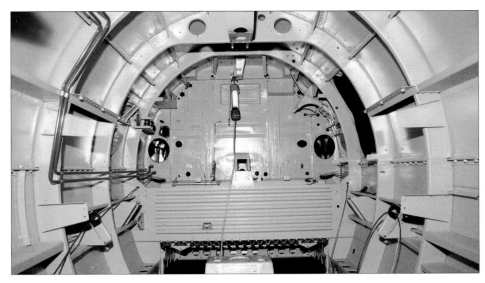

This view inside the fuselage reveals that restoration of the internal part of the airframe is important to ensure the long-term survival of the aircraft. Thierry Thomassin

Neal Melton in P-47D 44-90460/N9246B high above the clouds on a photographic sortie for the photographer Uwe Glaser. Neal Melton is now embarking on another P-47 restoration project.

flying hours in a North American T-6 Texan trainer, and read all he could about flying the high-performance tailwheel aircraft. He also underwent five hours of intensive flight training in a P-51 Mustang in Florida and was checked out in his T-28 Trojan by an examiner representing the FAA. Only then did he feel able to fly his own P-47D Thunderbolt.

Preparations were complete by 3rd September 1999; the time had finally arrived for the owner to climb into *Hun Hunter XVI* for his first flight. I asked Neal for his impressions on flying the aircraft: 'The *Hun Hunter* has really been trouble-free over the past three and a half years. I try to fly it weekly and have averaged about 70 hours a year. I have a total of 340 hours since restoration took place. The R-2800 engine burns about 80 gallons (303 litres) per hour and uses about 1½ gallons (5.7 litres) of oil per hour. The turbocharger is operational and works fine. You don't need it for take-off at the weight I operate at (around 12,000 lb; 5,443kg), but it is needed past altitudes of 8,000ft (2,438m) at a climb power setting. I have flown it past 18,000ft (5,486m), but I am sure would she would go on up in the upper thirties or even into the 40,000ft (12,192m) bracket.

'As far as flying the aircraft is concerned, it is the most forgiving tailwheel aircraft I have been in. On take-off, after getting it straight on the runway and locking the tailwheel, just increase the throttle to 30 inches, release brakes, go to full throttle (about 45 inches without turbo, 52 inches with), and it 'goes'. It tracks down the runway straight and is very easy to control with slight rudder movement. Visibility from the cockpit is good but you can't see over the nose until the tail comes up. At about 110mph (177km/h) indicated, you do have to pull it off the runway and make it fly. It does seem very sluggish for the first 500ft (152m), but after the gear comes up, things get better and smoother.

'In cruise, the aircraft is pure fun to fly. It handles great, has a fast roll rate, dives like no other, and you feel secure with all that mass around you. I know why the guys that flew the P-47 in combat loved them.

'To land the Thunderbolt is simple, just don't get too slow; no turns below 135mph (217km/h). With the gear down and full flaps, you can bring the speed on back to 120mph (193km/h) and down to 105mph (169km/h) when you know you can make the field. Pull the throttle back to the stop and flare to land, either mains first or three-point. It does not bounce, swerve, or balloon, it just stops flying. It does, however, want to roll to the other end, so a little brake is needed most of the time.

'I think the P-47 is one of the greatest fighters of all time.' Few would not echo that sentiment.

25

Curtiss P-40C Warhawk
41-13390/N2689

For the author at least, this aircraft is one of the greatest finds in the history of the warbirds movement; and it is testimony to its original owner, The Fighter Collection, that it was properly restored to its airworthy status without completely removing the patina.

What really makes this aircraft interesting is its traceable history. Manufactured to order number W-535, account 15802, at a unit cost to the US Government of $40,148.00, the Curtiss Wright Model 81A-3 was on the production lines between March and June 1941. One hundred and ninety-three Curtiss P-40Cs with manufacturer's serial numbers in the range 16104 to 16296 were finished during this period. The subject of this entry, the 90th P-40C manufactured at the main Curtiss factory in Buffalo, New York, was completed in March 1941 and allocated the serial 41-13390. Initial assignment was to Holabird, Central District, on 9th April 1941. However, it appears the aircraft remained in store for a short time period. There is no documentary evidence to suggest it had any USAAC service (the recovered airframe did not bear any previous markings or paint marks to suggest it had).

Purchased by the British Government, it was to be included in its order for 1,180 Tomahawk IIBs, but on 11th June 1941 it was diverted to the Office of Defense Aid. Just three months later, in September 1941, 41-13390 was allocated to the Defense Aid Program, destined for Russia. Scant details are available on the aircraft's Russian service.

In September 1941 the Russians took delivery of 47 Tomahawks IIBs in what must have been a substantial boost to their local air power. Assembled by an RAF team detached to Yagodnik, Archangel, the aircraft were air-tested by USAAC pilots Lieutenants Zemke and Alison. In early October 1941 the first two aircraft, AK300 and AK232 were physically transferred to the Russian Air Force. Ominously, both aircraft were the subject of emergency landings just 30 minutes into their Russian service. Investigations revealed that both aircraft had endured generator drive gear and accessory drive gear failure. The generator drive gear on these aircraft had not been upgraded before shipment to Russia, an omission that would result in a trail of aircraft failures in the following month. Reluctantly, the Soviets grounded all Tomahawks until they could be modified to incorporate changes to the gear assemblies.

According to official records, 41-13390 arrived at Murmansk early in 1942, delivered by ship. It was then assembled and air-tested at Yagodnik before assignment to an IAP unit. The Russian Air Force documented Defense Aid P-40s using the last three digits of their manufacturer's serial numbers, which in the case of 41-13390 was '194'. This number was painted on the back of the pilot's back armour and also stamped on the lower left longeron. (Aircraft delivered via the United Kingdom were recorded by their RAF serial.) Russian records show the first entry for '194' relating the following information:

P-40 '194' was issued new to the 14th Fighter Regiment, 14th Army early in 1942. P-40 '194' suffered engine failure and forced landing, undercart up, at Murmashi airfield, south of Murmansk, on 5th February 1942. Classified 'medium damage'. Pilot S-Lt N V Jurilin survived unhurt.

The aircraft was repaired and a new engine installed, before assignment to the 20gvIAP in July 1942. This unit had 20 P-40s on strength, of which 16 were operational.

The Soviet War Diary shows that on 27th September 1942 '194' took part in a skirmish worthy of mention. From 1617-1732hrs, five Hurricanes assigned to the 837th IAP flew air patrols over their base while nine P-40s of the 20gvIAP and a single Bell P-39 Airacobra from the 19gvIAP engaged with 18 Messerschmitt Bf 109s. The ensuing dogfight lasted for almost half an hour and resulted in the Russians claiming the destruction of three

The long-nosed Allison V-1710-33 engine is shown to advantage with the huge radiators/ oil coolers in the Fighter Rebuilders shop.
Thierry Thomassin

The cockpit of P-40C 41-13390 provides an interesting comparison with that of the P-40E illustrated on page 75 of this book.
Thierry Thomassin

Then owned by The Fighter Collection, the P-40C was rebuilt by Fighter Rebuilders Inc at Chino, California. Thierry Thomassin

September 1998 and Steve Hinton runs the long-nosed Allison V-1710-33 powerplant which was prepared by JRS Enterprises in Minneapolis, Minnesota. Thierry Thomassin

Bf 109s. Russian losses included Lieutenant N A Fikjunin (killed in a Hurricane), Staff Sergeant P K Prochan (forced to land his Hurricane two miles (3.2km) east of Shonguj) and Sergeant A P Pakov (parachuted to safety from his stricken P-40).

Another P-40 was lost that day when Major Ermakov was forced to belly-land his stricken fighter. The aircraft in question was none other than '194'. Consequently, '194' was struck off charge with the 20gvIAP on 5th January 1944. A mere 52 years later, examination of satellite photographs revealed the same P-40 sat in a desolate part of Russia. This was a truly exciting find. Eventually the rare warbird was recovered from within the confines of a rail depot at Murmashi.

As the aircraft details were researched both in the United Kingdom (by Mark Sheppherd) and in Russia, the story began to be pieced together. Apparently Major Ermakov was forced to land, wheels retracted, on uneven ground. Incredibly, very little damage occurred except for the radiator chin cowl assembly, which took the brunt of the impact. As if by miracle, the 'war prize' sat at the same location for the next half-century! Indeed it was one of two that lay in the snow south of Murmansk. When helicopters made their first attempt at recovering the other aircraft, the disturbance caused unexpended ordnance to detonate, destroying the P-40, the helicopter, and killing the helicopter's crew.

Patina Ltd, based in the Channel Islands, financed the recovery of '194'. The derelict hulk was airlifted from the crash site by helicopter, dismantled and shipped to the United Kingdom where plans were being drawn up to restore the aircraft at The Fighter Collection's base at Duxford, Cambridgeshire. The serial number located on the tailwheel oleo confirmed this was a P-40C-CU Model 81A-3, serial 44-13390. As related earlier, the fuselage longerons and back armour were stamped with the abbreviated manufacturer's construction number '194'.

Clearly marked with code number '53' on the faded camouflage, the upper surfaces of the aircraft had been weathered almost to bare metal by over 50 years of exposure to the harsh local climate. Faintly visible on the fuselage sides was the old-style American insignia; lettering spelling U.S. ARMY on the underside of the wings was much more in evidence. As expected, the undersides of the wings bore the red star insignia of the Russian Air Force. Some parts of the engine cowling were not original to this aircraft and

appeared to come from a British Tomahawk (they showed traces of green and brown paint). This change of parts could have taken place during an engine change, perhaps during combat operations.

The P-40C showed clear signs of combat damage. Small-calibre bullet holes were discovered along the fuselage and wings and the oil tank was holed – likely to have

been the chief factor in the loss of the aircraft. There were also signs of crude repair work, probably battle damage repair undertaken by Russians in the field. Detailed examination of the engine recovered with the airframe revealed United Kingdom War Office stamps and that it was a documented British-ordered 1,040-hp (776-kW) Allison V-1710-33.

The early P-40C looks much more a warplane than its successors, largely due to the aggressive but functional front end, emphasised in this side view.
Thierry Thomassin

Shortly before being sold to the Seattle-based Flying Heritage Collection (now Flying Heritage Inc), the rare P-40C was painted in the markings of AVG 'Flying Tiger' Erik Shilling and flown by Steve Hinton. Frank B Mormillo

After its arrival in the United Kingdom, the airframe sat for some months whilst it was evaluated for restoration. As the aircraft was in remarkably good condition, it was planned to do the absolute minimum as far as replacing skins and major structure was concerned, to keep the beautiful Tomahawk as original as possible. The caveat was that the aircraft should be restored to airworthiness.

This was the first early-model P-40 to be restored to flying condition. Though Project Tomahawk had two airframes being worked on in California, P-40C '194' was fairly complete when it was discovered (except for the all but written-off chin cowl, which gives the Tomahawk its characteristic and unmistakable look). Metal master Bob Cunningham, who also did a lot of the other complex curved metalwork on the airframe, fabricated a new chin cowl. The huge casting at the front of the cowl, which also formed part of the air intake, was produced in the United States.

After the preliminary work and some sourcing of parts, it was decided to despatch the rare P-40 to Steve Hinton's Fighter Rebuilders Inc at Chino, California, for restoration to flying condition. Some work had already been done on the airframe. The wings were shipped first in April 1994, followed by the fuselage.

After many years of research and restoration work on the airframe, the rare long-nosed Allison engine, restored by Sam Torvik and Bill Moja at JRS Enterprises in Minneapolis, Minnesota, was installed in the airframe and engine runs undertaken. On 1st September 1998, with the engine having passed its tests, Steve Hinton took the aircraft (by now registered N80FR) into the skies above Chino on its post-restoration first flight.

Shortly thereafter the aircraft was flown painted in the markings of a 'Flying Tigers' Tomahawk assigned to American Volunteer Group pilot Erik Shilling, who was present at Chino for the aircraft's first flight. It was planned to paint the aircraft in RAF markings as a 'Desert Air Force' Tomahawk and register it G-TOMA, but in 1999 the aircraft was sold to the Flying Heritage Collection in Seattle, Washington, and reregistered to its new owners as N2689 in August of that year.

Principal Piston-Engined Warbird Aircraft Recoveries

Curtiss P-40E   1947   (11)   Canada
Fred Dyson, Boeing Field, Seattle, Washington, USA; others by individuals from Patricia Island, Vancouver Bay, Canada

Curtiss P-40E   1950s   (5)   New Zealand
Recovered from the Asplin's Supplies scrap yard, Rukahia

Vought F4U-1 Corsair   1950s   (2)   New Zealand
Recovered from the Asplin's Supplies scrap yard, Rukahia

Lockheed P-38 Lightning   1960   (3)   Honduras
Bob Bean, Blythe, California, USA

Bell P-63E Kingcobra   1963   (3)   Honduras
Bob Bean, Hawthorne, California, USA

North American P-51D Mustang   1963   (14)   Nicaragua
MACO Sales Financial Corporation, Chicago, Illinois, USA

Hispano HA-1112 Buchon   1966   (24)   Spain
T.G. 'Hamish' Mahaddie, London (for *Battle of Britain* film)

CASA 2.111   1966   (2)   Spain
T.G. 'Hamish' Mahaddie, London (for *Battle of Britain* film)

Republic P-47D Thunderbolt   1969   (6)   Peru
Vintage Aircraft International, Nyack, New York, USA

Westland Lysander   1970s   (5)   Canada
Wes Agnew, Hartney, Manitoba, Canada

Fairchild Bolingbroke   1970s   (15)   Canada
Wes Agnew, Hartney, Manitoba, Canada

North American P-51D Mustang   1972   (7)   Guatemala
Don Hull, Sugarland, Texas, USA

Goodyear FG-1D Corsair   1973   (2)   El Salvador
Bob Hood

Bell P-39 Airacobra   1974   (14)   Papua New Guinea
Charles Darby, David Tallichet and Monty Armstrong

Curtiss P-40N   1974   (9)   Papua New Guinea
Charles Darby, David Tallichet and Monty Armstrong for Yesterday's Air Force

North American P-51D Mustang   1974   (8)   El Salvador
Flaherty Factors, Monterey, California, USA

Goodyear FG-1D Corsair   1974   (2)   El Salvador
Terry Randall and Bill Harrison of Har-Ran Aviation, Tulsa, Oklahoma, USA

Douglas AD-4 Skyraider   1977   (7)   France
Jack Spanich, Detroit, Michigan, USA

NAA/Cavalier P-51D Mustang   1977   (5)   Bolivia
Arny Carnegie, Edmonton, Alberta, Canada

NAA/Cavalier P-51D Mustang   1978   (at least 16)   Indonesia
Stephen Johnson, VanPac Carriers, Oakland, California, USA

Supermarine Spitfire   1978   (10)   India
Ormond and Wensley Haydon-Baillie, Duxford, Cambridgeshire, UK

Douglas AD-6 Skyraider   1980   (4)   Thailand
Yesterday's Air Force, Long Beach, California, USA

Hawker ISS Fury   1979   (29)   Iraq
Ed Jurist and David Tallichet

Hawker Tempest   1979   (7)   India
Douglas Arnold, Warbirds of Great Britain Ltd, Blackbushe, Hampshire, UK

Vought F4U Corsair   1979-   (16)   Honduras
George Heaven, Jim Nettle (of Hollywood Wings), Terry Randall and Howard Pardue

North American P-51D Mustang   1984   (9)   Dominica
Brian O'Farrell, Hollywood, Florida, USA

Douglas AD-4 Skyraider   1984-85   (4)   Gabon
French collectors

Yakovlev/LET C-11   1985   40   Egypt
Raymond and Alain Capel, Jean Salis, La Ferte Alais, France

Supermarine Spitfire   1987   (5)   United Kingdom
Tim Routsis, Historic Flying Ltd, Audley End, Essex, UK

Douglas AD-4 Skyraider   1988   (5)   Chad
Didier Chable, Melun, France

Curtiss P-40B   1989   (3)   Hawaii, USA
Curtiss Wright Historical Association, Torrance, California, USA

Curtiss P-40F   1989   (2)   Vanuatu
Robert Grienert and Martin Mednis, Sydney, New South Wales, Australia

Republic P-47D Thunderbolt   1991   (4)   Brazil
Airplane Sales International Corporation, Beverly Hills, California, USA

Fairey Firefly   1990s   (3)   Ethiopia
John Sayers, South Africa

Fairey Firefly   1993   (2)   Ethiopia
Canadian Armed Forces

North American B-25 Mitchell   1993   (3)   Venezuela
Steven A Detch, Alpharetta, Georgia, USA

Supermarine Spitfire   1999   (3)   Myanmar (Burma)
David Goldsmith, Golden Aviation, Colorado, USA

Supermarine Seafire   1999   (1)   Myanmar (Burma)
David Goldsmith, Golden Aviation, Colorado, USA

Curtiss P-40E AK979 (ex-RCAF1064) was relinquished by the RCAF to the civilian market in 1947 as N5672N. Seen here in an unmodified state at Merced, California, in June 1963, the aircraft is currently registered to the Federal Express Corporation in Memphis, Tennessee. Warbird Index

Curtiss P-40E RCAF1052 as CF-OGZ in August 1965. It is now registered N40PE with Rudy Frasca of Champaign, Illinois. Warbird Index

Hispano HA-1112-M1L C4K-172 was ground-looped at Waco, Texas, in 1977. The damaged aircraft was acquired by Robert J 'Robs' Lamplough and restored by Norman Chapman and his team at Duxford. Sadly the aircraft (registered G-BJZZ) was ground-looped again at Biggin Hill shortly after this photo was taken on 15th May 1982. It is now airworthy with the Cavanaugh Flight Museum in Addison, Texas. Warbird Index

P-47D-30-RA Thunderbolt 45-49181 when registered N151LF to Lester Friend of Carlsbad, California, in 1977. Bill Painter, Kalamazoo Air Zoo

Several Mustangs were recovered from Guatemala and El Salvador. The latter country yielded this Cavalier version, P-51K 44-11153 (FAS 409), which has been resurrected several times since and has recently flown for the first time after restoration for the Banta Aviation Corporation as N451TB. Dick Phillips

Several Bolivian Air Force Mustangs were 'sprung' from that country in 1977 when a group of Canadians exchanged several Canadair CT-133 Silver Star jets for the precious Cavalier conscripts. All of the Mustangs are still flying today in one form or another. Warbird Index

Cavalier processed a genuine Temco TF-51D Mustang (44-84658) for export to Indonesia where it was used for a number of years before being purchased in the great Stephen Johnson Mustang 'coup' of 1978. John MacGuire of Texas purchased the aircraft from Johnson and had Mustang restoration expert Darrell Skurich of Vintage Aircraft Limited undertake a restoration to flying condition as N51TF. John MacGuire

Warbird collectors have always regarded the Spitfire VIII as a 'difficult one to get'; MT719 was retrieved from India by the late Ormond Haydon-Baillie circa 1978 and was sold to Franco Actis of Turin, Italy. It was owned briefly by Reynard Racing Cars but was sold to the Cavanaugh Flight Museum in 1993. The aircraft was photographed at Duxford in 1988 during filming for the controversial TV series Piece of Cake. Michael Shreeve

A now famous shot of five Iraqi Single Seat (ISS) Hawker Furies at Langley just prior to export. The recent conflict in Iraq has thrown up a number of interesting but (at the time of writing) unsubstantiated reports of the hulks of at least two such aircraft close to Baghdad. Hawker Siddeley Aviation

One of the last ex-Iraqi Air Force ISS Furies in store with David Tallichet of the Military Aircraft Restoration Corporation in June 1993. Thierry Thomassin

In December 1981 Henry Haigh purchased this ex-Iraqi Air Force Fury and put it into restoration with Nelson Ezell at Breckenridge, Texas. It is seen here in 1989. Author

Warbirds of Great Britain operated Spitfire FR.XVIIIe SM969, appropriately registered as G-BRAF and seen here at Biggin Hill in July 1991. The aircraft is currently in store with Wizzard Investments. The Warbird Index

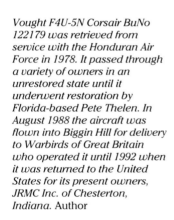

Vought F4U-5N Corsair BuNo 122179 was retrieved from service with the Honduran Air Force in 1978. It passed through a variety of owners in an unrestored state until it underwent restoration by Florida-based Pete Thelen. In August 1988 the aircraft was flown into Biggin Hill for delivery to Warbirds of Great Britain who operated it until 1992 when it was returned to the United States for its present owners, JRMC Inc. of Chesterton, Indiana. Author

Tyrolean Jet Service operate the one and only Austrian-registered F4U-4 Corsair, BuNo 96995/OE-EAS, an ex-Honduran Air Force airframe recovered in 1978. It was rebuilt by Ezell Aviation for Austrian Siegfried Angerer who enjoys the sponsorship of Red Bull energy drinks. Erich Gandet

Vought F4U-5NL Corsair BuNo 124724 is another ex-Honduran Air Force airframe that was retrieved by Hollywood Wings. Amicale Jean Baptiste Salis of La Ferte Alais took delivery of the aircraft in December 1986 and it was registered F-AZEG shortly afterwards. Warbird Index

A Dominican Air Force Mustang on Inspection and Repair as Necessary (IRAN) in 1983. The first Mustangs to come out of the country went through this process before passing into civilian hands, making them technically airworthy when they arrived in Florida. However, all of the customers undertook their own restoration work to get them certificated in the US.

An ex-Brazilian Air Force Republic P-47D at Santa Monica in May 1990. Both Warbird Index

A pair of ex-Egyptian AF LET C.11 wings at La Ferte Alais in the late 1980s. Author

The LET C.11 (a Czech-built version of the Yak-11) has become an extremely popular warbird since over 40 airframes were recovered from Egypt by Raymond and Alain Capel in Association with Jean Salis. The last few airframes are seen here in store at La Ferte Alais near Paris in the late 1980s. Author

The Dominican Air Force is the longest recorded military user of the Mustang (though rumours continue to abound of a Cavalier Mustang in Indonesia that is run regularly) and Brian O'Farrell recovered nine aircraft and several tons of spares in the early 1980s. When the author inspected the first Mustang to come out of that country in 1983, it was evident that the Dominican Air Force had been most frugal with their spare parts; a move that would later benefit civilian owners as the spares were released into the civil Mustang community. Warbird Index

This apparently battered and vandalised P-40F fuselage was recovered from Vanuatu by Martin Mednis, Rob Greinhert and Ian Whitney. Now registered VH-HWK to Judith Pay of Tyabb, Victoria, the aircraft is being rebuilt to fly. Warbird Index

The hulk of this rare P-40F, 41-14112, one of two recovered from Vanuatu in November 1989, has formed the basis of a restoration to airworthy condition in Australia where it is registered VH-HWK. Warbird Index

One of the most fascinating warbird recoveries of the last century has to be the retrieval of Lockheed P-38F 41-7630 from beneath the ice by the Greenland Expedition Society in the spring and summer of 1992. The aircraft, along with five other P-38s and a B-17, had force-landed while flying to England. Incredibly, ten years after its retrieval, the restored aircraft took to the air for the first time on 26th October 2002 at the hands of test pilot Steve Hinton. Wayne Gomes

Collections and Restorers

WARBIRD COLLECTIONS

Alpine Fighter Collection
Ray Mulqueen
Wanaka, New Zealand
+64 3 443 1451
+64 3 443 1452
www.skyshow.co.
afc@skshow.co.nz

American Airpower Museum
Farmingdale, New York, USA
631 293 6398
www.americanairpowermuseum.com
info@americanairpowermuseum.com

Amicale Jean-Baptiste Salis
Aerodrome de Cerny – La Ferte Alais
France
01 64 57 55 85

Association Aeroretro
Aerodrome Saint Rambert D'Albon
France
+33 04 75 03 03 58
+33 04 75 03 03 58
www.chez.com/aeroretro/

Battle of Britain Memorial Flight
RAF Coningsby
Lincolnshire, UK

Canadian Warplane Heritage
Mount Hope, Ontario, Canada
905 679 4183
www.warplane.com
museum@warplane.com

Cavanaugh Flight Museum
Addison Airport
Texas, USA
972 380 8800
972 248 0907
www.cavanaughflightmuseum.com

Chino Warbirds
Tom Friedkin
Chino, California, USA

Fantasy of Flight
Polk City, Florida, USA
863 984 3500
www.fantasyofflight.com
receptionist@fantasyofflight.com

The Fighter Collection
Duxford Airfield
Cambridgeshire, UK
01223 834973
www.fighter-collection.com

The Flying Bulls
Austria
+43 (0) 662 85 80 95 34
+43 (0) 662 85 80 95 00
www.flyingbulls.at
info@flyingbulls.at

Flying Heritage Inc
Seattle, Washington, USA
www.flyingheritage.com

Historic Aircraft Collection
Guy Black
Rye, East Sussex, UK
01580 830215
01580 830875
www.historicaircraftcollection.ltd.uk
hac@aerovintage.co.uk

Lone Star Flight Museum
Galveston, Texas, USA
www.lsfm.org
flight@lsfm.org

Museum of Flight
Seattle, Washington, USA
206-764-5720
www.museumofflight.org

New Zealand Fighter Pilot's Museum
Ian Brodie
Wanaka, New Zealand
+64 (0)3 443 7010
+64 (0)3 443 7011
www.nzfpm.co.nz
info@nzfpm.co.nz

The Old Flying Machine Company
Nigel Lamb
Duxford Airfield, Cambridgeshire, UK
01223 836705
01223 834117
www.ofmc.co.uk
info@ofmc.co.uk
Film and TV work, display flying

Olympic Flight Museum
Olympia, Washington, USA
360 705 3925
www.olympicflightmuseum.com
info@olympicflightmuseum.com

Planes of Fame
Chino, California, USA
909 597 3722
www.planesoffame.org

Royal Navy Historic Flight
RNAS Yeovilton, Somerset, UK
www.flynavyheritage.org.uk

Scandinavian Historic Flight
Anders K Saether
Oslo, Norway
+47 22 50 23 65
+47 22 52 14 89
www.shf.as
publicrelations@shf.as

The Shuttleworth Collection
Old Warden, Bedfordshire, UK
01767 627228
01767 626229
www.shuttleworth.org
collection@shuttleworth.org

Temora Aviation Museum
Temora, New South Wales, Australia
+61 (0)2 6977 1088
+61 (0)2 6977 1288
www.aviationmuseum.com.au

The Vormezeele Collection
Brasschaat, Belgium
geocities.com/vormezeelecollection/
frederic.vormezeele@skynet.be

Vulcan Warbirds
Seattle, Washington, USA

WARBIRD RESTORERS

Aero Trader
Tony Ritzman and Carl Scholl
Chino, California, USA
909 597 4020
www.aerotrader.net
All warbirds, bombers a speciality

Aero Vintage
Guy Black
Rye, East Sussex, UK
01580 830215
01580 830875
www.aerovintage.co.uk
info@aerovintage.co.uk
Hawker biplanes

Aerocrafters
Steve Penning
Santa Rosa, California, USA
707 527 8480
707 527 7524
www.aerocrafters.com
acrafter@sonic.net

Aerotec Queensland Pty Ltd
Lynette Zuccoli
Wilsonton Airport
Toowoomba, Australia
+61 (0) 7 4633 1315
+61 (0) 7 4634 5574
aeotec@bigpond.com

Aircraft Restoration Company
John Romain
Duxford Airfield
Cambridgeshire, UK
01223 835313
01223 837290
ange@arc-duxford.co.uk
All warbirds

Airframe Assemblies
Steve Vizard
Ryde, Isle of Wight, UK
01983 404462
01983 408662
www.airframes.co.uk
info@airframes.co.uk
All warbirds, major and minor structures

Airmotive Specialties
Dave Teeters
Salinas, California, USA
831 757 7154
707 222 7623
DTP51bldr@jps.net
P-51 Mustang

Airpower Unlimited
John Lane
Jerome, Idaho, USA
208 324 3650
208 324 3950
www.airpowerunlimited.com
Mainly F4U; other warbirds too

American Aero Services
Gary Norville
New Smyrna Beach, Florida, USA
386 423 3650
386 423 0622
www.americanaeroservices
All warbirds

American Warbirds
Dennis Buehn
Carson City, Nevada, USA
775 887 1231
T-6, T-28 and HU-16

ATW Aviation
Bill Muszala
Marana, Arizona, USA
520 616 0545
520 682 2301
atwinc@uswest.net
All warbirds

Avia Restoration
Boris Osyatinsky
Nikulinskaya str. 31, room 68
Moscow 119602, Russia
007 (095) 232 7388
007 (095) 746 1799
avia16@dol.ru
Russian-made aircraft to flying condition

C&J Sales
Chuck Smith
Camarillo, California, USA
800 828 3597
805 484 5840 (outside USA)
www.t28sales.com
t28flys@west.net
T-28 (all marks)

Cal Pacific Airmotive
Art Teeters
Salinas, California, USA
408 422 6860
P-51 Mustang major structures and restoration

Charleston Aviation Services
Craig Charleston
Colchester, Essex, UK
Bf 109E, Spitfire and others

Courtesy Aircraft
Mark Clark and John Kramer
Rockford, Illinois, USA
815 229 5112
815 229 1815
www.courtesyaircraft.com
sales@courtesyaircraft.com
Sales and maintenance (all warbirds)

Ezell Aviation
Nelson Ezell
Breckenridge, Texas, USA
254 559 3051/3651
254 559 3052
www.ezellaviation.com
info@ezellaviation.com
F4U, P-51, Sea Fury and others

Fighter Factory
Ken McBride
San Martin, California, USA
408-683-2602
info@fighterfactory.com
P-51 structures and spares, restoration

Fighter Rebuilders
Steve Hinton
Chino Airport, California, USA
909 597 3514
www.planesoffame.org
All warbirds

Flug Werk
Clauss Colling
Gammelsdorf, Germany
+49 (0) 8766 939 878
+49 (0) 8766 939 879
www.flugwerk.de
colling@flugwerk.de
Fw 190 new airframes and support

GossHawk Unlimited
Dave Goss
Mesa, Arizona, USA
480 396 9644
www.gosshawkunlimited.com
P-51, T-6, T-28

Hawker Restorations Ltd
Tony Ditheridge
Milden, Suffolk, UK
01449 741496
01449 741584
www.hawker-restorations-ltd.co.uk
Hurricane

Historic Flying Ltd
John Romain
Duxford Airfield, Cambridgeshire, UK
01223 839455
www.historicflying.com
Spitfire

Midwest Aero Restorations
Mike VadeBonCoeur
Danville, Illinois, USA
217 431 1998
217 431 8989
t6flier@aol.com
F4U, P-47, P-51 and others

Mosquito Aircraft Restorations Ltd
Glyn Powell
Drury, New Zealand
+64 9 294 8701
+64 9 294 8761
Mosquito new structures

Pacific Fighters
John Muszala
Idaho Falls, Idaho, USA
208 522 3502
www.pacificfighters.com
All warbirds

Panama Jacks Vintage Aircraft Co
Rob Poynton
Canning Bridge
Western Australia, Australia
+61 8 9414 1051
+61 8 9414 1052
www.panamajacks.co.au
rob@panamajacks.com.au

Pete Regina Aviation
Pete Regina
Granada Hills, California, USA
818 360 2613
All warbirds

Pioneer Aero Restorations
Garth Hogan
Ardmore Airport
Papakura, New Zealand
+64 (0)9 2968913
+64 (0)9 2968943
www.pioneeraero.co.nz
pioneeraero@xtra.co.nz
P-40 and others

Pride Aircraft
John Morgan
Rockford, Illinois, USA
815 229 7743
815 229 0120
prideboss@aol.com
T-28 and others

QG Aviation of America
Ray Middleton
Fort Collins, Colorado, USA
970 221 5461
All warbirds

Retro Track & Air (UK) Ltd
Upthorpe Iron Works
Upthorpe Lane, Dursley
Gloucestershire, UK
01453 545360
01453 544617
www.retroair.co.uk
retrotrackandair@aol.com
Merlin engine restoration, airframe work

Richard Goode Aerobatics
Richard Goode
Almelely, Herefordshire, UK
01544 322200
01544 322208
www.russianaeros.com
Yak-9

Sanders Aviation
Ruth or Dennis Sanders
Ione, California, USA
209 274 2955
209 274 2954
www.sandersaviation.com
info@sandersaviation.com
Hawker Fury and others

Sherman Aircraft Sales
Denny Sherman
Palm Beach, Florida, USA
561 799 1919
561 799 1920
www.shermanaircraftsales.com
Sales and maintenance (all warbirds)

Stars & Bars Aircraft
Paul and Diane Redlich
Huntington, Indiana, USA
219 356 6500
219 356 6500
www.starsandbarsaircraft.com
t6fixer@ctlnet.com
T-6 and other warbirds

Tab Air
Sam Taber
East Troy, Wisconsin, USA
414 642 4515
P-51 and others

Texas Airplane Factory
George Tischler
Fort Worth, Texas, USA
817 626 9834
817 626 7354
gtisch_taf@birch.net

Tom Reilly Vintage Aircraft Inc
Tom Reilly
Kissimmee, Florida, USA
407 847 7477
407 933 7843
www.warbirdmuseum.com
reilly@warbirdmuseum.com
B-17, B-25; mainly bombers

Tulsa Warbirds
Tom Dodson
916 742 0482
Russian aeroplanes and engines

Victoria Air Maintenance
Russ Popel
Sidney, Victoria
British Columbia, Canada
604 656 7600
www.vicair.net
T-28 and others

Vintage Aircraft Limited
Darrell Skurich
Fort Collins, Colorado, USA
970 533 8688
All warbirds

Vintage Fabrics
Clive and Linda Denney
Braintree, Essex, UK
01376 550553
01376 550553
www.vintagefabrics.co.uk

Yak UK
Mark Jefferies
Little Gransden Airfield
Bedfordshire, UK
01767 651 156
01767 651 157
www.yakuk.co.uk
Yaks

ENGINE REBUILDERS

Air Sparrow Merlin Service
Mike Barrow (owner)
5560 Pacheco Pass, Gilroy, CA, USA
831 902 5978
772 382 5798
sparrow@direcway.com
Rolls-Royce and Packard Merlins

Aircraft Cylinder & Turbine
Bill Jones
Sun Valley, California, USA
818 767 5000
818 504 1108
www.acftcyl.com/
sales@AcftCyl.com
Repair and overhaul of all round engines

Allison Competition Engines
Bud Wheeler
Latrobe, Pennsylvania, USA
724 539 0241
v1710@adelphia.net
Allison engines

Covington Aircraft Engines
Paul Abbot
Okmulgee, Oklahoma, USA
800 324 8320
918 756 8320
918 756 0923
www.covingtonaircraft.com
Pratt & Whitney R-983 and R-1340

Hovey Machine Products
Jack Hovey
Ione, California, USA
209 274 4422
Rolls-Royce and Packard Merlins

Mystery Aire
Dwight Thorn
Gilroy, California, USA
408 848 3431
847 537 1624
www.mysteryaire.com
Rolls-Royce and Packard Merlins

Precision Engines Corporation
Dave Cort
Everett, Washington, USA
425 347 2800
425 353 9431
www.precisionengines.com
All Curtiss-Wright and Pratt & Whitney round engines

Rick Shanholtzer
Addison, Texas, USA
972 347 2630
Rolls-Royce and Packard Merlins

Rudy Blakey Inc
Rudy Blakey
Perry, Florida, USA
850 578 2800
850 578 2333
www.rudyblakey.com
All Curtiss-Wright and Pratt & Whitney round engines

Tulsa Aircraft Engines
Sam Thompson
Tulsa, Oklahoma, USA
918 838 8532
918 838 1659
Pratt & Whitney R-985 and R-1340

Universal Airmotive
Riverwoods, Illinois, USA
847 537 4464
847 537 1624
Rolls-Royce Merlin and Griffon

Vintage Engine Technology Ltd
Mike Vaisey
Little Gransden Airfield
Bedfordshire, UK
01767 651794
01767 651794
Vintage aircraft engine overhaul

Vintage V12's
Mike Nixon
Tehachapi, California, USA
661 822 3112
661 822 3120
Rolls-Royce Merlin and Griffon, Daimler Benz DB605

We hope you enjoyed this book . . .

Midland Publishing titles are edited and designed by an experienced and enthusiastic team of specialists.

We always welcome ideas from authors or readers for books they would like to see published.

In addition, our associate, Midland Counties Publications, offers an exceptionally wide range of aviation, military, naval and transport books and videos for sale by mail-order worldwide.

For a copy of the appropriate catalogue, or to order further copies of this book, and any other Midland Publishing titles, please write, telephone, fax or e-mail to:

Midland Counties Publications
4 Watling Drive, Hinckley,
Leics, LE10 3EY, England
Tel: (+44) 01455 254 450
Fax: (+44) 01455 233 737
E-mail: midlandbooks@compuserve.com
www.midlandcountiessuperstore.com

US distribution by Specialty Press –
see page 2.

On this page are selected titles from the Red Star series; for details of the other volumes still available please see our full catalogues.

Red Star Volume 3
POLIKARPOV'S I-16 FIGHTER

Yefim Gordon and Keith Dexter

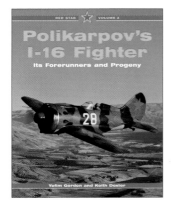

Often dismissed because it did not fare well against its more modern adversaries in the Second World War, Nikolay Polikarpov's I-16 was nevertheless an outstanding fighter – among other things, because it was the world's first monoplane fighter with a retractable undercarriage. Its capabilities were demonstrated effectively during the Spanish Civil War. Covers every variant, from development, unbuilt projects and the later designs that evolved from it.

Sbk, 280 x 215 mm, 128 pages,
185 b/w photographs, 17 pages of
colour artworks, plus line drawings
1 85780 131 8 **£18.99**

Red Star Volume 4
EARLY SOVIET JET FIGHTERS

Yefim Gordon

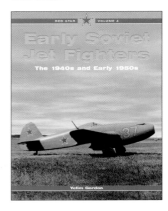

This charts the development and service history of the first-generation Soviet jet fighters designed by such renowned 'fighter makers' as Mikoyan, Yakovlev and Sukhoi, as well as design bureaux no longer in existence – the Lavochkin and Alekseyev OKBs, during the 1940s and early 1950s. Each type is detailed and compared to other contemporary jet fighters. As ever the extensive photo coverage includes much which is previously unseen.

Sbk, 280 x 215 mm, 144 pages
240 b/w and 9 colour photos,
8 pages of colour artworks
1 85780 139 3 **£19.99**

Red Star Volume 5
YAKOVLEV'S PISTON-ENGINED FIGHTERS

Yefim Gordon & Dmitriy Khazanov

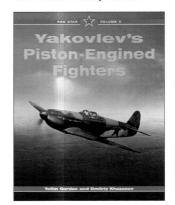

This authoritative monograph describes this entire family from the simple but rugged and agile Yak-1 through the Yak-7 (born as a trainer but eventually developed into a fighter) and the prolific and versatile Yak-9 to the most capable of the line, the Yak-3 with which even the aces of the Luftwaffe were reluctant to tangle. Yak piston fighters also served outside Russia and several examples can be seen in flying condition in the west.

Sbk, 280 x 215 mm, 144 pages,
313 b/w and 2 col photos, 7pp of
colour artworks, 8pp of line drawings
1 85780 140 7 **£19.99/**

Red Star Volume 6
POLIKARPOV'S BIPLANE FIGHTERS

Yefim Gordon and Keith Dexter

The development of Polikarpov's fighting biplanes including the 2I-N1, the I-3, and I-5, which paved the way for the I-15 which earned fame as the Chato during the Spanish Civil War and saw action against the Japanese; the I-15*bis* and the famous I-153 Chaika retractable gear gull-wing biplane. Details of combat use are given, plus structural descriptions, details of the ill-starred I-190, and of privately owned I-15*bis* and I-153s restored to fly.

Softback, 280 x 215 mm, 128 pages
c250 b/w and colour photos; three-view drawings, 60 + colour side views
1 85780 141 5 **£18.99**

Red Star Volume 10
LAVOCHKIN'S PISTON-ENGINED FIGHTERS

Yefim Gordon

Covers the formation and early years of OKB-301, the design bureau created by Lavochkin, Gorbunov and Goodkov, shortly before the Great Patriotic War.

It describes all of their piston-engined fighters starting with the LaGG-3 and continues with the legendary La-5 and La-7. Concluding chapters deal with the La-9 and La-11, which saw combat in China and Korea in the 1940/50s.

Illustrated with numerous rare and previously unpublished photos drawn from Russian military archives.

Sbk, 280 x 215 mm, 144pp, 274 b/w &
10 col photos, 9pp col views, plus dwgs
1 85780 151 2 **£19.99**

Red Star Volume 13
MIKOYAN'S PISTON-ENGINED FIGHTERS

Yefim Gordon and Keith Dexter

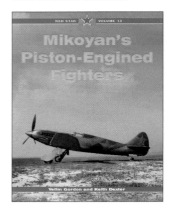

Describes the early history of the famous Mikoyan OKB and the aircraft that were developed. The first was the I-200 of 1940 which entered limited production in 1941 as the MiG-1 and was developed into the MiG-3 high-altitude interceptor. Experimental versions covered include the MiG-9, the I-220/225 series and I-230 series. A separate chapter deals with the I-200 (DIS or MiG-5) long-range heavy escort fighter.

Softback, 280 x 215 mm, 128 pages
195 b/w photos, 6pp of colour artwork,
10pp of line drawings.
1 85780 160 1 **£18.99**

Red Star Volume 15
ANTONOV AN-2
Annushka, Maid of All Work

Yefim Gordon and Dmitriy Komissarov

Initially derided as 'obsolete at the moment of birth' due to its biplane layout, this aircraft has put the sceptics to shame. It may lack the glamour of the fast jets, but it has proved itself time and time again as an indispensable and long-serving workhorse. The An-2, which first flew in 1947, has been operated by more than 40 nations.

The An-2 is the only biplane transport which remained in service long enough to pass into the 21st century!

Softback, 280 x 215 mm, 128 pages
c200 b/w and 28 colour photographs,
plus line drawings.
1 85780 162 8 **£18.99**

ROYAL AIR FORCE GERMANY Since 1945

Bill Taylor

This detailed survey takes the lid off RAF operations within Germany and provides a detailed valediction of its exploits from the establishment of the British Air Forces of Occupation in July 1945 to the tense days of the Berlin Airlift and the establishment of NATO and its tripwire strategy which placed Germany firmly in the front line via its Forward Defence policy. This book, acclaimed for its original research, serves as a timely study of a hitherto thinly documented era of RAF history.

Hbk, 282 x 213 mm, 240 pages
295 b/w and 59 colour photographs
1 85780 034 6 **£35.00**

BRITISH SECRET PROJECTS
Jet Fighters Since 1950

Tony Buttler

A huge number of fighter projects have been drawn by British companies over the last 50 years, in particular prior to the 1957 White Paper, but with few turned into hardware, little has been published about these fascinating 'might-have-beens'. Emphasis is placed on some of the events which led to certain aircraft either being cancelled or produced. Some of the varied types included are the Hawker P.1103/P.1136/P.1121 series, and the Fairey 'Delta III'

Hbk, 282 x 213 mm, 176 pages
130 b/w photos; 140 three-views, and an 8-page colour section
1 85780 095 8 **£24.95**

BRITISH SECRET PROJECTS
Jet Bombers Since 1949

Tony Buttler

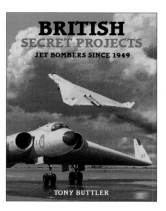

This long-awaited title forms a natural successor to the author's successful volume on fighters. The design and development of the British bomber since World War II is covered in similar depth and again the emphasis is placed on the tender design competitions between projects from different companies. The design backgrounds to the V-Bomber programme, Canberra, Buccaneer, Avro 730, TSR.2, Harrier, Jaguar and Tornado are revealed.

Hbk, 282 x 213 mm, 224 pages
160 b/w photos; 3-view drawings
9-page colour section
1 85780 130 X **£24.99**

BRITISH SECRET PROJECTS
Fighters & Bombers 1935-1950

Tony Buttler

This new volume will again place the emphasis on unbuilt designs that competed with those that flew, and covers aircraft influenced by World War 2 – projects that were prepared from the mid-1930s in the knowledge that war was coming through to some which appeared after the war was over. The latter will include early jets such as the Attacker, Sea Hawk and Venom which all flew post-war but to wartime or just post-war requirements.

Hbk, 282 x 213 mm, c208 pages
c160 b/w photos; 3-view drawings and a colour section
1 85780 179 2 May 2004 c**£24.99**

WAR PRIZES

Phil Butler
Foreword: Capt E.M. 'Winkle' Brown, RN

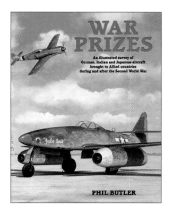

Meticulously researched study of the many German, Italian, and Japanese aircraft taken to Allied countries or flown by the Allies during and after the Second World War. The coverage includes civilian aircraft and sailplanes as well as military types; post-war production of German designs and details of surviving aircraft in museums. Appendices include German and Japanese aircraft designation and marking systems.

Hbk, 282 x 213 mm, 320 pages
450 b/w photographs
0 904597 86 5 **£29.95**

AIR ARSENAL NORTH AMERICA Aircraft for the Allies 1938-1945 – Purchases & Lend-Lease

Phil Butler with Dan Hagedorn

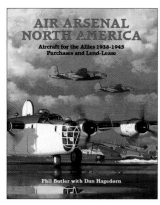

A detailed analysis of aircraft purchases made in North America by the British Commonwealth and European democracies during 1938-1945 and the subsequent operation of the Lend-Lease Acts and Canadian Mutual Aid.

All of the many aircraft types are described and illustrated; supplemented by sections covering their operation by each of the countries involved, including aircraft serials, delivery routes, and various appendices.

Hbk, 282 x 213 mm, c320 pages
c600 b/w photos, some colour
1 85780 163 6 August 2004 c**£40.00**

MUSTANG SURVIVORS

Paul Coggan

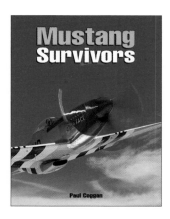

Informative and visual celebration of nearly 300 Mustang Survivors in 2002, including the A-36A, P-51 (NAA & CAC), the Cavalier and the F-82 Twin Mustang. Chapters cover airframes, powerplants, the specialised restoration industry, painting & finishing, insurance, owning a Mustang, and flying a TF-51. The final chapter comprises 285 biographies and includes military serial, civilian registration(s), last restorer, current status and a potted history of the airframe.

Sbk, 280 x 215 mm, 176 pages
330 colour and 25 b/w photos
1 85780 135 0 **£19.99**

WRECKS & RELICS THE ALBUM

Ken Ellis

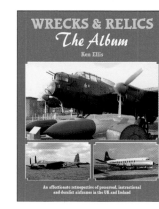

The continuing popularity of *Wrecks & Relics*, recording preserved, instructional and derelict airframes in the UK and Ireland is well known. Following a brief introductory narrative covering *W&R* itself, and the general preservation scene over the years, the body of the book is a gloriously nostalgic collection of photos with extended captions explaining the histories and linking the themes. An outstanding overview of the UK preservation scene.

Sbk, 280 x 215 mm, 128 pages
340 mostly colour photographs
1 85780 166 0 **£16.99**

Robert Bean of Hereford, Arizona, was the first civilian owner of F4U-4 Corsair BuNo 97264 in 1959. Its last American owner, Chuck Hall, sold the aircraft to Corsair Warbird Ltd of Marsannay La Cote, France, in 1996, at which time it was registered F-AZVJ. Thierry Thomassin